Two week loan
Benthyciad pythefnos

Please return on or before the due date to avoid overdue charges
*A wnewch chi ddychwelyd ar neu cyn y dyddiad a nodir ar eich llyfr os
gwelwch yn dda, er mwyn osgoi taliadau*

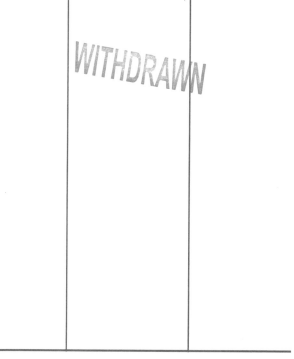

Organizational Change in Post-Communist Europe

Recent transitional developments in the former communist countries have aroused considerable interest among economists and political scientists alike. Yet relatively little attention has focused upon the ways in which these significant changes have impacted the micro realities of life within the transforming state-owned enterprises.

Organizational Change in Post-Communist Europe provides a unique and detailed examination of the complex processes of transformation in former state-owned enterprises in the Czech Republic. Drawing on in-depth case studies of organizational transformation, this book adopts a social-institutionalist approach to the study of organizational change, applying it in order to develop an explanation of organizational restructuring and management redefinition during the early transition period of 1990–1996. In particular, the authors highlight how these processes have been shaped by continuing historical state-socialist legacies and the powerful role played by senior managers in their efforts to fashion the new privatized organizations in their own interests.

By successfully re-balancing the prevailing disposition towards macro-economic research into the post-communist transition in Central and Eastern Europe, this volume constitutes an important work for all those interested in human resource management, organizational behaviour and the management of change.

Ed Clark is Principal Lecturer in Organisational Behaviour at Nottingham Business School, Nottingham Trent University. **Anna Soulsby** is a Senior Lecturer in Organisational Behaviour at the same institution. Their joint work on the post-communist transition has been published extensively in European and American journals, including *Organization Studies*, *The Journal of Socio-Economics* and the *International Journal of Human Resource Management*.

ROUTLEDGE STUDIES OF SOCIETIES IN TRANSITION

Organizational Change in Post-Communist Europe

Management and transformation in the Czech Republic

Ed Clark and Anna Soulsby

London and New York

First published 1999 by Routledge
11 New Fetter Lane, London EC4P 4EE

Simultaneously published in the USA and Canada
by Routledge
29 West 35th Street, New York, NY 10001

Typeset in Baskerville by
BC Typesetting, Bristol
Printed and bound in Great Britain by
Biddles Ltd, Guildford and King's Lynn

British Library Cataloguing in Publication Data
A catalogue record for this book is available from the British Library

Library of Congress Cataloging in Publication Data
Clark, Ed (Edward David)
    Organizational change in post-communist Europe:
management and transformation in the Czech Republic/
Ed Clark and Anna Soulsby.
    (Routledge studies of societies in transition; 11)
    Includes bibliographical references and index.
    1. Management – Czech Republic.   2. Organizational
change – Czech Republic.   I. Soulsby, Anna.
II. Title.   III. Series.
HD70.C89C555   1998
658'.0094371–dc21   98-35445

ISBN 0–415–20333–3

Contents

Figures

Tables

Preface and acknowledgements

> Serendipity: 'always making discoveries, by accidents and sagacity, of things [you are] ... not in quest of.'
>
> (Horace Walpole, *The Princes of Serendip*, 1754)

In November 1991, two years after the revolutionary events in Central and Eastern Europe had shaken the precarious global status quo, the authors went to Poland and to Czechoslovakia in order to complete the delivery of a postgraduate module in an MBA package. In the summer of that year, quite by chance, we had been approached by the staff responsible for British Know-How Fund contracts in Nottingham Business School at Nottingham Trent University to design and teach a module on organizational analysis at institutions in those two countries. The MBA was being used as a vehicle for passing on the conventional wisdom of market-economic management to senior academics in the two universities, with the further intention that they would establish business school-type structures through which *they* could then 'cascade' the knowledge to non-academics and the business community. Having delivered the first two-thirds of the module in Nottingham to twenty enthusiastic but critical Polish and Czech academics, we found ourselves in Poznań and Brno to complete the workshop elements of the module.

As part of the hospitality, our new Polish and Czech colleagues arranged visits to businesses in the respective cities. In Poznań, we were taken to two new, small service firms to meet up and coming members of the business community. Their offices were chic, equipped with expensive leather furniture and populated by young, modern, smartly dressed staff – we could have been in any bank or computer firm anywhere in the Western world. Their values and objectives were profit-focused, and the language was informed by Western business and management jargon. In Brno, on the other hand, our hosts drove us out to a huge, old-fashioned factory site, which was strewn with large, rusting metal objects which had obviously one day had pretensions to being useful industrial products. We had a long and fascinating meeting with the enterprise directors in a large boardroom, which was fitted out with the standard state socialist boardroom furniture and decor. We mused over the latest attempt to redraw the organization chart, sympathized with the unenviable challenge of changing the enterprise's internal culture and were stunned by the routineness of the everyday economic drama of having to find new customers for products previously designed for Soviet partners. All these problems and their tentative remedies were aimed at just one thing – the immediate survival of the enterprise and its 5000 employees.

These two contrasting experiences say much about the nature of the post-communist economic transition: about the diverse problems and difficulties of small and large enterprises; the predisposition of small capital to flood into the easier industries of service provision, and the investment difficulties of manufacturing; the distinctive priorities and values of small and large business managers towards markets, finances and their communities; the different problems of foreign trade for old and new business. Yet, at the same time, there were profound similarities. Notably, in each case the senior managers had only two years before had significant managerial responsibilities under a command economy, and had to conform to the institutional requirements of their respective systems. Yet by November 1991, it was clear that, to a surprising degree, these managers had gained access to and control of the rhetoric, the words if not the meanings, of Western management discourse; and they had done so probably to the same extent that they had participated in the concepts and practices of state socialist management just two years earlier. It was this conundrum that was to drive the enthusiasm – colleagues and families might call it the obsession – for the research that has resulted in this book. How could we account for the continuing presence and importance of former state enterprise managers in the emerging market conditions that economists call the economic transition? How can we understand the apparent facility with which they were able to convert themselves almost instantly from seemingly dyed-in-the-wool *nomenklatura* communists into enthusiastic capitalists?

At the end of our teaching in Brno and just before heading off to catch the flight home, we were taken to the top of a hill overlooking the city by a few of our Czech colleagues, who said that they looked forward to our next visit to Brno. Seeing the doubt in our expressions, they insisted that we would return. Within four months, they had found a state enterprise – called Vols in this book – which was pleased to play host to the obsessed researchers we had become.

Our approach to studying the economic transition has been the product of our circumstances. One trained as a sociologist, the other educated as an historian, we both work in the field of organizational behaviour and analysis in a university business school. After initial wider reading of the emergent literature, dominated as it was by economists, we began to feel that the key questions arising in our field with respect to the transition lay in understanding the ways in which managers, as key economic actors, had evolved new values and practices, and how these extensions to their repertoires of knowledge and technique were reflected in the enterprises themselves, in their structures, their cultures and their systems. By adopting the case study approach in the tradition of business and management research, we sought to identify socio-economic explanations which were rooted in the historical and current circumstances of societal and organizational transformation, and in the personal motives of the individuals in question. The book therefore examines the socio-economic transition from the perspective of enterprise managers, and explores the changes that have been occurring in the Czech Republic since 1989 as they have affected the enterprise. Its central concerns are with the processes of transition and transformation at the enterprise level, with questions of continuity and discontinuity with the past, with the ambiguities and uncertainties that arise within the transition process and with the management of the external and internal changes that have impacted upon economic life in the enterprise.

In sum, our intention is to contribute to the understanding of important empirical and theoretical themes. On the first front, we aim to describe and analyse the specific conditions of the economic transition of post-communist society in the early 1990s, and the resultant changes in enterprise and management patterns. Second, the book confronts two fundamental theoretical questions, using these changes in the Czech Republic as the empirical location: these are the relationship between institutional stability and change, and the social and institutional (re-)construction of socio-economic reality.

The reading for and the writing of the book has involved coming to terms with a research field that has attracted the attention of researchers working in many diverse academic disciplines and traditions – these include economists, historians, social anthropologists and sociologists, as well as other area studies specialists and (former) sovietologists. We believe that this book extends knowledge in a way which spans the interests of all these academic groups, but in terms of subject matter there are three distinctive audiences: organization and management theorists, transition economists and area studies specialists. We consider the book to be first and foremost a contribution to the theory of organization and management change and therefore we want our work to appeal to organization theorists independent of whether they are interested in post-communism. Second, the book adds to the understanding of the post-communist economic transition by examining the concrete behaviour of enterprise managers responsible for realizing moves towards a 'market economy'. We hope that transition economists will find the evidence and arguments useful in constituting the micro foundations of their theoretical propositions, which often seem to be divorced from the real world of economic decision-making and decision-makers. Third, specialists in the Czech Republic in particular and the Central European region generally should find complementary value in our empirical findings on, for example, the lives and conduct of post-communist managers and the changing role of the enterprise in local communities.

It has been difficult to write a book that can communicate with each of these audiences in an efficient way. As a starting-point, we have assumed no awareness of the historical and contemporary Czech context, as would be likely for most students of management and organization. Thus, it was necessary to write quite detailed contextual chapters (3, 4 and 6), which many regional specialists and some transition economists may find familiar. These latter readers may wish to skim-read only these chapters. After much thought, and again in recognition of the needs of most readers, we have decided to minimize the use of Czech terms in the writing of the book. Where appropriate, we have cited Czech terms on the first appearance in the text of a structure or institution, so that area specialists can know exactly what we are referring to, and we have compiled a glossary of the most important terms and abbreviations that occur throughout the book.

This book is the result of the collaboration of many Czech colleagues at the Technical University of Brno, in Moravia. In particular we would like to thank Miloš Drdla, Hana Škyvarová, Aleš Vladik, Mirka Čermáková, Thaddeus Mallya, Jan Hobl, Subodh Kumar, Alena Keřkovská and Irena Navrátilová, all of whom offered careful and sensitive interpretation skills which opened up the world of Czech management for our examination. Miloš Keřkovský, the first Dean of the newly established Faculty of Business and Management at the university, offered us unlimited support and has been a good friend in all aspects of our work. It is only when we hear the stories from British colleagues about their difficulties in gaining and maintaining good access to large and small enterprises that we realise how lucky we have been in having such cooperative and well-connected friends and colleagues in Brno. The quality of our research materials is a manifestation not only of the excellence of the contacts of our academic colleagues, but also of the openness and honesty of the enterprise managers who participated in the project. Each manager in his or her own way has made this book possible, providing us with research materials that have proved to be highly versatile and flexible. Although they have remained anonymous throughout, these managers are very real and vibrant people, and their enterprises are the lifeline for the future of many Czechs. Our respondents will not all agree with our composite version of events in their enterprises, and a few may be shocked by some of our inferences and conclusions; but we feel confident that each will recognize his or her version somewhere in the telling of the story.

Our first opportunity to visit the then Czechoslovakia was offered by Robin Ward, then Head of the European Business Centre at Nottingham Business School. He had thought that our work might suit the training needs of the European contract with Brno Technical University, and he continued to encourage our research until his untimely death in 1995. Robin has been sorely missed in both Nottingham and Brno. Various colleagues at Nottingham Business School have been strong supporters of our research: in particular, Francis Terry (then Head of Research), Jim McGoldrick (now at University of Abertay, Dundee) and Lynette Harris managed to organize both time and money for us to continue.

So many people in the UK have offered help in the way of vocal encouragement or introductions to important networks that it would be impossible to thank everyone. But the following is an attempt to rebalance the books. Anna Pollert, Simon Clarke, Peter Fairbrother (all at the University of Warwick) and Paul Thompson (now at the University of Edinburgh) were the first ones to tell us that we were really doing something worthwhile, and that first encouragement was special and important; and John Child's sensitive and thorough editorship of *Organization Studies* was a significant formative influence as we struggled to pitch the reporting of the research at the right level. We have received support and advice from many colleagues in ways that may appear small to them, but were significant to us in terms of morale and confidence. George Kolankiewicz (University of Essex), then directing the ESRC East–West Programme, kept inviting us as outsiders to workshops where we met many other like-minded colleagues. We would also mention Hugo Radice (University of Leeds), Nigel Swain (University of Liverpool), Richard Scase (University of Kent), Jeff Henderson and Richard Whitley (both University of Manchester). We are especially grateful to Miloš Keřkovský (Technical University, Brno), Anne Mills (Buckinghamshire College of Higher Education), and Martin Myant (University of Paisley) for their comments on earlier drafts. The book was originally commissioned by Tony Elger and Peter Fairbrother (University of Warwick), who each read the draft manuscript minutely and whose suggestions have improved the quality and accuracy of the final version. Their encouragement and support were invaluable. Any errors of argument or detail that remain do so because of our oversight, or because we have insisted on being wrong in spite of good advice.

Finally, we are both grateful to our families, who have tolerated our many absences in order to conduct fieldwork. Chris Soulsby, Mary-Anne Clark, Joanna Clark and Tom Clark have been so supportive throughout the past six years.

Glossary of terms

a.s.	*akciová společnost*, or joint stock company
CEE	Central and Eastern Europe
CP	Communist Party of Czechoslovakia
ČSSR	Československá Socialistická Republika
CMEA	Council for Mutual Economic Assistance
corporatization	turning state enterprises into 100 per cent state-owned joint stock companies in order to commercialize enterprise decision making
FDI	foreign direct investment
FTO	Foreign Trade Organization (Podnik zahraničního obchodu), enterprises organizing the monopoly of importing and exporting, usually by industrial branch
IC	investment company, which runs one or more investment privatization funds; often themselves owned by banks or other financial institutions
IPF	*investiční privatizacní fond*, or investment privatization fund, established in the privatization legislation to collect and 'spend' voucher points
kč	Czech crown (currency after January 1993)
kčs	Czechoslovak crown (currency before January 1993)
konkurs	the process of competitive appointment
Konsolidační banka	Consolidation Bank, established in 1991 to take on the bad debts and rotating credits of large commercial banks and enterprises
KSČ	Kommunistická strana Československa (Communist Party of Czechoslovakia)
Lustration (*lustrace*) Act	also known as the Screening Act, passed in 1991; it determined that people who had held certain influential positions in the Communist Party, its organs and institutions should not be permitted to hold certain levels of public office
men of '68	those individuals, usually former CP members,

	whose careers and lives had been affected by their refusal to sanction the Warsaw Pact invasion of 1968
milice	the people's militia, which was a military-style unit based at the enterprise to defend the gains of socialist production
monobank	the system of state socialist banking based on one central state bank
normalization	the period following the Warsaw Pact invasion of 1968 when neo-Stalinist political and economic structures were reimposed
národní podnik	national enterprise, the major legal form of state-owned enterprise until 1988
NPF	National Property Fund, established in 1991 to accumulate state assets and to manage their transfer to the private sector
ODS	Občanská demokratická strana, the Civic Democratic Party of the dominant political leader of the period, Václav Klaus
OF	Občanské forum, the Civic Forum anti-communist coalition forged by Václav Havel, and instrumental in organizing the Velvet Revolution
přestavba	restructuring of the economic system, the Czechoslovak equivalent of Gorbachev's *perestroika*
Screening Act (1991)	*see* Lustration Act
SPK	Státní plánovací komise, or State Planning Commission, the economic super-ministry responsible for top economic decisions
s.r.o.	*společnost s ručením omezeným*, or small private limited liability firm
státní podnik	state enterprise, into which legal form, with greater autonomy, state-owned enterprises were transformed after 1988
TR	transferable ruble, the nominal unit of account in CMEA trading
VHJ	*vyrobní hospodářská jednotka*, or production economic unit; usually the 'leading enterprise' in an industrial branch, and intermediary level of economic management in the central planning hierarchy, superordinate to state-owned enterprises
voucher privatization	*kuponová privatizace*, the main method of mass privatization, organized as the majority part of the two privatization waves
závod	plant or factory unit of organization, the lowest element in the command economy, normally with little significant responsibility

Part I

Backgrounds and contexts

1 Studying organization and management change in the Czech Republic

The Czech transition in perspective

The changes that have spread across Central and Eastern Europe (CEE) since 1989 have been as dramatic as they have been far-reaching. They raise so many practical issues at so many levels and in so many spheres of social life that the degree of interest shown by social scientists in researching the region during the early post-communist period can come as no surprise. In the former communist countries, they see opportunities for examining social change in all its richness. In a situation where the scope for research is so wide, it is our impression that social scientific interest in the socio-economic transition has been overwhelmingly dominated, in both Central and Eastern European and Western social science, by the politics and the economics of the post-communist transformation. Moreover, this concern has been played out especially at the macro level, as researchers have examined the transformation of political systems, structures and processes from the authoritarian, centralized, totalitarianism of state socialism, to the democratic, devolved, pluralism associated with Western-style societies; or considered the changes involved in the move from hierarchical, centralized, state-ownership systems of command planning, to an economy which is essentially decentralized, market-driven and founded on private property relations.

Within this context, the social transition in the Czech Republic has been of particular interest. As part of the Czechoslovak Socialist Republic (ČSSR), it approached the post-communist era from an extreme form of state socialism, having endured many years of strong, autocratic rule by a disliked Communist Party, over which time the command economy had remained fairly obdurate to market-oriented changes. However, it has rapidly developed (or redeveloped) democratic political institutions, and, alone among the former communist nations in Europe, has up to and following the June 1996 elections resisted any temptation to revive the political ambitions of the successor parties of the Communist Party of Czechoslovakia (KSČ). Equally irrefutable has been the nation's commitment to a transition towards a liberal market economy, having accepted the application of stringent economic policies, and the adoption of radical programmes of mass privatization, at the centre of which has been the much debated voucher system. It is our contention that any explanation of social and economic processes in the 'post-communist' period is necessarily predicated upon a sound understanding of historical influences and legacies. The book therefore devotes considerable space and argument to the consideration of Czechoslovak state socialism in the 1980s, and the various processes of socio-economic and institutional development over the forty-one years of communism in the country.

However, history goes back and then back some more, and it is difficult to avoid being caught in an infinite historical regress in the ideal pursuit of comprehensive social scientific explanation. To remedy this tendency we have defined the limits of historical detail as 1948, when, in February, the KSČ assumed control over the political and economic levers of society – which story we pick up in Chapter 3. Czech culture and traditions do have a much longer chronology, and, in contrast to their Central European neighbours, the Czech lands were not newcomers to the practices of democracy and market economics. It is therefore relevant to appreciate the broader historical context in which Czech communism was rooted.[1]

The Czech Republic in the 1990s is a small nation of 10.3 million people, and its situation at the very heart of Europe has been defining of its history, as it will be of its future. It comprises two historical parts: Bohemia forms the western half of the country and abuts the new enlarged Germany to the west, Poland to the north and Austria to the south; Moravia, the eastern half, borders Poland to the north Austria to the south and Slovakia to the east. Its immediate history was closely tied up with Slovakia, with which, for most of the previous three-quarters of a century, it had constituted the single state of Czechoslovakia. The latter country was established as recently as 1918, when it was formed from the devastation of the First World War, until which time it had been a significant geographical region under the control of the Habsburg dynasty, rulers of the Austro-Hungarian Empire. Following struggles in the early seventeenth century, the Bohemian ruling class, its national leaders and cultural representatives, were eliminated, expropriated or exiled, and Czech culture and nationhood were subsumed under, and subordinated to, the monarchical authority emanating from Vienna.

During the nineteenth century, Czech industry developed rapidly, especially in the region bordering Germany, and by the end of the century the Czech lands had become one of the most advanced industrial areas of the Austro-Hungarian Empire, with a ready market for its products throughout the rest of the empire (Polišenský, 1947; Teichová, 1988, p. 17).

> The industries of the Czech lands were the major supplier of industrial products to a far-flung empire with a population of 60 million. The industries of the region prospered in this large market protected by formidable tariff barriers.
>
> (Klein, 1979, p. 147)

Klein goes on to describe the important growth of the Czech coal, steel, textiles, brewing and sugar-refining industries, and the would-be nation's comparative advantages in the literacy and general educational standards of the region.

Czechoslovakia inherited these industrial and economic legacies on its legal establishment in November 1918. Tomáš G. Masaryk was elected the first president of the new republic, and he and his provisional government set about planning a constitutional democracy, with a strong parliament as the sovereign power. These arrangements – based on a two-house, elected National Assembly – were consolidated into the 1920 constitution of the First Republic. In addition to the Czechs and Slovaks, the newly defined boundaries included substantial minorities of Germans in the western and northern Bohemian region, Hungarians in southern Slovakia, Ruthenians near the eastern borders and Poles in Silesia (see, for example, Wiskemann, 1967; Anderle, 1979). All minorities, including the Jewish community, were ascribed social and civil rights to an enlightened degree for the time. Twenty years of political democracy and continuing economic development were brought to an abrupt end in 1938, when the growth of intense nationalism in Germany spilt over into territorial claims by Hitler on the German-speaking parts of Sudeten Czechoslovakia. The failure of France and Britain to support the small democracy, symbolized by the so-called Munich Agreement, ultimately paved the way for the military invasion in March 1939, when Bohemia and Moravia were overrun by German troops. Thereafter, the Czech lands were brought into the German Reich as a protectorate, and their natural and industrial resources were used to good effect in supplying the German war machine;[2] meanwhile, a puppet government loyal to Berlin was established in Slovakia (e.g. Seton-Watson, 1956, pp. 70ff; Taborsky, 1979).

Following liberation, an interim post-war 'National Front' government was established under Edvard Beneš, who had succeeded Masaryk on his retirement from the presidency in 1935, but had spent the war years in exile in London. The new government was based on principles resolved at a convention held in April 1945 in the Slovak town of Košice, when Beneš's London-based political exiles met Czechoslovak communists who had spent periods of the war in Moscow. In fact, dialogue between the two groups had taken place since 1941, though the common 'Košice Programme' for the reconstruction of post-war Czechoslovakia was signed on Czechoslovak territory (see Kaser and Zieliński, 1970; Hasager, 1986, p. 19). Beneš included communists and their sympathizers in significant positions in his National Front government, while limiting the scope of political pluralism. The Košice agreement included an extensive plan to nationalize major industries, including banking and finance. Starting in September 1945 and going through a number of phases, by early 1948 over 80 per cent of industrial assets had been confiscated (especially from Germans and Hungarians), come under national administration or passed into public ownership – these accounted for virtually all enterprises with more than fifty employees (Hasager, 1986, p. 25). Democratic institutions were reintroduced, and in the first post-war democratic elections of 1946, the Communist Party attracted 38 per cent of the votes cast, and its leader, Klement Gottwald, became Prime Minister. But, beyond their formal democratic success, the communists had also constructed a very solid grass-roots organization: they were very strong in local government, in the police force, in the trade unions and in workplaces, where they established armed worker militia units (the *milice*) to 'protect' the factories. Facing pressure from Moscow to consolidate the political position of the party, and in the face of doubts about its possible success in the next elections, in February 1948 Gottwald made an effective move to seize power and to eliminate the influence of political opposition (see, for example, Seton-Watson, 1960, pp. 248ff; Taborsky, 1979; Suda, 1980; Teichová, 1988; Kaplan, 1989).

The Czechoslovak economy had undoubtedly suffered during the war, particularly in agriculture, light engineering and consumer goods, which were sacrificed in favour of the contribution of heavy engineering to the German war effort. Many factories were selected as targets for allied bombing in the latter stages of the conflict, but it is probable that Czechoslovak industry suffered far less than that of other European countries, and some parts of it may actually have been enhanced through German war investments (Kieżun, 1991, p. 270). Moreover, after the war, industry recovered far more quickly than most comparable countries. But the biases that had been introduced into the industrial structure – particularly in the development of heavy and mechanical engineering – were compatible with the economic plans of the Communist Party, based as they were on extensive, Stalinist, industrialization. In Chapter 3 we explore the dominant features of the resulting economic and industrial structure during the communist era, in preparation for our more extensive analysis of the management and organization of manufacturing enterprises both during and after that period.

The four enterprises

The four former state enterprises that form the location of the research reported in the book were all, in one way or another, born out of political motivation to build a heavy mechanical engineering base to the post-war Czechoslovak economy (see Table 1.1, p. 8). Each has its own unique history, yet all operated under broadly the same institutional conditions that developed under state socialism. Drawing upon both secondary sources, including internal enterprise documents, and the memories of the managers whom we interviewed, we can put together pictures of the enterprises, describing how they were influenced by the flows of history. The economic development of the enterprises has to be understood in the context of the principles and institutions of central planning, which are discussed more expansively in Chapter 3.

The decision to build a mechanical engineering and metallurgical plant at Volna was taken soon after the Communist Party assumed power in Czechoslovakia in February 1948. Although the hills around Volna had been a traditional site for iron-working, which went back to the fourteenth century, these resources had long ago been considered inadequate for modern metallurgical production with its huge raw material requirements. The development of *Volnské Strojírny a Slévárny* (or *Vols*, for short) was therefore essentially a political decision, resulting from the need to develop heavy and military engineering quickly and cheaply to respond to the international post-war situation, and its location was based on social reasoning, to bring skilled, industrial employment to a rural region which had high levels of unemployment and a relatively low standard of living.

Starting the construction in 1949, Vols was inaugurated as a state-owned enterprise (*národní podnik*) and produced its earliest steel in the summer of 1951. The first industrial machines were manufactured in 1953, in the still-unfinished plant. For the near-forty years of its existence under state socialism, Vols produced metallurgical products, including steel castings of various quality and forgings of diverse weights. In its mechanical engineering activities, which use forgings and excess energy from metallurgical operations, Vols manufactured rolling mills – traditionally its most valuable product – and forming machines; the latter are in turn employed in the forging workshops. This production programme was of enormous importance to the 'iron and steel concept' (Renner, 1989, p. 21) of industrialization that dominated the Stalinist definition of socialist development (see Chapter 3). Vols's industrial machinery contributed to the construction plans for Soviet military equipment such as tanks and armoured vehicles, and so enjoyed great exporting success to the socialist world. Likewise, its rolling mills, which enabled the mass production of wire and rails, were sold to developing nations of both the socialist and the non-socialist world, especially where, in the latter case, purchase was aided by politically inspired trade credits.

After 1958, Vols's domestic markets were organized on its behalf by the lead enterprise in its industry, realizing state plans to expand particular industries or enterprises, and accounted for about 35 per cent of its production programme, while the remainder was exported primarily to socialist countries. Around 40 per cent of all output would be transported to the Soviet Union (its biggest customer); 6 per cent to other Council for Mutual Economic Assistance (CMEA) countries; 16 per cent to developing nations (like Iran, Iraq, India and Syria); and the remainder to the industrialized world. These exporting activities were facilitated by three state exporting organizations, each specializing in a different product line. Its commercial activities were straightforward, because, being based on centralized plans, all but the smallest proportion of its work was contracted for up to five-year periods, with some of the larger projects lasting even longer. These contracts were the main instruments for connecting with partners in the Soviet Union and the European socialist region.

Table 1.1 The four Czech enterprises

Feature	Vols	Montáže Jesenice	Jesenické Strojírny	Agstroj
Date established	Legally founded in 1951	Founded as *národní podnik* in 1953	Founded as a plant (*závod*) of larger national enterprise in 1948	Opened as plant (*závod*) of larger national enterprise in 1948
Location	Rural town of Volna	Large rural town of Jesenice, but dispersed workforce	Large rural town of Jesenice	Stroměsto, a large city
Industry	Heavy mechanical engineering	Heavy mechanical engineering	Heavy mechanical engineering	Mechanical engineering
Primary task	Manufacture of industrial presses, rolling mills and metallurgical products	Assembly, repair and maintenance of industrial plant and machinery	Manufacture of industrial machinery and investment plant (e.g. cement works projects)	Manufacture of agricultural machinery, metallurgical products and ball-bearings
Former markets	Mostly Soviet Union, CMEA and Soviet Third World contacts	Mostly Soviet Union, CMEA and Soviet Third World contacts	Mostly Soviet Union, CMEA and Soviet Third World contacts	70 per cent to 'Western' capitalist markets; 25 per cent to CMEA; 5 per cent domestic
Hierarchical status	National, state-owned enterprise (*národní podnik*) till 1989; then a state enterprise (*státní podnik*)	Subsumed under Jesenické Strojírny's leadership in 1958, and became a subsidiary plant (*závod*) in 1965. Became independent *státní podnik* in 1990	In 1951, became *národní podnik*, till 1958, when it took on role as leading enterprise. 1965: became subsidiary to VVV in Prague. *Státní podnik* in 1988	From 1950, *národní podnik*; in 1983, took role as leading enterprise in branch (*koncerní podnik*). *Státní podnik* in 1989
Structure	Standard functional form	Standard functional form	Standard functional form	Standard functional form
Pre-1989 size	Large: 5600 employees	1150 as part of Jesenické Strojírny	Large: 7000 employees	Very large: 10,000 employees

Some 80 kilometres from the nearest city of any consequence, Volna in 1948 was a small, isolated village of 3500 inhabitants, whose lives were almost entirely linked with agricultural work. Since the arrival of Vols, this rural community has grown to 25,000 people, mostly in response to its expansion needs. The factory site of approximately 74 hectares is situated about 500 metres from the old village centre and dominates the south-western fringes of the town. On the cobbled track which leads to the factory gatehouse stands the statue of a socialist foundry worker, which, together with the heavy concrete symbol of Vols, is a strong iconic reminder of the important role of heavy industry in the communist bloc before 1989. The town itself is visibly divided into two architectural halves: the old centre gathers around a large square and a church, while, across a main road and behind the square, the apartment blocks of the great years of expansion point skywards, and the dull grey shopping, hotel and office facilities associated with the urban development extend blandly to the town limits. The size of the community, its relative isolation from cosmopolitan influence and the domination of the community by Vols, with its military connections, combined to give Volna the reputation of being a 'communist town', a stronghold in terms of values and ideology.

Vols was physically and socially connected to Volna in many ways (see Soulsby and Clark, 1995; Clark and Soulsby, 1998). Over the forty years of state socialism, the enterprise built many of the major social, cultural, accommodation and recreational facilities of Volna, and it also supplied, at a cost that was never calculated, hot water and energy that was surplus to production requirements. Vols provided kindergartens, crèches and holiday camps for employees' children virtually free of charge. Recreation and sports facilities, including a first-class winter stadium for ice hockey, were subsidized, as were canteen and factory grocery shops, for which Vols paid staff wages and part of the cost of the food. Reflecting a special concern, foundry workers received priority in obtaining medical assistance, which was free for all employees. Vols built a cinema, and invested in a major cultural complex comprising a huge ballroom, a discotheque and a restaurant. All, in effect, were available to everyone who lived in Volna. Beside this complex stood the enterprise's own hostel and hotel, which offered subsidized rooms for single workers, as well as comfortable apartments for visiting guests from the Communist Party. Vols owned blocks of apartments, which were rented to employees at subsidized prices and for which services and repairs were free. During the 1980s, Vols employed about 5600 of Volna's inhabitants, so the enterprise's tentacles reached into virtually every home in the region. So intertwined are the enterprise and the town that it is commonplace to hear phrases like 'Volna is Vols', and 'the factory is our life and home'.

By virtue of its production activities, its ageing technology and its symbolic role in 'socialist development', in many ways the story of Vols is also that of the Czechoslovakia as told by economic historians. Its exports to the communist bloc were successful only at a price, which the central planning procedures and bureaucracy glossed over. Vols was a massive consumer of energy and raw materials which had to be imported, and the lack of central investment in modern technology and the resistance of the planners to real industrial and enterprise restructuring (particularly in the 1960s and 1980s) left Vols in dire straits after the events of 1989.

Unlike the other enterprises, *Agstroj* is located on the outskirts of a large city, which we have called Stroměsto. Since 1952, the enterprise has manufactured agricultural machinery of repute in the CEE region, which is also fairly well known elsewhere. However, its origins lie in other products, and in another era. It was the occupying German forces that first constructed an industrial plant on the present site in 1942 in order to make aeroplane engines to supply the war effort. In 1944, the site was abandoned following massive Anglo-American bombing raids which left only 10 to 15 per cent of the factory's walls standing. The liberating Soviet army returned the factory to the post-war Czechoslovak state in 1946, and the Cyrillic messages that the Red Army left on the walls were ritualistically repainted throughout the communist era. In 1947, the renovated plant began production of textile machinery and various kinds of ball-bearing, which were to become its staple product and contribution to the major economic programme of Stalinist industrialization that followed the communist take-over in 1948. At this stage, the plant was just a numbered site of a much larger enterprise known as Vojenská Stroměstská, which had started manufacturing agricultural machinery in 1945 at one of its other sites.

At the beginning of 1950, the plant took on its own legal status as a *národní podnik*, and was baptized with the bland nondescript name 'Enterprise for Special Engineering', which typified the new kind of state-owned enterprise. In 1952, much of the production of agricultural machinery, sold under the brand name Agstroj, was transferred from Vojenská Stroměstská to the new enterprise. As this activity expanded, the manufacture of textile machines was returned to Vojenská Stroměstská, and, after 1968, the production of the ball-bearings was gradually reduced. The Agstroj site retained only the more specialized engineered items, and more routinized work was transferred to Slovakian sub-plants. In order to increase its autonomy, a new metallurgy plant had been established in 1963, by which time it had become virtually the only supplier of certain kinds of agricultural machinery in Czechoslovakia. The enterprise finally adopted the name Agstroj, so that it could benefit from being directly associated with the reputation of its products. From 1983 to 1989, its domestic commercial activities were handled by Agrov, the leading enterprise in the industry, which was based at Agstroj and organized the activities of the industry's ten or so key players.

The exporting activities of Agstroj were mediated by its foreign trade organization, located in Prague, whose many foreign branches acted as general dealerships and sold its machines to many clients. Agstroj proved to be a great success, its foreign sales spreading across more than eighty countries.

In spite of the innovatory design and technology of its machinery, the vicissitudes of the socialist trading bloc meant that Czechoslovak farmers were only able to buy between 5 and 10 per cent of the enterprise's output, having to make do with lower-quality Polish imports. Poland and East Germany, on the other hand, imported Agstroj products, with a handful going to the Soviet Union. In the 1970s, Agstroj exported 90 per cent of its production, of which 60 to 65 per cent went to non-socialist countries, earning substantial amounts of hard currency for the state. Responding to this success, the central plan supported substantial investment programmes, which included the installation of advanced West German and Italian machinery, and by the early 1980s Agstroj's production capacity had increased substantially. Its exports continued to be oriented to Western markets at a time when there was a national drive to correct the trade and currency imbalances with the non-socialist world, and thereby contributed to the Party's determination to resist dependence on Western financial institutions (see Myant, 1989, pp. 191–3). By 1989, Agstroj had regular markets in forty countries, and approximately 80 per cent of its output was exported. During these last two decades of communism, Agstroj and similar enterprises were strategically crucial to Czechoslovak economic planning.

As Agstroj grew, it developed a number of satellite companies around Stroměsto, and many of its ball-bearing operations were relocated to subsidiary plants in the large heavy industrial areas that grew up in Slovakia; even some of its new lines of agricultural machinery were grudgingly moved away eastwards. These decisions often followed the political logic of 'industrializing' the Slovak republic, and of satisfying the demands of the ruling coalition in the Communist Party, but created resentment within the enterprise's management. Taking all these activities into account, Agstroj was, at its peak, responsible for over 20,000 employees, though employment at the Agstroj site fluctuated around 10,000 to 10,500. Following legislative changes in 1988, Agstroj became a *státní podnik* (state enterprise), with formally more devolved powers and greater independence from the pared down centralized planning structures.

Stroměsto is a large Moravian city with a strong tradition in and reputation for mechanical engineering. It is the location for a number of other very large mechanical engineering enterprises, including Vojenská Stroměstská. Unlike the much smaller towns of Volna and Jesenice (see below), it had a huge central shopping centre, suburban shops and well-developed municipal recreation and entertainment facilities. Agstroj is located on a 120-hectare site some three miles from the centre, in a suburb which is dominated by its physical presence. The enterprise is surrounded by the familiar high-rise blocks of apartments, over 1000 of which it constructed and ran for its own employees. Many of its employees lived in these housing schemes, and walked to work for a six o'clock start along a complex series of criss-crossing walkways. Others would arrive using excellent local bus and tram services, which terminated outside the factory gatehouse. Like the other enterprises, Agstroj took its local social responsibilities seriously, building and maintaining facilities for the provision of a variety of social and welfare services. In addition to its housing, it ran a training college, and had a number of holiday camps and vacation hotels to which its employees had subsidized access, as well as sports facilities and grounds across the city. The enterprise – or rather its trade union – ran a social club for workers, though it was never well-frequented because of the attractions of bars and other entertainments that were part of the large city environment.

Metal-working and engineering have had an important presence in the Jesenice region, coexisting successfully with the more traditional agricultural way of life for more than 150 years. A factory site was established as a new plant in the first flush of communist industrial development in 1948. Named after one of Czechoslovakia's new communist leaders, it belonged to a large national enterprise in Stroměsto, some 80 kilometres away. Its purpose was to manufacture equipment and plant for making cement, bricks and other building materials, which were in turn so crucial for the construction industry in its strategic role to build the foundations for the socialist development of Czechoslovakia. Smaller engineering workshops, some of which dated back to the nineteenth century and the industrial expansion in the early 1900s, and which had been nationalized after the war, were absorbed into the newly created *Jesenické Strojírny* when it was declared a national enterprise in 1951.

Jesenické Strojírny increased in size and influence within its heavy engineering sector, and in 1958 was nominated to act as one of the new intermediary economic associations in the government's early attempts to 'decentralise' the economy (see Chapter 3). Jesenické Strojírny organized three large construction engineering enterprises, which complemented its own production activities. Jesenické Strojírny lost its hierarchical status when the planning structures were refined in 1965, and became one of the production enterprises of a huge, diversified engineering concern based in Prague (VVV), which took all the major commercial, financial and production decisions for its subsidiary. In 1988, Jesenické Strojírny took on the new legal status of a state enterprise, and began to operate with greater independence than at any earlier time.

Since 1948, Jesenické Strojírny had grown by both 'legal acquisition' and internal development, becoming the biggest of the four large national enterprises which dominated the town of Jesenice. By 1989, it employed over 7000 people from a regional population of about 50,000. Its size and its exporting prowess gave it enormous economic power. According to one employee, 'Nothing could happen in the region without Jesenické Strojírny'. Jesenice itself is an old industrial town in Moravia, and has an old castle and a charming though dilapidated town square. The town grew in response to the needs of the engineering and pharmaceutical enterprises that had been located on its periphery. But as the residential areas spread to accommodate the workforce that migrated from local rural areas and further flung regions, the industrial sites were more fully incorporated into Jesenice proper. In the centre, many old nineteenth-century and earlier buildings decayed through lack of attention; the new housing developments, comprising the familiar concrete, high-rise blocks of apartments, likewise deteriorated. The town became heavily polluted, with the large plants belching smoke into the air and emitting effluent into the river that flows through the centre.

Like other national enterprises, Jesenické Strojírny invested heavily in social and welfare facilities, from which the town and its region directly benefited. Jesenické Strojírny supported Jesenice's social activities, owning over 600 apartments and providing hotel and hostel accommodation for employees and visitors, as well as supplying many of Jesenice's important local dignitaries. In order to perform its welfare and non-work services, the management and trade union agreed in their annual collective agreements to make available more than the legal minimum in order to contribute to the enterprise's cultural and social fund. Jesenické Strojírny provided many of the same facilities as Vols and Agstroj for its employees, including a technical training school for apprentices and a commercial education centre. Moreover, it had three very good recreation facilities (hotels and holiday resorts) in the Moravian mountains, and more locally. The enterprise owned an exquisite 700-year-old building in Jesenice, which had been specially bought and restored for use as a social and cultural centre for employees. A particular feature of Jesenické Strojírny's social provision was the excellent sports facilities it financed in Jesenice, and the support of first-class enterprise teams. Managers estimated that up to 15 per cent of the formally allocated social funds were spent on supporting sporting activities and recreation facilities. Jesenické Strojírny contributed to the construction of an Olympic-size swimming pool, a winter stadium, a football stadium and a tennis court complex, at which national tennis competitions were held in the late 1970s.

As participant in or as leader of building consortia from the industry, Jesenické Strojírny manufactured the machinery for large, turnkey investment projects like the building of plant for cement (its main expertise), brick and ceramics. It also supplied one-off equipment like crushing machines and industrial gearboxes, and, like many heavy engineering enterprises, developed its own metallurgy capacity. But its most profitable work has always been the large integrated projects, of which by 1990 it had completed more than 300 worldwide. Exports were distributed to 35 countries, with the overwhelming balance being to socialist countries or to developing countries which enjoyed the patronage of the Soviet Union and its satellite states. Of the large-scale investment projects Jesenické Strojírny completed between 1948 and 1990, 43 per cent were for the domestic markets and 27 per cent were constructed in the socialist countries (12 per cent in the USSR). A further 27 per cent were realized in developing countries, dispersed quite evenly across the Asian, African and South American continents, though with strong representation in India, Iran and Brazil. The vast majority of these deliveries were realized either through trade credits arranged and guaranteed by the state as a policy directive, or through nationally or locally arranged product exchange. Only 2 per cent of the completions were in the Western developed world and resulted in the earning of hard currency. In 1989, fewer than 9 per cent of deliveries, by value, earned hard currency for Jesenické Strojírny; over two-thirds by value of completed production was destined for the home market, and the remainder was exported to countries with non-convertible currencies.

Jesenické Strojírny enjoyed particular success in the USSR, because of the strength of VVV Praha's connections in Moscow. In fact, some 70 per cent of its industrial gearbox production normally went to this region. In 1986, Jesenické Strojírny acquired a nine billion crown share of a prestigious joint investment project (the SOVREP project), which was agreed by CMEA members as part of its 1986 to 1990 Concerted Plan, and for which it acquired a multi-billion crown credit from the State Bank. SOVREP was a huge iron ore extraction development located in a Soviet republic, with a completion date in the early 1990s. The project was thus as certain as it could be, planned by the highest economic organ of the socialist world, with guaranteed payments from the Czechoslovak state. Further, this extraction development contributed to securing access to raw materials into the long term for the Czechoslovak heavy metallurgical, steel and engineering sectors. On the basis of this project, the management of VVV and Jesenické Strojírny invested in the necessary technologies and started production, knowing that they could commit a large proportion of the enterprise's resources to supply and install the machinery, and earn a good return. Before 1989, in one respondent's view, Jesenické Strojírny had an 'image of goodwill, prosperity and security', much of which came from its strong exporting performance.

The service unit that now constitutes the company *Montáže Jesenice* was until 1990 the assembly and maintenance plant (*závod*) of the state enterprise which we have described above as Jesenické Strojírny. It had started as a separate national enterprise in 1953, a specialist in the assembly of ceramics works in Stroměsto, providing its services to, among others, the newly operational Jesenické Strojírny. In 1958, it was amalgamated with Jesenické Strojírny in its new capacity as a leading enterprise, and was later integrated structurally as one of Jesenické Strojírny's functional plants in 1965, when VVV Praha took over the economic management of Jesenické Strojírny.

While its history has not been formally separate from its superordinate structure since 1965, it has always had a rather special independence that has overridden any formalities. This in part derives from its particular activities. The majority of its employees have never lived in Jesenice, because the tasks of assembling cement, ceramic, brick factories and other investment complexes took place on the building sites of clients all over Czechoslovakia, across the socialist bloc and, to a lesser extent, elsewhere, where it was a practical policy to send an enterprise assembly supervisor and hire local workers. The work has always been very skilled as well as hard, with workers having to live away from home, in hostels or dormitories, for various periods of time. These factors created a distinctive worker culture, as the site employees, invariably men, lived a close, cooperative lifestyle that mirrored in many respects the ideal of the socialist worker.

In reality, only the head office of the plant was located in Jesenice, in a building near the centre of the town, some two kilometres from the main site of Jesenické Strojírny. The production programme of the department was directly related to that of Jesenické Strojírny, whose management sent the latest projects to the function's senior management, who would also have their own economic targets for assembly, repair and maintenance work. Before 1989, about 90 per cent of Montáže Jesenice's work derived from the contracts initiated by Jesenické Strojírny. At head office, the business was run very autocratically and bureaucratically, but at each site – or group of sites – the assembly supervisor would manage the work and the workers with a good deal of autonomy. As can be inferred from the description of Jesenické Strojírny's project work, contracts tended to be medium to long term, allowing a high level of security to be built into the function.

Employment in the plant used to be about 1150 workers, of which 850 to 900 were site assembly workers, and the rest were locally employed managers and administrators in Jesenice. The workers enjoyed salaries that reflected their skilled worker status, often exceeding the amount paid to professional employees. Although the higher managers were usually recruited with university engineering qualifications, it was also a pattern for middle managers to spend long periods of time working as assemblers or 'pipe-workers' – perhaps as enterprise policy, maybe because of the relatively high remuneration – before rising to administrative jobs based in Jesenice.

For long periods of its existence, Montáže Jesenice enjoyed relative autonomy in operating its social and welfare provision. At these times, the plant had its own trade union structures, and its own cultural and social fund, and it arranged holidays in its own recreation facilities, one of which was located at a Bulgarian Black Sea resort. Even when its trade union was formally absorbed into that of Jesenické Strojírny, it effectively managed its own social facilities. In principle, the two entities shared their facilities to provide mutual benefits, but most of the site assembly workers preferred to stay at home at holiday time with their families because they spent so much work time away, so they rarely took advantage of the available holiday and recreation facilities.

The economic transition and enterprise behaviour

In the following pages we examine the processes and problems of economic transformation and transition[3] in the now Czech Republic, but this is not another book on the economics of transition (e.g. Köves, 1992; Earle *et al.*, 1993; Frydman *et al.*, 1993; Estrin, 1994a; Gros and Steinherr, 1995; Lavigne, 1995; Svejnar, 1995a). The arguments developed in the following pages are committed to expanding the social science of the economic transition beyond a set of economic outcomes which can be described or analysed in purely aggregate terms. Instead, we theorize economic transformation as social and behavioural processes constituted by motivated economic actors surviving in the complex and ambiguous social reality that is the transitional environment. We wish to ground the transitional process in what has been happening in concrete economic situations which typify, or carry typical features of, the economic transition at large. This is not to diminish the work of transitional economists, whose work highlights major economic features and results of the transition which any social scientist needs to be aware of, and, further, to interpret and understand. The macro-structural findings and arguments of economists inevitably raise a whole raft of theoretical questions, but the kinds of answers offered are necessarily of a similar structural kind. We would argue that the important economic questions are rarely satisfactorily answered in this manner. When economists' work raises issues about overall patterns of corporate governance in former state-owned companies, about transitional levels of unemployment or about the rapid reorientation of foreign trade, it usually begs important questions about, for example, entrepreneurial behaviour, capital accumulation in small, private businesses, lending policies of financial enterprises, the degree to which enterprise managements are becoming more market-oriented, strategically minded, professional and so on. Underlying the structural discourse on the economic transition are critical *behavioural* matters, but neither their theoretical frameworks or models nor the methods of research they typically adopt allow them to move beyond theoretically and empirically contestable inferences. By virtue of economists' professional interests and methodologies, much of the emerging social science of economic transition has had to be based upon logical deduction about economic behaviour at the level of the production unit, or enterprise, rather than upon enterprise level observations and discussions about concrete instances of economic action and process.

Like the macroeconomist, we are interested in the nature of the post-communist economic transition, but we have opted to approach the topic from the bottom up, collecting materials about and from real economic actors who have had to confront and solve concrete problems arising from the wider context of transition. They know, as do we, that the ways in which they respond, successfully or otherwise, to the everyday, micro problems that face them, inescapably, in their own managerial work will shape the micro-economic transition that is their and their enterprise's life. Their decisions and solutions in turn influence the 'behaviour' of their enterprises; which in turn, with the behaviour of other enterprises, aggregates to the behaviour of the pertinent industrial sector or market; which in turn influences economic indicators at a yet more aggregated level. The performance, outcomes and results that constitute the economic transition as observed through the eyes of the macroeconomist are thus the consequences of the motivated actions of many economic actors within concrete economic situations, such as business organizations.

Research that examines the economic transition at the level of organization and management adds in vital ways to the revealing of the whole picture: it locates the apparently fairly abstract phenomenon of the economic transition in a complex nexus of real human motive and conduct. It therefore offers the opportunity to develop a social scientific explanation that postulates economic processes as being socially constructed, rather than the result of objective, impersonal, independent 'variables'. In this book, we aim to develop a theoretical framework that allows these two discourses of objective structure, favoured by economists, and of human agency, advocated by micro-sociologists, to be bridged in some degree. Our approach takes as its central focus the interplay between macro systems and micro behaviour, and it derives from a methodology which places the emphasis on the concrete behaviour of actors in real socio-economic situations, but always locates such behaviour in the wider social, institutional and historical context. We shall briefly introduce both the institutional arguments which form the book's theoretical core and the case study method which is the mainstay of the empirical work.

Developing institutional theory

One of our aims is to make a contribution to social-institutionalist theory by developing a greater conceptual flexibility in relation to two major unresolved tensions in the framework of such analysis. The first tension concerns the relationship between macro-institutional systems of a society and micro-institutionalized practices or conduct. Our proposed emphasis on studying the economic transition through the behaviour of enterprise managers demands a theoretical counterbalance to the institutionalist's preference for investigating social systems at an abstract, sometimes formal, level of analysis, with a focus on structures and normative systems rather than social interactions and practices. There is also a second, perhaps stronger, tension in institutional theory as the search for principles of social persistence has involved the relative neglect of the institutional bases of social change. The circumstances of the Czech post-communist transformation make it a perfect situation for evolving and evaluating possible explanations of processes of fundamental change.

Western research has considered the effects of social change on organization and management, but researchers have tended to have their focus restricted by the normal socio-economic contexts in which they work to alterations in public opinion, legal conditions and similar discontinuities *within* social structures (see Tushman and Romanelli, 1985, p. 205). The post-communist transition, however, provides a setting that is very different in its characteristics, one in which discontinuities are more fundamental, and change is less constrained by institutional frameworks which are themselves not merely destabilized, but even in the process of demolition. The economic transition describes a social process in which a complex set of normative and operating principles, embodied in historical structures, systems and practices, becomes replaced by another alternative, albeit unknown, set. The change from hierarchical economic planning and administration through command directives, to a situation in which the responsibility for economic decision-making lies with local enterprise managers responding to market signals — although the concrete features of this future alternative are disputed — is so radical that it demands a perspective which captures its dramatic, revolution-ary nature. In essence, these structural changes are deeply *institutional*, with implications on a different scale to the structural amendments which are the topic of studies of organizational change in the West. Such a change of societal form is so fundamental in its effects on the macro systems and structures that the everyday experience of social life takes on an entirely different appear-ance. It is thus rightly called trans*form*ation, being a radical change that permeates society both systemically and socially (Clark and Soulsby, 1995).

We propose that the task of understanding the socio-economic transforma-tion of the post-communist period is facilitated by conceptualizing it in terms of institutional change which occurs as simultaneous but reciprocal macro-system and micro-social processes. In taking this approach, certain basic questions need addressing. First, the essential features of the starting-point of the economic transformation (namely, the societal-economic form of Czech state socialism) have to be captured in institutional terms, and the ways in which they were reproduced in stable organizational and managerial patterns at the enterprise level need to be understood. Second, there should be a credible account of what triggered the move from the pre-1989 stable form. Third, the relationships between this prior stable form, the point or trigger of change, and the processes of change which involve the search for a new stable form must be explored. This is the very stuff of transformation, which includes the actual processes of transition themselves — the structure and con-tent of the changes undergone during the move to a new institutional future. We will thus speak of institutional inertia, deinstitutionalization and reinsti-tutionalization as constituent processes of transformation as institutional change. Finally, as implied above, this approach entails the establishment of links between the macro changes in the socio-economic systems and the micro changes of enterprise restructuring and management redefinition, a task that draws attention to both the theoretical and the empirical relation-ships between structures (formal institutions) and social action (institu-tionalized practices).

We thus hope to demonstrate the benefits of institutional analysis for under-standing the post-communist transition at the level of the work organization. The approach focuses analysis on the processes which destabilize a system whose institutionalized features give it a predisposition towards persistence. It directs consideration to the problems of rebuilding an institutional base, when existing and hitherto accepted principles of human conduct no longer provide the baseline clues. It highlights the inherent instabilities and uncertainties of the interim transitional period – what Giddens (1984, p. 244) calls the 'process of institutional transmutation' – between the deposing of one set of principles and the introduction and establishment, or routinizing acceptance, of the new, radically different set.

Terminological caveats

Before we go any further, it is necessary to clarify several terms, whose unreflective use may be seen to signify certain unintended theoretical and conceptual meanings. So far, we have spoken freely of economic *transition* and *transformation*, which some social scientists have taken to indicate rather different processes. Whitley (1995) and Whitley *et al.* (1995) have expressed a preference for the terminology of transformation, and reject the term 'transition' because of the simplistic theoretical notions and implicit ideological baggage which comes with it. In short, the argument is that the concept of transition has been claimed by uncritical economists to connote a presumed move between 'simple dichotomies of highly general and abstract socioeconomic forms' (Whitley, 1995, p. 12) – from the command economy towards a Western-style market economy – and that the use of the term necessarily has such an ideological halo effect. On the other hand, the notion of transformation suggests nothing about the destination of the process of socioeconomic change, and emphasizes the variety and complexity of the process.

While the concept of transition may have been unjustly acquired by liberal economists, it is difficult to see why it necessarily implies any greater sense of predestination than, say, the idea of transformation. While we feel more comfortable with the latter because it is less contaminated, the concept of transition has become so much part of the language of post-communism that it is a little late in the day to ban it. To make our position clear, unlike many economists' discussion of transition, we will not use it to imply a form of 'predestination' or any presumption that the future state of post-communism is a certain mode of market capitalism. On the contrary, our arguments will underscore the uncertainty and ambiguity of the transition/transformation process, suggesting that future Czech social and economic structures are developing towards a state unplanned by the ardent politicians and economists who have tried to direct it.

We have consciously adopted, and adhered throughout to, the term 'post-communism' to refer to the transitional state of the Czech Republic, and this reinforces our belief that it is too early to borrow or apply more conventional descriptors to the economic system or to the motives of people in it. Indeed, we take this position despite the enthusiastic urging of some of our Czech colleagues to apply the terminology of market economics in our discussion of organizational and management changes.[4] The arguments presented in Part Three, which point to the difference between the mastery of market-economic management rhetoric and its successful application in practice, support the view that the reality of the transition economy is still unfolding, and its final shape and nature remain debatable.

The research process

The research project has systematically examined organizational and managerial behaviour by looking in detail at the changes that have taken place in four enterprises since the demise of state socialism in 1989. Each enterprise entered the post-communist era with distinctive legacies drawn from its command-economic experiences, and has attempted, as organization, management and employees, to cope with the ambiguities and conflicts of the early transition period. This book tells the stories of the four industrial enterprises as filtered through selected theoretical and methodological lenses. Their histories are compiled from the recollections, perceptions, explanations, justifications and criticisms of managers and other employees, as well as from various internal and external documents. The stories are told over a historical time-scale and within wider structural contexts which are relevant to understanding the transformation process over the critical early years of the socio-economic transition, which we have defined as 1990 to 1995. Within this criterion of 'relevance', we include the state socialist inheritance of these enterprises, which is treated in three senses as a *critical resource* in accounting for the post-communist years. First, the sedimentation of history in the systems, structures and traditions of the enterprises ensured a continuing representation and role of the past in the early 1990s. Second, historical practices which had been consolidated in the repertoire of bona fide management have since been available to managers in order to cope with transitional problems. Third, the ingrained, recursive nature of socio-economic conduct over many years has ensured that state socialist management has remained integral to the social self, or the personal identity, of the individual manager, and has continued to be expressed and externalized into the world of post-1989 work.

Collection of material commenced in the spring of 1992, with the main ten-day field visit to Vols. Each of the other three enterprises was visited for a similar period of time: Montáže Jesenice in September 1992, Jesenické Strojírny in November 1993 and Agstroj in September 1994. Each enterprise has been regularly revisited for one-day meetings with senior managers in order to keep abreast of changes: Vols in September 1992, November 1993, September 1995 and February 1996; Montáže Jesenice in September 1993, September 1995 and May 1996; we spoke on a number of occasions to contacts from Jesenické Strojírny in 1994, and revisited the enterprise in September 1995 and September 1996; Agstroj was revisited in September 1995. The period of cooperation with each enterprise has differed, as has the degree of access achieved in each, so as a result of normal research experiences both the quantity and the quality of materials have varied between them.

However, such differences have been taken into consideration in the process of analysis and interpretation throughout the book. Our research visits were underpinned by a comprehensive research protocol document, in which we outlined our aims, our methods and the problems we foresaw (see Yin, 1989). We kept field notes about the physical, emotional and intellectual environments of the research work.

We adopted a case study approach with the intention of constructing a rich descriptive picture of each enterprise, but sought comparability by applying the same methods and seeking the same sorts of information. During our field visits and revisits we always accumulated as much enterprise documentation as we could, in both Czech and English where the latter was available. But such materials were in themselves not appropriate to our main aim, which was to build up a picture of actual management attitudes, behaviour and practices, both before and after 1989. Official in-company documents have always been seen as a source of 'objective' information in organizational research, but the reliability of such information in Czech enterprises, particularly before the revolution and during the early years of the transition, was to say the least suspect. Interviewing, our chief research method, offered some compensation for the poor reliability of secondary information, but also allowed us to gain access to the sorts of materials which could support or challenge the main arguments we were developing, i.e. materials recording managers' own perceptions of the past and the present, and how their own conduct related to the changing economic institutional structures.

For each research visit or revisit we worked closely with two colleagues from our partner university in Brno. In general, these colleagues were native Czechs with a very strong grasp of English language and idiom. They were business or economics students or junior lecturers who spoke good English, rather than language students, a matter which was of great importance for translating, explaining and interpreting the terminology of management and of organization. We each worked with one Czech colleague over a ten-day period, and met each evening to discuss, explore and record on computer the interviews of the day. On the four cases, we have worked with six colleagues, all of whom have been indispensable interpreters of language and decoders of cultural nuance.

We chose our interviewees according to a certain pattern; the aim was to interview as many senior managers or directors as was feasible, given our position as guests and their work schedules, which meant that some were away from the factory on business. Using an organization chart, we also selected for interview a sample of second level, or department, managers, so that the main enterprise functions of accounting and finance, personnel, commercial (sales and marketing), production and technical were represented. Finally, we requested interviews, on a token basis, with some representative of the shop floor and/or the trade union. Table 1.2 outlines the eventual sample. The numbers in the table illustrate the point made earlier about differential access – Agstroj was the most difficult enterprise to penetrate.

Table 1.2 The management sample

	Vols	MJ	JS	Agstroj	Totals
General directors	0	1	0	0	1
Directors	6	5	3	3	17
Department heads	8	9	11	7	35
Other employees	2	3	3	1	9
Total managers	14	15	14	10	53
Total interviewed	16	18	17	11	62

We interviewed each respondent for approximately two hours, usually in his or, very occasionally, her office. The process was designed to maximize the confidence the respondents had in us. We were always introduced as British academics, working in association with a Czech university which most of them knew. We guaranteed anonymity, took written notes rather than tape-recorded and smiled as often as possible! We always started an interview by asking interviewees to speak about themselves and showing impromptu interest in their personal stories, before moving chronologically through their pre-1989 experiences, and then changes in the organization and their work. Some managers were quite anxious about being interviewed, but most settled down during the session. Some managers demonstrated a remarkable ability to find reasons to avoid us, but most were very keen to put their version of reality on record. Once in the interview, only one or two respondents actually declined to answer certain questions, and another few hid behind the facade of the engineer, responding in a purely technical way about their work.

We had agreed that the identities of interviewees and enterprises would be anonymized because of the sensitivity of some of the questions and much of the information, and the book has been written with this in mind. We have chosen names that bear no resemblance to those of the actual enterprises, and any similarity to other existing Czech enterprises is purely accidental.[5] We have presented some of the information in such ways as to preserve this promise of confidentiality at the expense of complete accuracy, but where we have done so it does not affect the nature of the argument. This anonymity extends also to names and information about the towns and communities.

Although we are heavily dependent on personal accounts, what we present in the book is neither a historical narrative nor a pure description of events and changes as seen through the eyes of the respondents. Our methodology has allowed us to create a set of qualitative materials which have shown themselves to be highly flexible in usability and rich in texture, and which we have organized for theoretical purposes – to develop a mode of explanation of management and organizational conduct in which the managers themselves have a strong voice. While the managers do not have the only voice, their words, sentiments and rationalities have been the main resource at our disposal in the search for a coherent theoretical interpretation. The empirical base of the research is reported in Chapters 4, 7, 8 and 9, where the reader will be fully exposed to the words and views of the managers in the sample.

Our approach has raised a number of interesting methodological issues that we cannot address in a book of this nature, especially concerning the validity or accuracy of the interviewing materials that pass through the string of language 'interpretations' – from interviewer to translator to interviewee to translator to interviewer – before they reach their final version as statements recorded on a computer. Our main checks for validity and reliability have entailed intense discussion with translators, double or triple checking of responses where they conflict with previous or following statements and corroboration of 'facts' or opinions across interviews. Of course, as in any such research, there remain quandaries and irreconcilable contradictions, but we feel confident that these are mostly in the responses themselves, rather than in our interpretation of them. Throughout the book, we have drawn liberally upon the final records of our interviews for quotes to support our arguments. Unlike working with direct utterances from English-speaking respondents, such quotes can only be estimates of what was actually said, organized in a way to convey the meaning (which we believed was) actually intended. The methodological implications and complications of our approach merit further discussion in a more appropriate forum.

Moving on

These four former state-owned enterprises and the sixty-two interviewees provide us with the empirical context and resources to explore the nature of the economic transition from the level of organization and management. The remainder of the book is devoted to such an exploration, and is divided into three distinct parts. Part One, of which this chapter is the first half, is concerned with setting the general contexts of the discussion. In this chapter, we have outlined the major reference points and objectives of the book. In Chapter 2, we address the conceptual ideas and theoretical propositions that have served to order our thinking about the materials, problems and ambiguities raised by our fieldwork experiences. We examine the social-institutional approach which highlights the need to understand structural features of society as an ongoing process of social reproduction, in which the achievement of normative legitimacy is a central concern. In the chapter, we locate the possible sources of societal breakdown and institutional change in the relationship between the macro-world of institutional structures and the micro-world of human agency, and develop a conceptual and theoretical vocabulary that provides a framework for analysing and interpreting the socio-economic transition and organizational transformation.

Equipped with these conceptual tools, we approach the main body of the book. As we have explained above, the role of historical legacy – the continuing impact of social norms and institutionalized practices – is central to the understanding of the post-communist transition, so in Part Two we consider the nature of the state socialist world of organization and management. Chapter 3 outlines the formal institutional features of the Czechoslovak command economy, and places them within a historical perspective which accounts for the extreme hierarchical form of state socialism that prevailed in the late 1980s. Chapter 4 complements this examination of the formal institutional structures of Czechoslovak state socialism by investigating the ways in which state-owned enterprises were managed during this period. We analyse management values, styles and practices by drawing on the reported experiences of our respondents, and relating them to the economic and social problems faced by enterprise managers in their everyday work and social lives. In Chapter 5, the findings of Part Two are summarized, analysed and interpreted using the social-institutional theory developed in Part One. We conclude this part of the book by summarizing the nature and extent of the socio-economic transformation necessitated by the fall of the communist state.

Part Three continues this analysis into the post-1989 period, applying a similar logic to Part Two. In Chapter 6 the aim is to delineate the main ways in which the formal institutional structures have changed in the retreat from the command economy and in the pursuit of integration into the global market economy. The institutional changes are surveyed from the particular stance of understanding the contemporary context in which the former state socialist enterprises and managements have had to approach the issues of organizational, professional and personal survival. In Chapters 7, 8 and 9, we then focus in detail on the questions of management and organizational change as they have been experienced in the four case enterprises. We discuss the enterprise transformation during the early 1990s in institutionalist terms, and argue that management's search for post-communist legitimacy has been one of the driving motivational forces shaping the direction of the economic transition at the micro level.

Notes

1 There are several excellent histories of modern Czechoslovakia and the Czech Republic which are readily available. The following brief account draws on only some of them.
2 Teichová (1988, p. 84) suggests that during the war years the Czech lands contributed as much as 12 per cent of the industrial production of the enlarged German Reich.
3 We take up the question of the relationship between 'transition' and 'transformation' below.

4 More specifically, one of our Czech colleagues strongly suggested that we entitle Part Three 'The Emergence of Market-economic Management'. We feel that our findings are not compatible with, from his viewpoint, such an 'optimistic' title.

5 Over the period of research since we have had articles accepted for publication, we have become aware of one or two Czech enterprises with names very similar to the ones we had chosen more or less randomly. We felt it best to adhere to the names that have appeared in journals for the sake of consistency, and we apologize to managers of any enterprises which may in error be linked to our cases.

2 Institutions, organizations and management

Over time, societies and their constituent structures develop a certain predisposition towards relative stability, partly through characteristics of the structures themselves which are conducive to coherence and inertia, and partly as a result of the humanly motivated behaviours that serve, often unintendedly, to reinforce and reproduce these structures. Changes in stabilized, structured societies which take place within relatively predictable and routinized environments may be described as evolutionary movements, since they occur on a gradual, incrementalist scale which sustains societal forms within the parameters of certain organizing principles. The changes in CEE state socialist societies in 1989 were remarkable because they resulted in a rapid and dramatic collapse of structures, systems, rules and principles that had made human behaviour and social life rational and understandable for over forty years, leaving a vacuum of meaning and motivation. With the benefit of hindsight, it is possible to see historical processes for ten or twenty years inevitably pointing to the demise of state socialism, and there were, across the region, different degrees of suddenness in the changes and of institutional preparedness for them. In Czechoslovakia at least, the changes were experienced largely as an unpredicted surprise, breaking with the long period of relative stability since the Warsaw Pact invasion of 1968.

In this chapter, we expand our proposition that important aspects and elements of the socio-economic transformation in the Czech Republic can be understood by using the reasoning and adapting the concepts of an institutional approach. Three sets of issues are at the heart of our analysis of the post-communist Czech transformation: the processes of institutional order and change; the relationship between social structures and human agency in the reproduction and transformation of institutional structures; and the problems of legitimacy and legitimation, which we argue are of special significance in the Czechoslovak case. This chapter focuses specifically on the development of the institutional framework to cope with these themes. It starts by considering the theoretical logic of the conventional institutionalist approach, defining the key characteristics of the concept of institution and the processes of institutionalization, and examining the grounds for institutional stability, by considering questions of structural coherence and social support. We then locate the empirical focuses of the book – organization and management – within this theoretical framework, conceiving them as vital features of the institutional landscape of economic systems. We end the substantive discussion in the chapter by directing attention to the main theoretical theme of institutional change. We explore sources of instability and disruption within an institutionalized system and develop an understanding of the general processes of institutional change that can help us to analyse the post-communist transformation in the Czech Republic.

Underlying the arguments in this chapter is the general proposition that social phenomena such as organization and management can only be understood in relation to the wider contextual influences that surround them. Further, these influences do not just refer to the technical or economic factors which are the normal topic of investigation in orthodox systems approaches to microeconomic or organization theory (e.g. contingency theory). They also include socio-cultural processes which, by defining the prevailing nature of rationality, endow technical-economic factors with a normative force that renders them significant elements in an organization's environment. In brief, the institutional theorist argues that this normative force originates from the fact that societies are *institutionalized contexts*, so the explanation of the processes of economic organization and change must start from an understanding of the nature of institutions and the ways in which institutionalization influences concrete economic structures and activities.

Economists, structures and action

Transition economists have adopted a rather different perspective on the transformation process. The failure of the centrally planned economies and the rapid dismantlement of the structures which represented them have been portrayed by economists, from both the West and CEE, as heralding the emergence of new market economies. Western economists anticipated the need to fill the institutional space vacated by the end of the command economy with market-economic structures. They rushed to offer and proselytize policy analyses of the transition process that were required to move to a Western-type capitalist system, which was assumed to be the natural goal of post-communism. State socialism tended to fit the description of the inefficient hierarchy of economic planning mechanisms, integrated by the exercise of centralized authority; while capitalism was portrayed in stereotypical fashion as being constructed through free, decentralized economic relations governed by the allocative rationality of prices. It was an inevitable inference for conventional economists to conceive of the process of economic transition as a movement from one ideal type of economic structure ('hierarchy') to another ('market'), and much normative economic analysis has used this conceptual short-hand as the basis of a model for analysing, planning and evaluating the transformation (e.g. Hare, 1991; Clague, 1992; Murrell, 1992; Walters, 1992; Estrin, 1994b).

The normative economics of transition have therefore been directed towards the identification of the key market-economic institutions that need to be implemented, and debate about the efficient sequence in which they should be introduced. Authors working in such a tradition often show a casual awareness of the difficulties of imposing new, institutional structures on social situations with an ongoing history and on real social actors at the point of economic activity, but these problems cannot be seriously entertained within the theoretical framework employed. The predisposition of policy economists to adopt macro perspectives on economic systems or history has led to the treatment of the actual behaviour of economic agents such as managers or workers as residual – explaining by default or by fiat the micro details of the macroeconomic 'data'. Thus, in the Czech Republic, the continuing low rate of national unemployment has been commented upon with interest, but, without the examination of actual decision-making behaviour of managers at enterprise level, economists have resorted to guesses at generalized motives that can be attributed to 'enterprises'. In fact, unemployment, like inflation, productivity, profit or any other macroeconomic phenomenon, is the social accomplishment of social actors, often powerful ones, within the social system, whose motives may be varied, but are invariably considerably more complex than some generalized search for, say, utility maximization.

In this book, organizing and managing are treated as social processes which are pre-eminently the accomplishments (intentional or otherwise) of motivated social actors, and these are seen as the building blocks of the structures and performances of the economic system. Enterprises and their managers behave within and are inevitably influenced by the structured context of economic systems and history, but this is itself shaped by the decisions taken at enterprise level. Put more generally,

> there is no such entity as a distinctive type of 'structural explanation' in the social sciences: all explanations will involve at least implicit reference both to the purposive reasoning behaviour of agents and to its intersection with constraining and enabling features of the social and natural contexts of that behaviour . . . The only moving objects in human social relations are individual agents who employ resources to make things happen, intentionally or otherwise.
>
> (Giddens, 1984, pp. 179, 181)

If we accept that the most startling characteristic of the post-communist socio-economic journey which begun in late 1989 is the comprehensive *formal-institutional* collapse and the subsequent incipient reconstruction of society, both as economic system and as socio-cultural life-world, it is almost trivial to treat the development of new economic processes and behavioural patterns as an exercise in macroeconomic and microeconomic planning – the application of a kind of 'cookbook capitalism' (Stark, 1992, p. 18). The story must involve both larger questions of the general socio-historical changes in the countries in question, for it is such matters that situate the processes of economic transition, and more micro issues about how real social actors at the level of economic enterprises (and households and such units) relate to the processes of collapse and reconstruction. It is our contention that these questions can be most adequately understood within a framework which emphasizes the centrality of social institutions and institutional change.

Institutions, institutionalized forms and institutionalized practices

Institutions refer to patterns of behaviour or social entities which are imbued within the society in question with social value beyond the purely technical benefits of their consequences or purposes (see Selznick, 1949), and thus link generally culturally accepted values with the specific social actions that take place in any one of many concrete social situations. Berger and Luckmann (1971) demonstrate that institutions originate in concrete social encounters, but only derive their enduring force and significance by developing an 'existence' independent of ephemeral social interaction. They locate the source of social institutions in the habitualization of interaction patterns between concrete individual social actors who develop in their own social exchanges mutual expectations about future meetings. Such habitualization is an incipient feature of institutionalization, which occurs when behavioural patterns and their normative rationales extend across particular social actors and social situations. In short, an institution (or institutionalized pattern) allows habitualized social norms to be desituated and depersonalized, carrying their influence across time and space and urging certain types of social actor to engage in certain types of social action, without having to (re-)invent a meaning and motivation for their behaviour (Berger and Luckmann, 1971, p. 72).

In this formulation, the most evident features of institutions are their 'historicity' and 'attributed objectivity'. Historicity refers to the apparently irrefutable quality of stretching the past into the future through the present, i.e. having an ongoing history. As Giddens (1984, p. 24) claims, 'Institutions by definition are the most enduring features of social life'. But this temporal extension implicit in institutions has important consequences for the social characteristics of the world as experienced by people who share the concrete time and space of everyday social life: 'With the acquisition of historicity, these formations also acquire another crucial quality . . . this quality is objectivity' (Berger and Luckmann, 1971, p. 76). In other words, institutions are the accumulated, sedimented consequences of past social interactions, which are habitualized, desituated, routinized and objectified as part of the shared social world. They take on an existence separate from their concrete historical origins, and in their ideal form are presented to members of a social community as external objects to which they respond as part of their natural, unreflective attitude to the world (see Schutz, 1966). As an external entity, the pattern can be passed on as a 'natural', given part of objective, social reality, possessing recursive, self-perpetuating qualities.

Institutions (or institutional processes) can be understood as operating as behavioural definitions, which may take the form of either 'cultural accounts' or 'cultural rules'. Such definitions specify the typical and necessary ways of acting (or doing), and the types of actor (or ways of being), indicating the characteristics of what sort of person should do the doing (Berger and Luckmann, 1971; Scott, 1994a). Institutions always have a shared history, of which they are themselves the products, and always imply social control by virtue of their very existence. This distinction concentrates attention on what many theorists perceive as the core of the study of institutions: 'the essence of an institutional perspective resides in focusing on the cognitive and normative frameworks that provide meaning and stability to social life' (Scott, 1994b, p. 81). In other words, institutions are enduring, enabling structures which function as meta-rules, or rules of the game (North, 1990, p. 4), and provide the means and facilities for members of society to construct a sense of social order, both individually in terms of their life-career and collectively in terms of shared meaning (Berger and Luckmann, 1971, p. 110). Giddens (1979; 1984) similarly sees institutions as structures of possibility, rules and resources that can be drawn on by social actors to explain and justify social reality, or to make things happen in it.

As 'cultural accounts', the cognitive aspects of institutions are highlighted. In this respect, institutions offer members of a society 'descriptions of reality, explanations of what is and what is not, what can be and what cannot. They are accounts of how the social world works' (Meyer *et al.*, 1994, p. 24). Institutions are by their very existence invisible explanations of the mechanics of social reality, but also extend cultural resources to members of society, allowing them to assemble socially acceptable accounts which display qualities of plausibility, recognition and authority. In this way, institutions have cognitive elements which provide a basic framework of knowledge and belief about how some particular sphere of the social world operates, defining the existing real world or ruling alternative realities out of existence.

The second, and complementary, aspect of institutions is as 'cultural rules', which embody normative principles and social values, and ascribe to social entities and social action a sense of justification or rightness. The implication is not only that institutions prescribe and legitimate social actions in concrete social situations, but also that they define 'wrong' or deviant behaviour, and often the sanctions that are necessarily and routinely applied to those who do not behave appropriately, or who are not the right people to conduct the action.

As meta-rules, principles, values, norms, justifications and explanations, institutions develop a longevity, durability and perceived objectivity in time and space. Institutions not only inform and prescribe the motivations and practices of human agents across the wide range of concrete social situations, but also, as integrated 'clusters', delineate the boundaries and essential principles of existing societies (Giddens, 1984, p. 164). As abstract rules and accounts, they 'exist' in the minds of individuals who share experiences in social groups and communities. However, from a sociological viewpoint, institutions can be more clearly evidenced in the ways in which they are expressed in modern industrial society.

Institutions find expression in society through social constructions, such as events, structures, organizations, regulatory systems, procedures, artefacts and patterns of behaviour, to the extent that they convey the cultural rules and accounts into social processes and acts (compare Friedland and Alford, 1991, p. 249; Jepperson, 1991, pp. 150–1; Scott, 1994a, pp. 68ff). There are two general ways in which institutions are explicitly expressed and made visible in socio-economic life. First, they take the familiar form as formal structures, recognized in social entities such as organizations, formal regulatory systems and procedures, and codified laws; we shall refer to such expressions as *institutionalized forms*, but also use the more common, but looser term, *formal institutions*. Second, institutional rules are expressed in social conduct as processes of practical action, which we shall call *institutionalized practices*, though it is important to understand that such practices are at the same time *institutionalizing*. These two forms of institutional expression and their contingent interrelationship are central to comprehending the dynamics of social institutions as both persistence and transformation. In this conceptualization of a social institution, the abstract cultural level of cognitive and normative rule is connected with its concrete expressions at both the formal, structural level of organization and procedure, and the interactive processual level of everyday social practices.

In modern industrialized societies, the ways in which institutions are expressed, especially in the economic sphere, have been deeply affected by the rationalization of society and culture. Rationalization has been a continuing theme in the sociological literature since Weber's classical works (e.g. Weber, 1964), and is vital to the modern institutionalist perspective on organizations, as evidenced in Meyer and Rowan's (1991) seminal article. Institutionalist writers have shown how the process of rationalization has influenced the nature of modern organization and management. At the level of cultural rules and accounts, for example, industrial societies have become predisposed to accepting explanations and justifications that abide by the dominant 'myth' of formal rationality, and such abstract cognitive and normative principles of behaviour have found their normal expression in the formal structures, rules and procedures which underlie the logic of organization and management. To the extent that everyday social practices are institutionalized, they too express, reproduce and reinforce the cultural principles and formalized structures of the prevailing instrumental rationality. This premium on the institutional rules of technical efficiency and formal rationality permeates social life not only to explain the nature of, for example, appropriate economic action, but also to provide normative value and sanction to such behaviour. Thus, the formal institutional structures and concrete institutionalized practices of economic life do not just *exist* in such a rational form, it is *right* that they exist like this. Where formal and social institutional expressions do not conform to such a rational form, they may be considered as deviant or inappropriate, and further may be ruled as illegitimate or illegal – that is, without a right to exist. This ultimately leads to the strain that institutional theorists call 'institutional isomorphism' (e.g. DiMaggio and Powell, 1991) – that is, the tendency for certain forms and practices to be replicated within and across social and economic sectors.

In this predominantly structural view, institutions exist as 'external social constraints' (structures, procedures, rules, laws) which influence and channel human action and which present themselves as the technically efficient and rational way of achieving social performances (see, for example, Friedland and Alford, 1991, p. 232). In particular, it offers a credible account of the structural-normative impact of institutional environments on the social patterning of, for example, organization and management. The copying of institutional norms across organizations, industries and sectors constitutes one important explanation of the essential stability of societies, as degrees of homogeneity emerge over time (see later).

But this structural-institutional view points to another explanation of institutional order and stability, by identifying the tendency towards coherence within an institutional system. In any society, institutions do not exist as isolated social patterns, but as part of a relatively coherent clustering (Giddens, 1984, p. 164) of institutions. As Jepperson argues, 'A given institution is less likely to be vulnerable to intervention if it is more embedded in a framework of institutions' (Jepperson, 1991, p. 151). This embedded, interlocking quality is enhanced structurally to the extent that the clustering has a common history, that any institution is closer to the traditional, organizing principles and cultural accounts of the whole framework and that these central rules and accounts are drawn from 'socially exogenous (transcendental) moral authority or presumed laws of nature', i.e. to principles that cannot be challenged in terms of social pragmatics (Jepperson, 1991, pp. 151–2; compare Berger and Luckmann, 1971, pp. 113ff). The persistence of institutions can be attributed to their 'multiple sources of support' (Scott, 1994a, p. 67), each of which is by itself capable of explaining a large part of that persistence. Borrowing from D'Andrade (1984, p. 98), Scott (1994a, p. 67) concludes that institutional stability results from the 'over-determined' quality of institutional systems.

This structural picture of a stable, highly institutionalized system is one that prevails within mainstream institutional theory, whose main contribution has been accounting for 'stable, repetitive and enduring activities' (Oliver, 1992, p. 563). It is clear, however, that this offers more of a sketched caricature than a detailed oil painting of the institutional landscape. To gain a richer picture, we need also to unlock further two interrelated sets of institutional issues: the first concerns the *social* basis of institutional order, or the social construction of institutions; the second involves understanding the essential precariousness of institutions and the ways in which they change. We now turn to these tasks.

Legitimation, social support and institutional reproduction

To complement the dominant thread of structuralism present in the institutionalist theory of organizations, we advocate the formulation of ideas which emphasize the role of individuals and social groups in the construction of social institutions. From this *social*-institutional perspective, an institution is a social process rather than a social entity, and it exists only in so far as it continues to be socially reproduced, and, to a greater or lesser degree, legitimated in everyday conduct (Jepperson, 1991, p. 158). As we have already seen above, institutions are in some way experienced by members of society in everyday concrete situations, and therefore find expression *through members' interpretations* in the latters' daily social practices. This mode of institutional expression adds to the formal-structural expression mentioned above by seeing institutions and institutional order as the outcome of humanly meaningful action (see Zucker, 1991).

We can identify four different views of how institutional order may be reproduced through the actions of concrete social actors (viz. individuals and social groups), and each may be related to a central process of social support. At the heart of the structural-institutionalist approach are the assumed processes of *passive* support through mundane reproduction and *normative* support through the positive attribution of social legitimacy. Other institutionalists, particularly those who write within an industrial relations tradition, have focused on how, through their incorporation within the formal-institutional process, organized interests develop a *negotiated* support. Finally, often seen as a last resort when legitimation processes fail, there is *coerced* support through forced compliance. In each case we use the term 'support' to refer primarily to the consequence of these patterns of social response – namely, continued participation in the institutional order which is thereby effectively reproduced – rather than to a necessary state of voluntary or positive consent. We first turn to the question of legitimation, which underpins the notion of institutional stability.

The long-term sustainability of an institutional pattern depends upon processes whereby members of society come to accept it as not only necessary, but also right: that is, a general process of legitimation. Indeed, as we shall argue later, legitimation, or relegitimation, becomes an even more crucial issue during institutional change. As we have seen, institutions are constituted through two component processes: explanation, whereby a social object (institution, social structure, type of person) is rendered objectively available to, or cognitively valid for, members of society; and justification, which makes the social object subjectively plausible, by integrating the social object into the actor's own meaningful world and thereby 'dignifying' any social actions that an actor must subsequently perform (Berger and Luckmann, 1971, p. 111; Scott, 1991, p. 169). As a result, one member of society can offer any other member a sensible account of what he or she has done, and how he or she has done it, which in turn reflexively gives the institutional pattern in question a degree of social support that contributes to its own accountability.

The general process of legitimation mediates the reciprocal relationships between the institution, its institutionalized form and the social practices of human agents which enact its behavioural implications. There are two sides to this process. *Legitimacy acquisition* refers to those processes whereby institutions (or institutionalized patterns), by their existence or through active strategies, persuade social actors of their subjective meaningfulness and plausibility. *Legitimacy attribution* is the reciprocation of acquisition, occurring when social actors concede the existential influence and/or normative rightness of institutions. These processes of legitimation have direct implications for processes of social support which sustain institutions.

Looking at the first view of social support, the reproduction of institutions may be achieved through passive, unthinking, taken-for-granted processes of acceptance. It is axiomatic in much institutionalist theory that institutions are at their strongest and most enduring when they are accepted as part of the natural order of things, and are unquestioningly reproduced in the institutionalized practices that are enacted in everyday social life. The concept of an institution has been defined as a pattern or process that has a 'rule-like status in social thought and action' (Meyer and Rowan, 1991, p. 42), and is routinely and 'chronically reproduced' (Jepperson, 1991, p. 145) because it has a 'natural' and unchallengeable appearance. When the social accomplishments of social actors in their mundane worldly activities reflect the objectively and historically given cognitive and normative principles of an institution and follow the precepts laid down in the organized rules and procedures structured into a formal institution, these social practices are both institutionalized and institutionalizing. In other words, the social action flows from the social institution and its formal expressions, and flows back into them, reproducing them anew, with little or no reflection. An institution retains its taken-for-grantedness as the objectified product of social interactions as long as its inherent recursiveness, and thus precariousness, goes consciously unrecognized.

To the extent that the relationship between institutionalized forms and institutionalized practices is mutually reinforcing, the underlying cultural rules and accounts that constitute the institution at a level of social meaningfulness will be reproduced, and continue in a state of objective and historical immunity. This social-structural recursiveness, wherein social institutions are in their essence self-explaining and self-justifying, offers a major processual explanation of the *institutional inertia* that provides for the essential stability of societies (see, for example, Meyer *et al.*, 1994, p. 10), and leads to a high degree of institutionalization. Mann's (1970, p. 425) conceptualization of 'pragmatic acceptance', whereby people simply cannot see an alternative to what they are doing, is a related idea, since stability is born from what Marx (cited in Abercrombie *et al.*, 1980, p. 166) dubbed the 'dull compulsion of economic relations' (see also Burawoy, 1985).

Moving to the second view, the relationship between legitimation and institutional order can also be explored in terms of normative support. Legitimation acquisition can be usefully seen as active, thoughtful, artful or calculated attempts by an institution's representatives to control or manipulate its meaningfulness; and the reciprocal process of legitimacy attribution then refers to ways in which social actors positively consent in their social practices to the plausibility and meaningfulness of the institution in question. Legitimation here refers to conscious, knowledgeable processes (see Habermas, 1976; Giddens, 1984) associated with justificatory claims to normative status. Normative support is achieved through the active processes of attributing a positive (moral) value to the institutions in question. In social action, legitimation works both as a *formal* process, in which institutional agents claim their right to act from the institutionalized forms that provide their legal and structural context; and as a *social* process, whereby institutional agents are conceded their legitimacy 'from below', from the social actors whose lives are affected by the agent-in-question's conduct. Managers, for example, can enjoy various combinations and degrees of formal and social legitimacy, and their ability to get things done will depend on whether they have acquired both kinds of legitimacy to a sufficient extent. From this perspective, legitimation secures normative consent and therefore connects institutions, institutionalized forms and institutionalized practices, and mediates between the social world as a structural system and as an everyday social accomplishment (Habermas, 1976, pp. 45ff; compare Giddens, 1979, pp. 76ff).

The third view, based on negotiated support, also connects legitimation to the processes of institutional reproduction, this time by encouraging social actors to participate in the institutions themselves. By negotiating and bargaining over contested issues in the political process, social actors (both individuals and groups) who hold different stakes and interests in the status quo reach compromise solutions which serve to perpetuate the (evolving) institutional order. Corporatist and neo-corporatist approaches may be taken to typify this view, portraying an institutional process whereby organized interest groups (such as trade unions and employers' associations) participate in macro-level formal institutions and share in the defining of institutions with the state (e.g. Crouch, 1979; Crouch and Dore, 1990; Fulcher, 1991). However, the negotiated basis of institutional order may take a more social-political form than that offered by corporatists[1] – indeed, such a view of legitimation and institutions is at the centre of the framework that is developed here. This view is already implicit in the discussion of the legitimacy acquisition behaviour of institutional agents, whose job is to devise and pursue *strategies* of legitimation, with the intention of confirming, revising or redefining existing institutions in order to reinforce or reclaim their social acceptability. In fact, the contestation of institutions is an essential conse-quence of considering the role of concrete social actors in reproducing a social order, and leads to an empirical project of identifying the motives and interests of social actors that result from their relationship to societal processes (see Lukes, 1974; Femia, 1975). It is necessary to evaluate institutional order as the outcome of negotiated support from this, rather than the more formal corporatist, perspective.

In some respects, the very existence of institutions implies a coercive, or potentially coercive, power, since it defines out of the range of possibility any real choices for social agents who are routinely subjected to them. However, the fourth view of institutional order, based on a concept of coerced support, is usually applied to those situations – often last resort ones in modern indus-trial societies – when the other processes of acceptance, consent and compro-mise fail to produce sufficient legitimacy and compliance for institutional continuity. The history of state socialist Czechoslovakia, and of the whole CEE region, is replete with examples of when appeals to legitimacy and order had to be reinforced with mechanisms of state repression. The underly-ing threat of coercion, whether internally or externally imposed, is in many ways the ultimate guarantor of institutional order in conditions when its social legitimacy is seriously questioned and opposed.

The arguments in this book recognize the importance of these different social processes that may support institutions, but for two related reasons take as their primary focus the problems and processes of legitimation. First, the general historical circumstances of the Czechoslovak Socialist Republic indicate that the regime and its representatives at all levels of the economic system suffered from a massive withdrawal of social legitimacy and normative support following the Warsaw Pact invasion of 1968, and that Czechoslovak state socialism never really recovered from the social consequences (see Part Two). Further, these inherited problems of legitimacy continued to plague post-communist enterprise managers during the post-communist tran-sition as they attempted to re-establish their (institutional) credentials (see Part Three). Before turning to the key issue of institutional change, we consider the nature of organization and management within the social-institutional framework.

Organization and management as economic institutions

In this book, the analysis of socio-economic transformation at the enterprise level depends on an adequate conceptualization of organization and manage-ment as both institutionalized forms and institutionalized social practices, as explained above. In our view, organization and management must be under-

stood as parts of the institutional system; they do not exist or operate independently, but reflect, reveal and reinforce cultural rules and accounts about
the nature of rational economic behaviour in particular, and social conduct
in general. It follows that organizing and managing are subject to the same
processes of institutional inertia and change as other formal structures and
social practices, and abide by the same technical criteria of rationality and
normative criteria of legitimacy as other elements of the system.

The institutionalized forms of management in any society logically and
normatively presuppose the existence of other institutionalized forms, such
as organization, which are in turn interdependent with other formally defined
economic structures, i.e. with what legally and formally passes for economic
behaviour in the society in question. As formal institutions, management
and organization are social constructs whose structural features persist only
to the extent that they are enacted – passively, normatively, coercively or
through negotiation – in social practices (see Murrell and Wang, 1993,
pp. 388–91). Using our earlier terminology, a multi-level institutional
environment, or organizational field (see Friedland and Alford, 1991,
p. 242; Scott, 1994a, p. 70), maintains its integrity through flows of legitimation. Formal legitimation circulates between macro formal institutions
(e.g. private property or social ownership; the free market or central planning) and micro formal institutions (e.g. management and organization).
Social legitimation flows from the institutionalized management and organizational practices in concrete economic situations (plant, enterprise, planning agencies). Such processes of legitimation, or non-legitimation, support,
adjust or oppose the cultural rules and accounts of the economic order,
which in principle reflect and reinforce the 'organizing principles' (Habermas, 1976) of the society in question – whether capitalist–free market or state
socialist–central planning.

Institutionalized environments are the source of both technical and
normative influences on the individual organizations which constitute them
(DiMaggio and Powell, 1991; Scott and Meyer, 1991). Managements are
under social pressure to adopt or develop internal structures, procedures
and practices that enable them to run their organizations efficiently and/or
legitimately within an organizational environment with predominant
market, hierarchy or network characteristics, or some combination of them
(Williamson, 1975; Bradach and Eccles, 1991; Meyer and Rowan, 1991;
Powell, 1991; Scott, 1994a). Researchers who have been concerned to understand how institutional rules and features spread their influence across social
sectors and organizational fields have examined the mediating role of
formalized, organized entities, such as specialized professional bodies and
consultancy agencies. Such mediating entities not only conform in their con-
stitutions to the prevailing institutional rules of rational form, but further
express these rules in clearly formulated and codified theories, schemes and
methods. By acting as specialists in institutionalized knowledge and practices,

these agents carry, diffuse and promulgate the dominant institutional norms of rationality (e.g. Meyer and Rowan, 1991; DiMaggio and Powell, 1991; Huczynski, 1993; Strang and Meyer, 1994). At any one time, certain structures (e.g. divisionalized), systems (e.g. total quality management), technical methods (e.g. just-in-time) and schemes (e.g. performance-related pay) take on institutional force and become models, or patterns, for types of organization seeking both technical efficiency and institutional legitimacy (DiMaggio and Powell, 1991; Wilson, 1992, pp. 84ff). Patterns of organization thereby come to reflect the technical and institutional demands of the rational organization as an institutionalized form, itself embedded within, and formally legitimated by, its institutionally structured organizational field.

In institutional terms, management can be understood in similar ways, comprising, first, the cognitive ideas and beliefs which serve to define the technically effective and socially accepted range of methods and procedures that constitute its rationality; and, second, the normative rules and associated sanctions that prescribe 'good' management and justify derived management practices in terms of their formal and social legitimacy. As with other institutions, management is expressed both formally and socially. First, management as institutionalized form consists of a set of formal rights to act and decide, which are grounded in the higher level institutions that prescribe the social, political, legal and economic existence of business enterprise. Managing is to a large extent presupposed by its cultural (Globokar, 1994) and institutional (Willmott, 1987) context. Second, the conduct of management is a set of socially sanctioned practices, which are in part derived from the institutional descriptions and prescriptions accepted more widely, but also in part emergent from the real problems faced by typical managers in their complex, ongoing struggle to manage in local conditions. It is the interplay between these systemic and social processes which constitutes the actual nature of management at any one time (see Willmott, 1987, p. 260). The institutional stability of management is directly related to the stability of the institutional order in which it is embedded, and to the extent that the formal structures and social processes of management are mutually reinforcing.

Management and organization are influenced by many of the same institutional factors and processes, because in accepted modern usage, management as an activity, a function and a group is oriented to the rational (i.e. technical and economic) achievement of organizational ends, and includes the adoption and application of practices directly intended to design and mould the organization. The practices that have developed as part of the modern management repertoire involve techniques, systems and methods such as budgeting, quality control and just-in-time; and social practices like human resource management, social networking and leadership. Underlying such practices are the ideas and values which serve as assumptions about the nature of management, about its proper tasks in work organizations and about economic behaviour in society at any given time. These ideas not only act to provide a technical explanation of 'what managers do'; they also offer the grounds for current, ideological justifications of management, managers and the organizations for which they are responsible (Reed, 1984, p. 281).

It is misleading to understand management as a neutral, technical function within a value-free organizational context, because it operates ideologically and politically, and is enacted by real individuals with their own motives and agendas (Willmott, 1987). Assumptions regarding proper managerial work and bona fide managers incorporate normative definitions about access to management as a job and as a career, and circumscribe the relationship of management and managers to organizations and to their socio-economic environment. The credibility of those who are managers is linked to these conditions of legitimacy, while the institutional nature of management is associated with the social and technical qualifications and credentials of managers, who, by virtue of being the right sort of person and doing the right sorts of activities, are granted access to the rights and 'privileges' of the status. Management is therefore technically, socially and personally grounded in what passes for 'management knowledge' at any one time, i.e. what is accepted as appropriate ideas and practices.

Being normatively and practically embedded in the wider institutional order, it follows that fundamental changes, such as those involved in the transformation of the centrally planned economies of CEE, have dramatic implications for the nature and practice of organization and management. In brief, the practices of state socialist management were unlikely to be technically or normatively suitable to a post-communist economy which is an emergent institutional order based on different organizing principles. We now turn to the conceptualization of institutional change in order to develop the theoretical tools for the empirical tasks ahead.

Institutional change

Given the main aim of this volume – to examine the Czech socio-economic transformation, at both macro and micro levels, as institutional change – it is crucial to understand the processes and conditions that made problematic, eroded and undermined the country's state socialist institutions, which had appeared to be relatively stable over a period of time. At one level, the very strength of a coherent, structurally interlocking institutional system can be the source of its potential for fundamental change. Highly institutionalized systems may be stable over long periods of time, but are highly vulnerable to sudden internal challenges or external shocks that make irrelevant or unsustainable any one part, with subsequent systemic reverberations.

At the centre of our examination of the post-communist transformation in Part Three are two general processes of institutional change, namely de-institutionalization and reinstitutionalization. By *deinstitutionalization*, we mean the processes whereby an institution's elements lose credibility and the contingent nature of cultural accounts and rules are revealed, interrogated, contested, opposed, effectively challenged and, ultimately, overturned. The process may be gradual or sudden and may affect formal institutions and institutionalized practices at different rates. Deinstitutionalization is corrosive of social life because it takes away the certainty associated with institutionalized rules, attacks the meaningfulness of the social world and thereby reduces levels of social support and motivation. The parallel withdrawal of social legitimacy results from what is, in part, a process of demythologizing, and becomes a threat to the degree of social integration (see Jepperson, 1991, p. 145; Oliver, 1992, p. 654). *Reinstitutionalization* refers to the process of redefining and relegitimizing patterns and activities, using, in some degree, a framework of rationality and values which is different from that previously taken for granted. The construction of new formal institutions (laws, structures, procedures) may be effected very quickly, but their realization in new social practices occurs only very slowly, as the values and their underlying logic take time to become reproduced unquestioningly in routinized conduct. In this context, social transition may be understood as the period between the effective demise of one institutional system and the point at which another institutional system has been established and accepted on new cognitive and normative grounds. The transition *process* therefore refers to the social, economic and political processes that take place within that period to develop the new states of system and social integration. In institutional terms, this involves the playing out of the simultaneous processes of deinstitutionalization and reinstitutionalization, the consequent state of 'being in the middle' setting up conditions of *social transience*. Such circumstances create acute social and psychological problems for social actors as they try to adapt to the continuing pulls of the past and the new pushes of the present and future. We return to these problems in detail in Part Three.

Conceptually, it is possible to see deinstitutionalization occurring in stages. An institution becomes vulnerable to erosion as soon as it loses its taken-for-granted qualities, and its mere existence is not enough to sustain it. As implied above, once institutional representatives establish conscious legitimation strategies in order to expound and propagate normative justifications, members of society can feasibly conceive of alternative plausible social realities. The development of specialized structures and normative rules, such as professional associations and theorized ideologies dedicated to providing cultural support for existing patterns, may bolster the status quo in the short run, but at the same time suggests that the hitherto unquestioned social reality is in some way challengeable or contestable (see Berger and Luckmann, 1971; Habermas, 1976, p. 36; Suchman, 1995, p. 576).

Deinstitutionalization is related to changes and reductions in the flows of legitimacy throughout the institutional system, which make compliance with the formal rules and procedures of institutionalized forms problematic: 'the normative elements of social systems are contingent claims which have to be sustained and "made to count" through the effective mobilization of sanctions in the contexts of actual encounters' (Giddens, 1984, p. 30). When legitimation processes break down, and normative rules are no longer reliably reproduced by social actors in their everyday behaviour, the conditions exist for potential deinstitutionalization and subsequent institutional change. Institutional failure can arise in many ways, and it is not appropriate here to explore their origins in detail, but obvious examples include the effects of sudden exogenous shocks, and changes in social, political or economic conditions within a society.

In this discussion, we can usefully draw on the conceptual tools developed by Habermas (1976) and Giddens (1984). Although these are embedded in those authors' particular sociological perspectives and imbued with their specific theoretical interests, they none the less help to illuminate certain features of the deinstitutionalization process. Thus, while bearing in mind that institutional disintegration may be pre-empted by external crises, we focus on three related internal possibilities: failures of formal institutions (or system crises); failures of institutionalized practices (or social crises); and the hiatus between formal institutions and institutionalized practices.

Regarding the first source of deinstitutionalization, it can be argued that, despite their theoretical over-determination and consequent tendency towards inertia, institutions and institutional systems are never completely defined, internally consistent and mutually compatible. In reality, institutions exist in varying degrees of messiness and contradictoriness of organizing principles or of formal structures (Friedland and Alford, 1991), which lead to political and economic problems of defining consistent social goals, acquiring and allocating the resources necessary for material production and achieving economic objectives well enough to sustain the commitment and loyalty of the members of society. Habermas (1976) analyses the *system crises* created in advanced capitalism as arising from the contradictory demands placed upon the system's political and economic institutions. In order to sustain capitalist development in its advanced stages, he argues that contradictory institutional principles and processes have become expressed in the structural complexes surrounding, for example, oligarchic markets, representative democracy and social welfare provision. The resulting structural crises lead to attempted resolutions which simply relocate political and economic problems by shifting their negative consequences from one social sphere to another. Giddens (1984) similarly discusses the Marxian idea of structural contradiction as the logically irreconcilable tendencies of the political and the economic, arising from a 'Disjunction of structural principles of system organization' (Giddens, 1984, p. 198).

A second source of disintegration arises in the social world. As argued above, as soon as institutions are stripped of their unreflective taken-for-grantedness, they become vulnerable to change. When the social world is only confronted 'pre-theoretically' or legitimated by an overarching 'symbolic universe' (Berger and Luckmann, 1971, pp. 83, 113), the existing institutional system takes on characteristics of immutability and inevitability that are reinforced in passive support. In reality, however, especially in industrial society, the role of critical reason and the existence of diverse minority cultures allow, even encourage, the emergence of multiple realities based on different, often conflicting, cognitive and normative principles. Where social actors and social groups espouse openly hostile social theories and enact them partly or entirely in their divergent (even deviant) social practices, the ensuing conflict engenders a *social crisis*, threatening the withdrawal of legitimacy and adequate levels of motivation to support the extant institutional system (see Habermas, 1976). The expression of social conflicts and differences through political action and opposition becomes the main vehicle for change, unless it can be incorporated within the institutional system (negotiated consent) or repressed (coerced support).

While it is conceivable that social and systems crises operate independently, the reality is more complex. The really significant question in explaining the processes of institutional change concerns the emergent relationship between contradictions in the sphere of formal institutions and crises in the realm of institutionalized practice, the consequences of which may engulf the institutional system as a whole. At one level, formal institutional problems can express themselves as technical issues, such as the lack of political direction, decision-making inconsistencies, resource-allocative inefficiencies, trade deficits and economic underperformance. But in a rationalized industrial society, such problems of purposive and instrumental rationality also reach to the heart of the institutional process – namely, its social legitimacy. In short, technical deficiencies can easily translate themselves into deficits of legitimacy or meaning. Habermas (1976) clearly treats legitimation as the major vehicle whereby the technical crises emerging from the formal institutional system spill over into local social situations to create threats to the degree of consent and support forthcoming in everyday social behaviour.

When an institutionalized social pattern fails to be sufficiently subjectively meaningful and the normative demands of the formal institutional structures are ignored, overruled or 'reinterpreted', or where they otherwise become detached from the behaviour produced in the everyday social practices of human agents, we shall speak of an *institutional gap*. Institutionalized structures, rules, patterns, procedures and methods which satisfy neither technical criteria of instrumental rationality nor norms of legitimacy will tend not to be reproduced in social action, and hence be subject to erosion and change. In these circumstances, members of society may engage in deviant social practices which, over time and as collective action, can be the source of new social institutions. In Chapter 4, we show how management and business practices in Czechoslovak state enterprises became divorced from the procedures and regulations of command-economic institutions, and the consequent institutional gap not only threatened the continuity of the existing institutional structures, but was also the incipient source of those patterns that have subsequently emerged in the post-communist period (see Chapter 8).

In principle, then, the social processes emanating from the institutional gap encapsulate both processes of institutional change: deinstitutionalization and reinstitutionalization. New variants of social practices which begin to reshape rules and accounts may be contained within the bounds of the existing institutional establishment – what Jepperson (1991, p. 152) calls 'institutional development or elaboration' – or may form the basis of reinstitutionalization, as defined above. Processes of institutional development, which restrict change to within an institutional form, may happen in a number of ways, including the incorporation of conflicts and opposition within the system, or the adaptation of institutions. The institutional literature also identifies 'decoupling' as a major source for containment. In this case, social practices which in fact deviate from the prescriptions of external formal procedures are presented in ways that make them appear to be conforming (Meyer and Rowan, 1991, pp. 57–8). The reasons for deviance may be normative, based on principled disagreement; or, as in the case of Czechoslovak management in the 1980s, pragmatic, in that changed circumstances might render institutionalized practices inadequate for dealing with the 'real' managerial problems.

As mainstream institutional theorists have argued, formal institutions and structures can be sustained without being technically efficient as long as they have sufficient social support or are subject to strong processes of social legitimation (e.g. propaganda) that gloss the reality. Further, they can survive without social legitimacy as long as their technical efficiency generates sufficient material benefits to persuade members of society to be at least quiescent. However, if the above conditions do not exist, or if the institutional system neither produces technical efficiency nor acquires social legitimacy, the institutional status quo can only be safeguarded by the coercive exercise of power (Habermas, 1976, p. 96). Such repression merely stores up hostility in a latent social crisis, reduces further the stock of social legitimacy and presages a total institutional collapse – in this context, the persistence of formal institutions is a function of how repressive political leaders are willing to be in their efforts to sustain (the myth of) institutional definitions.

Reinstitutionalization is problematic because cultural rules and accounts, which new institutions comprise, cannot by definition be imposed, and can only emerge as stable social forms with historicity and objectivity if they are grounded in the shared experiences of the former, flawed institutions. In the modern, rationalized, international world, however, an institutional system can be assembled from institutional parts that are available, so to speak, off the global shelf. In practical terms, the economic transformation can be understood as first, the emergent redefinition of economic institutions using domestic, historical resources; and, second, the rational redesign of structures and practices assembled from borrowed ideas and knowledge from contemporary foreign origins (Meyer, 1994, pp. 52–3). These processes of 'international isomorphism' will concern us in Chapter 9.

Summary and conclusions

> The changes of political power in Eastern Europe have been sufficiently sweeping to usher in a new normative order . . . It is giving rise to a radical restructuring of the economic and social context within which organizations operate . . . What is taking place is therefore an institutional change in the full sense of that term, embracing both societal values and structures.
>
> (Child, 1993, p. 204)

We agree with Child in his view of the post-communist transition as a deeply institutional change, and in this chapter we have developed the conceptual and theoretical foundations for examining organizational and management transformation in such terms. Institutions are cultural accounts and justifications of prevailing patterns of social action which are expressed both formally (for example, in legal constructs) and socially in the concrete practices of members of society. Given the ideal conditions of institutionalization, socio-economic systems will tend towards an inertial state, which results from the conjunction of system integration and social integration, whereby social institutions benefit from the dual processes of formal and social legitimation. The failure of legitimation processes, or withdrawal of legitimacy from the system and from social life, leads to crises that undermine the presumed stability and persistence of institutions, because it reveals the social processes of power that underlie institutional order, subjects the ongoing definition of institutions to social contestation and leads to a hiatus between the formal-legal and the social-practical spheres of society.

This social-institutional analysis of the bases and processes of institutional order and change establishes important research questions. In the context of our discussion of the Czech Republic, this means that, throughout the book, our sights remain closely focused on certain themes: the interaction between formal institutions and institutionalized practices; the role of external structures and internal human agency; the processes of social and formal legitimation and institutional stability and change; the influence of historical experiences and practices on current behaviour; the contestation of institutional order and the deinstitutionalization of state socialism; and the motives and objectives of influential social actors – in our instance, enterprise managers – in their drive to control the definition of a new institutional order, i.e. to reinstitutionalize social structures and practices according to new post-communist values and rationalities. By grounding our empirical examination in detailed micro processes, we hope to demonstrate the theoretical benefits of exploring the Czech economic transformation from the practical social world of enterprise management and managers. We believe not only that the dramatic nature of the economic changes in the Czech Republic serves to demonstrate the usefulness of this extended institutional framework, but also that the latter offers a repository of concepts and propositions that permit insightful evaluation of post-communist enterprise and management.

In Part Two, we examine the nature of state socialist economies, employing the mode of analysis suggested in the above framework. In Chapter 3, we investigate the major formal institutional features of Czechoslovak state socialism as it developed and survived up to the Velvet Revolution of 1989. We argue that the hierarchical, centralized structures of the command economy provided a relatively highly interlocked and theoretically coherent institutional system, based on a mixture of passive and coerced support. In Chapter 4, attention shifts to the institutionalized practices of enterprise managers, when we draw upon the experiences and memories of our respondents to examine the ways in which they made sense of, reproduced and modified the formal demands of the economic system. The problems of social legitimacy that Czech communist managers faced, and the institutional gap they created between everyday management life and the institutions of centralized economic control, were fundamental to the collapse of state socialism as an economic system, while paradoxically their institutionalized management practices had sustained the faltering system over many years. We develop these propositions in more detail in Chapter 5, which also serves to summarise the arguments of Part Two and to make the theoretical and empirical bridge to Part Three.

Our major contribution, however, resides in considering the socio-economic transformation as institutional change – at both the formal institutional level and the level of everyday enterprise management. Conventionally, the strength of institutional theory has been its ability to account for social persistence and resistance to change, but we have described above how an institutional analysis can be developed to incorporate the issues of radical change. The concepts of deinstitutionalization and reinstitutionalization direct theoretical attention to the formal-legal aspects of the economic transition, while emphasizing the essential role of human agency in the restructuring and redefining processes at the level of concrete economic action. These issues of institutional change are taken up in detail in Part Three. Chapter 6 considers the formal aspects of the rapid deinstitutionalization of the command economy, and the Czech(oslovak) route to economic restructuring, involving legal actions to introduce new organizing principles. In the following three chapters (7, 8 and 9), we return to our case study materials in order to examine the unfolding experiences of institutional change at the level of organization, and the new values and motives that have guided and driven the emergence of new management rhetoric and practices in the enterprises we have studied.

Notes

1 In fact, the corporatist approach as it is normally presented has not proven very helpful in the present analysis, at least at this stage of the transition. State socialism

was unitary in its institutional structure, and, although there was a superficial appearance of corporatism at state and enterprise level, the 'organized interests' were all effectively part of the communist apparatus. Since 1989, there have been formal-institutional developments at the national and enterprise levels which suggest greater involvement of, for example, trade unions and employers' representatives in the governance structures. However, the effective degree and depth of corporatism in the Czech Republic, relative to Poland or Hungary, has been influenced by the dominant free-market political ideology, and the relative strength of the enterprise management *vis-à-vis* trade unions (see Brewster, 1992; Héthy, 1994; Pollert and Hradecká, 1994; Cziria, 1995; Hegewisch *et al.*, 1995; Tatur, 1995).

Part II

Enterprise and management under state socialism

3   The Czechoslovak state socialist economy

Czechoslovakia was founded following the First World War, and established democratic institutions during the inter-war period, which collapsed only with the invasion of Hitler's forces in 1938. Indeed, of those that came within the Soviet sphere of influence, Czechoslovakia was the only CEE state to have a democratic tradition – a fact of which Czechs are understandably proud, and which is an important part of the post-communist context. Czechoslovakia also had strong industrial manufacturing traditions, especially in light engineering, and before the war was one of the world's top ten industrial economies (Glenny, 1993, p. 27), with a per capita national income 10 per cent higher than Austria's; by 1990, the Austrian per capita gross domestic product was more than 30 per cent higher than Czechoslovakia's, after the latter's years of industrial development under state socialist management (Jeffries, 1993, p. 245). It is against this democratic and industrialized background that the 1945 'National Front' coalition under President Edvard Beneš agreed a policy under which an extensive nationalization of industry took place. By February 1948, when the Communist Party of Czechoslovakia (KSČ) took power, over 80 per cent of productive assets were state owned, and these accounted for two-thirds of net material product (Mejstřik, 1993, p. 125; Dlouhý and Mládek, 1994, p. 159). The communist state proceeded with the socialization of private property, and established institutions to govern the economy according to command principles.

The early post-communist transformation of Czech enterprises has been strongly influenced by the enduring legacies of the 1948–89 period, in particular the legacies embodied in the institutions of central planning and of state socialist management. To some extent, these structures and experiences were replicated across the whole of CEE, reflecting the success of common and persistent internationalist themes in the Soviet doctrines imposed on the region by Stalin in the late 1940s, and renewed under Brezhnev in the late 1960s and 1970s. The Soviet model of economic management was exported to and broadly implemented in socialist Europe, and this produced certain typical features of economic process and performance throughout the region. However, concrete socio-economic forms varied quite broadly around such common themes. Over the years and in various ways, there emerged a more diversified approach to socialist development. Yugoslavia planned its third road at an early stage; several countries created some distinctiveness over longer periods (e.g. Hungary since the late 1960s), while others retained independence on certain issues (e.g. Poland's resistance to farm collectivization) or for short bursts (notably, Czechoslovakia in 1967–8; see Golan, 1973; Ulč, 1974; Skilling, 1976). In that state socialism was not a uniform structure, process or experience throughout the former East European bloc, by 1989 the former communist societies found themselves in different states and ready to move out of the communist era in different ways and at different paces (see Lane, 1976; Koźmiński, 1990; Batt, 1991; Kieżun, 1991; Clague, 1992; Deacon, 1992; Mickler, 1992; Frydman *et al.*, 1993). We shall argue in this book that, while there were important and enduring institutional similarities between the countries of Central Europe, Czechoslovakia (and the Czech Republic) offers a particularly interesting case for researching economic transformation in relation to its neighbours. Poland and Hungary had experienced gradual formal and informal experimentation with decentralized, market-type reforms during the 1980s or before, while the post-1968 'normalization' experience in Czechoslovakia had left the country with a form of 'neo-Stalinism' (Batt, 1991, p. 17; Glenny, 1993, p. 22) that affected social, economic and political spheres of life. The institutional state of the Czechoslovak Socialist Republic (ČSSR) in 1989 therefore called for a more abrupt and radical approach to the socio-economic transformation.

In this chapter, we shall examine the major ingredients of the history of Czechoslovak state socialism as they affected the development of the command economy. The aim is not to present an exhaustive economic-historical account, which exists already in a number of publications (e.g. Teichová, 1988; Myant, 1989). The intention is rather to understand the economic and institutional context of managerial experiences in the pre-1989 period, in that these form the origins of the transition process, and it is in such legacies that we can isolate the roots of contemporary post-communist organization and management. We shall start by considering the main formal principles of the command economy, as they were espoused and applied after 1948; we shall then look more specifically at the phases of economic reform and retrenchment that were experienced in the ČSSR. We will conclude the chapter by outlining the main institutional structures of the Czechoslovak centrally planned economy, as they had evolved over the communist period. It is important to realize that we are not suggesting that these structures describe how the command economy actually worked, but that these were basic formal rules and procedures which *could* have been enacted, and were in varying degrees during the 1948 to 1989 period, in support of formally legitimate claims to power, authority, privilege etc. This point will become clearer in Chapter 4, where we shall examine how these historical and institutional processes influenced the actual experience and conduct of state enterprise management. Chapter 5 will draw out the implications of this analysis for Czechoslovak enterprise management as it approached the demands of the post-communist world.

The economic goals and institutional principles of communism

The aims and organizing principles of the Stalinist model of socialist economic development were imported into the new European communist regimes in the late 1940s, and derived from the precepts and practices of Marxist-Leninism in the Soviet Union. It was the responsibility of the Communist Party to decide upon economic goals and to plan for their achievement, and it devised institutional structures in all spheres and at all levels of society in order to assure the authority of its own influence. The scale and legality of such influence was formally consolidated in Article 4 of the 1960 Czechoslovak constitution, embodying the principle of the leading role of the Party (Suda, 1980, p. 287).

The strategic aim of (state) socialism was to achieve rapid economic growth by the full utilization of all human and material resources, and by the forced building of a broad-based industrial structure, founded upon an indigenous, self-sustaining capability. Extensive industrialization was understood as an end-in-itself, the achievement of which would establish the economic pre-conditions for the formation of a communist society. In countries which were typically agrarian in nature, such growth demanded giving priority to the development of basic metallurgical and steel production, and of the heavy engineering sector which enabled the creation of other industrial capacity. Although Czechoslovakia was a notable exception to the underdeveloped agrarian economies of the region, the application of Soviet socialist precepts led to a similar prioritizing of heavy engineering activities (Teichová, 1988, pp. 134ff). The commitment to the relative independence of the internal political economy from external pressures led to the elaboration and replication across the region of more or less autarkic economies (Brabant, 1991, pp. 69–72; Lavigne, 1991, pp. 7ff; Lewis, 1994, pp. 103ff).

Economists have identified a number of characteristics of the conventional Stalinist economic model which was adopted as the basis of the institutional structures of Central European communism (e.g. Hába, 1988, pp. 48–9; Brabant, 1991, p. 70; Lavigne, 1995). Table 3.1 provides a summary list of such features. The stated economic goals required a concerted, central direction which overruled the rationalities of any 'scarcity indicators' that might emerge from signals given by spontaneous market values. Growth strategy and targets were chosen because of given political presumptions, not on the basis of real economic opportunities. In addition, however, the values of communism demanded that economic progress be intrinsically linked to, and constrained by, desired socio-political qualities such as maintaining full employment, meeting social needs and enhancing social equality.

Table 3.1 Principles of the conventional socialist economy

Key features	Description
Central planning	Nearly all economic decisions taken at the centre, and the conduct of all economic agents strictly regulated.
National ownership	Socialized ownership of all significant factors of production – capital, natural resources, land (in most cases).
Economic autarky	National self-sufficiency, and the rigid protection of the domestic economy from foreign economic influences.
Labour resources	Allocation and pricing of labour resources controlled by planning authorities to ensure full employment and social equality.
Collectivized agriculture	Large-scale organization and control of farming by collectivization of agricultural activities.
Role of mandatory plans	Deliberate disregard of market-coordinative information, in favour of directive planning of physical details.
Monobank financing	State funding of operations and investments through an administrative State Bank, the single source of credit.
Administrative hierarchy	Bureaucratic control of economic decisions, governed by clear rules, regulations and procedures.
Nomenklatura appointments	Allocation of important posts according to political credentials.
Enterprise management	Strong constraints on local managerial freedom by the central plan, local supervision by party and related organs (e.g. trade union).

Main sources: Hába, 1988; Brabant, 1991; Lavigne, 1995.

The strategic selection of development targets and the allocation of resources to fulfil these targets as effectively as possible thus took little account of economic costs or other values. The planning objectives and instruments were determined by a small elite group of the Communist Party, usually the Politburo, sometimes known in the ČSSR as the Executive Committee of the Presidium (Kaser and Zieliński, 1970, p. 35; Suda, 1980). Production and distribution were planned in detail and by quantity, obviating the need for other independent relations between economic agents, such as enterprises at lower levels of the planning hierarchy (Brabant, 1991, pp. 73–4). Even the financing at enterprise level was administered through the 'monobanking system', with the State or National Bank acting to channel monies in the form of credits (in reality, subsidized and often rotating) from the state budget for necessary capital investment or normal operating costs to meet a production plan. In this way, the main economic decision-making responsibilities lay at the apex of the command economy, and the decisions that emanated from this apparatus were administered by 'managers' at the local levels of productive activity. The Communist Party and its various local organs (e.g. party sections, trade unions, the youth movement) were mobilized to motivate and discipline the workforce, and to oversee the attainment of enterprise targets (Myant, 1993, p. 60; Wolchik, 1991, p. 97).

The principles of economic development reinforced the desirability of a high degree of economic autarky, or self-sufficiency, which led to what Jeffries (1993, p. 25) called a 'trade aversion'. There was a clear distinction between the operation of domestic production and foreign markets, whose relationship was managed by the state control of the foreign trade and exchange systems. Like the domestic planning of production, the planning and control of foreign trade were channelled through the central institutions. 'A monopoly of foreign trade was expressly instituted to neutralize all influences from abroad, whether positive or disruptive, and thus to further domestic policy autonomy' (Brabant, 1991, p. 77).

Within the autarkic economy, foreign trade was seen as a 'residue' (Lavigne, 1991, p. 19). The planning of domestic production was the key economic activity (Brabant, 1991, p. 77), and the device of 'material balances' was used to match the planned internal production ('supply') of and the planned internal uses ('demand') for products. Material imbalances that emerged in the process of estimating gaps between demand and supply were met through internal adjustments, and/or foreign trade (Jeffries, 1993, p. 24). In most cases, it was presumed more desirable to produce domestically than to import, because the latter involved arrangements for payments (Brabant, 1991, p. 78). In this model, there was no aspiration or incentive to take advantage of any economic trade opportunities that might arise independently of domestic economic planning needs, as all eyes were on the goals of internal economic development. Foreign trade took place initially to source domestic shortfalls in input materials, but this model incorporated a pecking order of preferred trading partners, mostly reflecting political priorities, and subsequent economic benefits arising from trading in kind and by barter, rather than through monetary values. Dealing with other CMEA countries was an evident first choice, followed by other socialist countries, then non-socialist countries.

The main political precept underpinning the goals of the rapid social and economic development was the 'leading role of the communist party' (Jancar, 1971, pp. 17ff; White *et al.*, 1990, p. 130; Lewis, 1994, p. 84). In order to assure that the social, economic and political system worked according to the ideological priorities of the party, all the post-war communist countries imported, as part of the Soviet blueprint, the 'cadre policy', or *kádrování* (Jancar, 1971, pp. 29–31; Kaplan, 1987, pp. 151ff), which became known throughout the region as the *nomenklatura* system. 'Jobs of any importance in the administration, economy and social organizations were invariably . . . taken by party members' (Lewis, 1994, p. 84).

In order to secure communist policies in practice, local cadre policy was applied to make sure that all applicants for such jobs possessed the 'political, professional and moral prerequisites for the post' (1988 Law on State Enterprises, Article 27 (2): see *Czechoslovak Economic Digest*, 1988, p. 22).

> The nomenklatura is first of all a series of posts which cannot be filled without the special scrutiny of some special organs . . . The . . . categories of the party-nomenklatura are by far the most important. They contain all the main 'responsible posts'.
>
> (Ionescu, 1967, p. 61)

By having control over access to the *nomenklatura* posts, the Communist Party, at central, regional or local levels, sustained a senior group of trusted comrades and practised an 'effective monopoly over appointments to key positions at all levels of society' (White *et al.*, 1990, p. 148).

The *nomenklatura* lists included all the senior managerial posts in the economic planning apparatus (see examples in Ionescu, 1967, pp. 61ff; Waller, 1993, pp. 257ff). Applicants for posts in the central institutions as well as for management positions in the more important state-owned enterprises, such as those in military manufacturing sectors and key engineering enterprises, required approval at the most senior levels of the party. Within the enterprise, applicants for managerial jobs which involved foreign travel (e.g. commercial posts) or gave access to vital information (such as financial or personnel posts) also needed party dispensation, though for the most part at a lower level of authorization, often within the enterprise itself (Lavigne, 1995, p. 5). With senior enterprise posts only available to approved individuals, aspiring career managers, as well as committed communists, were attracted to membership of the various institutions of the Communist Party – such as the party itself or its youth association (*Československý svaz mládeže* was the equivalent of the Soviet *komsomol*).

Although the reality of the *nomenklatura* system has to be evaluated with great caution, given the diverse motives[1] of those who benefited from it, as a social institution it served a number of functions: it enabled the party to exercise control over the functioning of the various economic institutions; it allocated reliable and trustworthy individuals to important jobs; and, more unintentionally, it acted as the institutional medium for the development and sustenance of a new social elite or ruling class, integrated by common membership, shared values and similar interests in maintaining their own privilege and power (Djilas, 1957; Lane, 1976, p. 109).

By 1952 or 1953, these principles had been more or less fully adopted across the region, despite some evidence that local leaders tried to adapt them to national circumstances (Rychetník, 1981, p. 114; Lewis, 1994, pp. 79–80). Within five or six years of the communist coup of February 1948, the Stalinist model of command-economic planning had been gradually but effectively introduced into Czechoslovak conditions. State investments favoured new patterns of trade and investment, which altered economic structures over the first Five Year Plan (1948 to 1953). There was not only a significant restructuring of Czechoslovak productive capacity from light engineering towards the heavy and construction industries (Teichová, 1988, pp. 126–7; Wolchik, 1991, p. 218; Lewis, 1994, p. 105), but also a rapid redirecting of trade to the new socialist bloc in general, and to the USSR in particular (Myant, 1989, pp. 17ff; Wolchik, 1991, pp. 258–60). Further nationalizations completed the socialization of industrial assets which had begun under the Beneš postwar presidency, leading, by 1952, to some 98 per cent of industrial assets having been taken into state ownership (Lewis, 1994, p. 98). New institutional structures were created in 1948–9 which consolidated the idea of the binding central plan. Binding targets were set and organized in new central institutions at ministerial level, and imposed on factories via a hierarchical-administrative system, in the same way as in the Soviet Union. The number of such targets increased from 100 in 1949 to 1100 in 1951, when they covered nearly 70 per cent of the volume of industrial production (e.g. Hasager, 1986, pp. 57ff).

The economic reform processes in the ČSSR

Soon after Stalin's death in 1953, the CEE socialist states began to undergo a series of economic reform phases, during which attempts were made to adjust the extreme features of the system. By then, however, the economic structures and institutions were well bedded down. The institutions that were established and the industrial structures that were shaped in this early period were to have fundamental and long-lasting consequences for the economic development of the ČSSR, and have largely withstood the intervening attempts to reform and restructure (Hába, 1988, p. 49).

Throughout the region, economic reform took on a general pattern of limited decentralization, followed by recentralization, and then further decentralization. Reform phases were responses by economic planners and politicians to the perceived economic problems and crises that resulted from the historical experiences of countries at different times, and from practical alternatives deriving from diverse economic theories that prevailed and were allowed to spread across the region. These factors led to large differences between the countries in the actual socio-economic developments (see Myant, 1989, p. 248; Brabant, 1991, p. 68), in the exact timing of decentralizing and recentralizing phases and in the degrees to which reforms in economic structures, instruments and institutions took root. In Hungary, for example, the processes of decentralization penetrated more deeply than elsewhere into the structures of planning and into the mentalities of planners.

In Czechoslovakia, it is possible to identify four phases of economic reform between 1948 and 1989, each one, until 1989, followed by processes of retrenchment (Wolchik, 1991, p. 239; see also Hasager, 1986; Hába, 1988; Dyba and Kouba, 1989). The leading actors in the Czechoslovak reforms were motivated by the particular economic conditions and political climates of each period, but ultimately were 'constrained by the need to confine changes to modifications within the framework of the socialist economy' (Wolchik, 1991, p. 239). Measures outlined at the 1956 Communist Party conference were implemented during 1957–8, increasing the emphasis of the centre on what was called 'perspective planning' (qualitative, long-term or scenario planning), rather than on the detailed planning of physical output. New instruments and institutions were introduced to increase the degree of devolved decision-making in the conventional Stalinist system. For example, more operational authority and control was decentralized to a new form of economic association of industrial plants, called *výrobní hospodářská jednotka* (VHJ). The VHJ was an intermediary structure between the ministry and the productive enterprise, which was to take on more detailed aspects of the planning process and hence relieve the central planners of impossible informational burdens (Suda, 1980, pp. 283–5; Rychetník, 1981, p. 114; Teichová, 1988, p. 148; Myant, 1989, p. 82; Jeffries, 1993, p. 246; and see below, pp. 62–3). These new larger national enterprises effectively consolidated enterprise-level management into larger units, with over 1400 enterprises being regrouped under 383 new ones (Hasager, 1986, p. 87). As a number of commentators have made clear, these changes in fact left the core of the central planning system untouched (e.g. Hába, 1988, pp. 50–1; Wolchik, 1991, p. 240).

The Czechoslovak economy performed very badly in the early 1960s, reaching an all time low in 1963, and leading to the enforced revision of the third National Plan (1961–5). Senior politicians explained poor economic performance in terms of the consequences of the 1958 'decentralizing' reforms and the 'anarchy' created by the now uncoordinated and unconstrained decision-making that was happening at enterprise level (Myant, 1989, p. 101). Consequently, much of the devolution was halted or reversed, and effective economic control was recentralized in the central planning structures by the end of 1962 (Rychetník, 1981, p. 115; Hasager, 1986, p. 103; Hába, 1988, p. 51).

In January 1965, the Central Committee of the Communist Party approved a document entitled 'Principles of Improvement of the Management System' (Eliás and Netík, 1966, pp. 270ff). In its implementation, the number of VHJs was decreased, and their size and influence increased, thereby enlarging their conglomerate and monopoly status (Myant, 1989, p. 122; Jeffries, 1993, pp. 246–7). A wave of genuine economic decentralization and marketization proceeded alongside the political processes leading up to the Prague Spring of 1968, when the economic theorems of Ota Šik (see Myant, 1989, pp. 110ff; Wolchik, 1991, p. 241) held some authority. The 1967–8 period is evaluated by many as, with the possible exceptions of Yugoslavian self-management and Hungary's New Economic Mechanism, the most radical attempt to reform and decentralize socialist economic decision-making, and to introduce market elements into the process of economic coordination (Teichová, 1988, p. 151; Kosta, 1989; Brabant, 1991, p. 90; Wolchik, 1991, p. 241; Jeffries, 1993, p. 246). This second period of Czechoslovak economic experimentation was brought to an end after the invasion of the Warsaw Pact armies in August 1968, as a military response to political changes of Dubček's Prague Spring. The Soviet occupying forces sought to re-establish the former political and economic institutions of Czechoslovakia, and in April 1969 they installed a new political regime, led by Gustav Husák, to oversee this 'normalization' process. The essential theme of the new politico-economic system derived from what eventually became known as the Brezhnev doctrine, which reformulated the Stalinist position of the single route to socialism, with each socialist state having obligations to defend socialism in other 'fraternal' states.

Over the early 1970s, the normalization process re-established directive control and planning at the political and economic centres, by cleansing the party of elements which were untrustworthy because of their links with Dubček's liberalization policies, and by placing reliable communist apparatchiks at the top of economic and political institutions (see, for example, Šimečka, 1984; Renner, 1989, pp. 86ff; Wheaton and Kavan, 1992, pp. 6ff). While some have argued that the process of economic normalization did not entirely turn the clocks back (see Rychetník, 1981, p. 114), most commentators see the 1970s as gradually refreezing the central planning institutions into a more or less pure-type, hierarchical form, which remained intact until the middle-to-late 1980s (Ulč, 1978; Batt, 1991, pp. 16ff; Kieżun, 1991).

> it is true that a number of financial indicators were retained. In practice, however, these were of little relevance and were easily swamped by the re-emergence of 'old-fashioned success indicators' around binding annual plans in 1971. As these were soon given a firm ideological justification, full return to the essence of the old system was practically inevitable.
> (Myant, 1989, pp. 184–5)

A further attempt at economic reform was made in the early 1980s, aiming once more to focus central planning agents on longer-term, perspective planning and to let economic management at the level of the VHJ take care of short-term, operational planning. However, meeting plan targets rather than making market responses remained the main formal objectives of local enterprises (Rychetník, 1981; Myant, 1989, p. 210). Wolchik (1991, p. 243) argues that the role of binding plans was reaffirmed in these reforms, and any attempts at greater production efficiencies at the level of the enterprise were quietly set aside, as they served no one's interests. Following 1968, Czechs and Slovaks had to wait till the last three years of state socialism for the regime to attempt a serious reform of the economic institutions in a way that genuinely recognized the need to push decision-making closer to the point of production (see Červinka, 1987; Janeba, 1988; Kerner, 1988). In the late 1980s, economists and officials spoke openly about the need for fundamental change for the first time since 1968 (Wolchik, 1991, p. 245), but changes were to be introduced very slowly. The Czechoslovak communist leaders took their time before deciding to 'mimic Soviet economic reforms' (Myant, 1989, p. 251) of *perestroika* with their own version of *přestavba*. This took the form of several acts of legislation which dissolved the VHJs, redefined more autonomous state-owned enterprises with control based on financial principles, re-established the principle of worker councils and freed some elements of foreign trade from state control. The new laws changed the legal status of the old national enterprises to state enterprises, which had more concrete 'founding owners' and which took on the responsible stewardship of the businesses' assets. Ministers announced these conversions in a great clamour of publicity (see Matejka, 1989), but by this time it was too late to affect economic mentalities and behavioural patterns in a way that could prepare people for the radical decentralization processes of the 1990s.

This was in contrast to the other Central European communist states. For example, by 1989, Hungary had experienced thirty years of 'Kádárism', which, pragmatically and incrementally, had introduced political and economic freedoms, had openly sanctioned markets and, for a number of years, had successfully attracted foreign capital to rejuvenate its tired economy. Over the 1980s, the Communist Party in Poland had also developed a greater openness towards the West, in spite of its continuing problems with Solidarity, and had borrowed from foreign sources to renew its ageing capital base. But to many, it appeared that the ultra-conservative Czechoslovak Communist leaders made only grudging concessions to economic reforms (Lavigne, 1991, p. 136). Having become thoroughly implicated in the normalization of Czechoslovakia, including the ritual denouncements of the Prague Spring, Husák and his party comrades were never able openly to espouse economic reforms which invoked memories of the Dubček era. Husák could not be a Kádár, and Miloš Jakeš, who replaced Husák as General Secretary in late 1987, only 'held out the promise of a cautious implementation of modest reforms' (Jeffries, 1993, p. 253; see also Dawisha, 1990, pp. 189–90).

Reforms, which were already restrained by anxious national communist leaders, were further frustrated by the entrenched interests of local communists and those in *nomenklatura* positions: 'centrally enacted policies were subject to being modified substantially as they were implemented by lower level administrators and professionals' (Wolchik, 1991, p. 247).

The practical activities of interested parties within the central planning machinery, which suppressed, resisted or subverted the implementation of reform legislation, made it impossible to effect real decentralization of the hierarchical, authoritarian form of the Czechoslovak command economy. It became clear that radical economic reforms could only proceed when key figures in the national and local establishments felt it would serve their interests. Writing in the final throes of Czechoslovak state socialism, Myant argued as follows:

> Centralised planning, within the existing political system, therefore now appears as a system offering immediate protection to threatened interests . . . The implication is that there is no specific social group with an immediate material interest in pushing for economic reform.
>
> (Myant, 1989, pp. 260–1)

It has been argued by Myant (1989) and others that the various reform programmes tended to address the 'wrong' problems, failing to identify the source of the ČSSR's economic woes in its industrial structure. The autarkic presumptions of socialist development had not suited Czechoslovakia, whose production activities in an already industrialized economy rendered it a heavy user of energy and raw materials, which were domestically in poor supply. As a consequence, the economy was disproportionately dependent on the import of such materials – mostly, in fact from the Soviet Union – and hence vulnerable to international, external conditions (Teichová, 1988, pp. 162–3; Wolchik, 1991, p. 262). This vulnerability was exacerbated when the Soviet Union began to divert its energy exports to hard currency markets in the 1980s, and by the input inefficiencies associated with the ageing stock of technology which was a feature of Czechoslovak industry. Instead, economic reforms, designed and controlled from the top, were targeted at the institutions of economic management, particularly at the lower, local levels, which were identified as causing the poor economic performance. The debates, when they arose, concerned the proper balance of decision-making authority and responsibility between the central planning institutions (the State Planning Commission and the industrial and foreign trade ministries) and the productive sphere of the enterprises; and the nature of the directive plans (e.g. physical or financial) that were to drive socialist development. By 1989, although enterprise managements were in theory given more discretion to conclude inter-enterprise contracts themselves and to participate in deals with foreign companies, the state plan was to continue to function as the basis of enterprise targets, especially in producer goods sectors.

Formal institutions in the Czechoslovak command economy

Many of the reforms introduced in enterprise law and institutional structures did not enter into real management practice, and, in the experience of many enterprise managers, were always likely to be either side-lined or rescinded by the reluctant reformers at the national levels of the party. In this section, we examine the economic structures which constituted the institutional environment of the productive enterprise in the late 1980s, and hence of the enterprise managers who, as we shall see, were to become the driving force of the post-communist transition.

Although the emphases of the economic structures had ebbed and flowed over the forty years of state socialism, their authority and directive nature remained intact until the end (see Figure 3.1). The small executive group of the Central Committee of the Communist Party, the Politburo, decided the strategic priorities and mechanisms of the Czechoslovak economy, and the State Planning Commission (SPK, or *Státní plánovací komise*), with the status

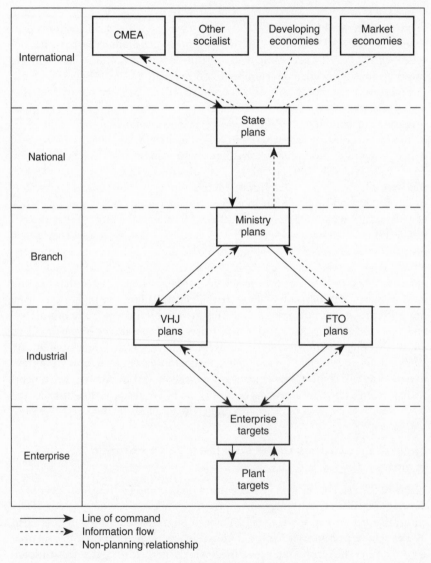

Figure 3.1 The structure of central planning in Czechoslovakia, 1980s

of a ministry, took control of fleshing out the details of the central plan. Different parts of the overall state plan were handed on to the various ministries, nominated by domestic industrial branch and by foreign trade. The early principles of physical quantity planning were supplemented gradually by more subtle financial targets related to profit and value added, but retained their mandatory role. The state plan was formulated for a five-year period, which was then broken down into annual targets for each industrial sector. The state plan would determine the degree of expansion or reduction of different sectors, itself reflecting the development needs of the domestic economy (e.g. construction of industrial plants, infrastructural enhancement, availability of consumer goods) and the external demands of fraternal economies, especially the industrial and military needs of the Soviet bloc. In establishing the production needs of the economy over the planning period, the state plan would attempt to ensure the availability of material resources at last resort, or through prearranged CMEA, usually bilateral, contracts, drawing upon foreign supplies. In this way, the industrial ministries would make decisions that eliminated the exercise of most commercial judgement at the level of the enterprise.

The CMEA was always dominated by the interests of the Soviet Union, not only because of its political influence, but also because international socialist economic forces inevitably rotated around and were attracted by the sheer size of the Soviet economy and by its critical significance as a supplier of raw material resources. The success of the CMEA at any time during its life therefore depended upon the USSR's prevailing attitude towards it (Lavigne, 1995, p. 76; Volgyes, 1995, p. 46). At its very inception in January 1949, Czechoslovak politicians had tried to define the institutions of the CMEA so as to support an international division of labour, helping it, for example, to procure the raw material and energy supplies that were the life-line for its domestic, industrialized economy. But Stalin preferred to deal with the new communist allies in a series of bilateral deals, hence allowing him to exert greater control over the economic relationships of the smaller countries (Myant, 1989, p. 15). Combined with the desire by most communist economies to optimize autarkic expansion, the failure of the CMEA to develop internal institutions for planning and international integration led to poor cooperation and very little multilateralism (Brabant, 1991, p. 96).

The ubiquity throughout the region of ČKD trams and Ikarus buses is evidence enough of a certain level of agreement on national specialization, and following the events of 1968, there was renewed interest in mutual regional cooperation and integration. In the 1970s, the CMEA became the focus of 'concerted plans' (Lavigne, 1991, pp. 88ff; Jeffries, 1993, p. 252), but even these projects tended to break down into more reliable bilateral agreements, which Lavigne (1991, pp. 76, 90) has variably labelled 'Soviet-centric bilateralism' or the 'radial pattern of intra-Comecon relations'. Bilateral agreements often led to sudden adjustments to the state plan, which communicated themselves down the hierarchy as unpredicted and unwanted increases in production targets. There were, however, attempts in the 1980s to build the economic demands of projected concerted plans into the national five-year plans.

At a national level, CMEA operated as a simple, unsophisticated trade clearing instrument, using the mechanism of the 'transferable ruble' (TR). This led to more irrational foreign trade decisions as, at the end of an accounting period, countries with a surplus of TRs would rush to do business with deficit countries. The impact of such sudden demands to clear trading imbalances served to distract enterprises in the deficit economies from their planned production schedules. The practical importance of CMEA for Czechoslovak industry was self-evident: 70 to 80 per cent of Czechoslovak trade was regularly conducted with CMEA partners, with raw materials and energy constituting some 75 per cent of its imports from the Soviet Union, and machinery and equipment being its major export to that country (Brabant, 1991, p. 115; Wolchik, 1991, p. 259; Jeffries, 1993, p. 252: Lewis, 1994, p. 218). Directly or indirectly, the CMEA was an important part of the general institutional economic context of state socialist enterprises, especially in the 1970s and 1980s. From the viewpoint of Czechoslovak heavy engineering industry, the CMEA could be the source of large-scale development projects, attracting investment and kudos to individual enterprises and plants. Within the existing international socialist division of labour, Czechoslovak engineering enterprises tended to fare well in the allocation of chunks of such projects, which were often located in the territory of the Soviet Union in order to exploit more fully the latter's enormous raw material resources (Lavigne, 1991).

The initial 1957/8 economic reforms had aimed to decentralize economic planning by establishing a new intermediate layer of economic management, the VHJ, which was to become a major feature of the organizational world (Myant, 1989, p. 82). The VHJ was an association of usually large enterprises and plants, mostly in the same field of industrial activity, which had the status of a national enterprise and served as a management framework to mediate the state plan, as elaborated at ministry level, and the production plans of its constituent economic subjects (national enterprises and subordinate plants). The VHJ was organized under the aegis and the name of an existing leading enterprise within its branch, and had the detailed task of translating the economic plan of the branch into a set of five-year and annual targets to be met by the managers of production units under its general direction.

By July 1966, the VHJs had been amalgamated and reduced to ninety-nine in number, with some organized by similarity of product and others by vertical integration (Hasager, 1986; Teichová, 1988, p. 148). On the pretext of increasing efficiency by specialization, this reform in fact further centralized 'market' structures by creating larger industrial monopolies (Myant, 1989, p. 122; Jeffries, 1993, pp. 246–7). For a short time, associated with the 1967–8 reforms, and lasting until normalization eventually put an end to the more localized decision-making autonomy, VHJs were allowed greater autonomy: to determine their own input–output mix, while maximizing net value added; to engage in some foreign trade directly with foreign partners; to administer the distribution of profits and subsidies to their constituent enterprises; and to borrow from the state bank against commercial criteria, rather than depending on state and ministerial budgets (Jeffries, 1993, pp. 246–7). While the central plan was less detailed for this short period of reform, the VHJ still had to bargain with the central institutions over questions of import limits, subsidies, credits and exemptions (Myant, 1989, p. 145).

The recentralization that followed normalization drastically reduced enterprise autonomy, and 'non-command planning' was no longer acceptable; by 1970, VHJs were required again to deliver specified goods to the state (Jeffries, 1993, p. 247). The 1980 reforms brought further refinement of the VHJ, defining three kinds of arrangement: the *koncern* (a large branch enterprise alone, or linked with much smaller ones), the *trust* (a merging of enterprises of comparable size) and the *kombinát* (the vertical integration of enterprises). It became the unit for taxation, a contributor to the state budget and the bearer of central plan targets; it was responsible for technical and economic development in its sphere of production and for applying principles of self-financing to its sub-enterprises (Rychetník, 1981, p. 117). The Law of the State Enterprise (1988) formally dissolved the VHJs, but by this time they were so well engrained in the institutional structures, and in enterprise managerial networks and practices, that many continued to exist by redefining themselves as new state enterprises, or acting in other support capacities to their former subjects (Rychetník, 1992, p. 114; MacDermott, 1993; Myant, 1993, p. 158; Cziria, 1995, p. 65).

All foreign trade contracts and arrangements were handled by Foreign Trade Organizations (FTOs), which had a monopoly of exchanges with clients both within and outside the socialist world. Their primary aim was to secure materials that were not domestically available and to administer the selling of domestic products in order to balance foreign trade. FTOs had their own planned targets that derived from the state plan, and tended to specialize in certain industrial or product groups (Lavigne, 1991, p. 128). In their work, they acted as a buffer between foreign partners and domestic manufacturers, thereby reinforcing the principle of autarky (Brabant, 1991, p. 79). The FTOs would purchase at domestic prices from home producers those products destined for export, and sell them for hard or non-convertible currency (including TRs) according to the client nation. Reciprocally, they would buy imported goods in the appropriate currency, and sell them on the local markets at domestic prices denominated in domestic currency. The differences between domestic and trade prices in domestic currency were offset by the 'price equalization account', which was part of the national budget (Brabant, 1991, p. 78; Jeffries, 1993, p. 24). This account gained from or subsidized the price differences, and thus passively absorbed the consequences of trade. Domestic producers and other economic agents were thereby restricted in their access to what was happening in terms of comparative costs and scarcities on the world market, and, with little incentive to develop new products or to be innovative in production methods and technologies, they gradually lost contact with industrial developments elsewhere.

The breaking down of the state monopoly of foreign trade had been a slow process in Czechoslovakia. When given the opportunities, few enterprises took advantage of any autonomy to trade directly with foreign clients (Lavigne, 1991, p. 78), since the skills, experience and knowledge were so concentrated in the FTOs. In the 1980 reforms, the Law on Economic Relations with Foreign Countries provided for certain experiments to be started, incorporating FTOs in the larger VHJs, or establishing contractual arrangements between the two formal institutions.[2] Some specialized producers of consumer goods were allowed to export directly (Lavigne, 1991, p. 135; Jeffries, 1993, p. 252). There was further decentralization of foreign trade from the ministry to production enterprises in 1986, and the state introduced new legislation allowing, under great restrictions, state enterprises to enter joint venture agreements with foreign companies. This legislation enjoyed little success in attracting foreign investment and technology, mostly because of the limited control it allowed foreign partners, and because of the complexity of the regulations, stretching back over decades, that governed such relationships. The legislation was extended in 1988 in order to increase interest, but the numbers of joint ventures established before 1990 was 'modest' (Wolchik, 1991, pp. 272ff; see also Jeffries, 1993, p. 252).

For most of the state socialist period in Czechoslovakia, the state-owned enterprise was legally known as a national enterprise (*národní podnik*) with associations of dependence and subordination (Rychetník, 1992, p. 113). Any devolution of decision-making responsibility had only happened briefly during the late 1960s and up to about 1972, at which time normalization finally struck at the lower levels of the economic system and reinstituted the hierarchical authority in central planning. The 1988 Law of the State Enterprise defined the greater independence of the local production unit following the dissolution of the VHJs, and changed the legal relationship of the management to the assets which provided the enterprise's productive base. State ownership was given a more concrete expression in the guise of a 'founder', which appointed the directorate of the state enterprise (*státní podnik*), the successor to the national enterprise. The 'all-people property' was placed under the stewardship of the management, who had the responsibility 'to reproduce and augment [it]' (Červinka, 1987, p. 8; Rychetník, 1992, p. 114). In principle, the enterprise management took on the authority and obligations that had hitherto resided in the VHJs or a more senior level. However, as before, the spirit of these changes was subjected to much resistance. The local enterprise managers who had received more formal responsibility for commercial, financial and investment decisions were able to frustrate the functioning of the employee councils recreated by the 1988 legislation because the basic power structures and objectives of the economic system had remained unchanged (Jeffries, 1993, pp. 249–50; Myant, 1993, p. 160). 'The fate of the Law on the State Enterprise was a typical example of how the entrenched bureaucracy could ensure that apparently radical measures ended up altering nothing' (Myant, 1993, p. 158). The state continued to exercise control over key economic constraints, like being able to impose limits on the use of scarce raw materials and on access to foreign currency (Jeffries, 1993, p. 249), and despite formal-legal changes enterprise management was still unable to exercise much discretion, being subordinated to plant and local party authorities (Wolchik, 1991, p. 221). Since many of the institutional changes were only due to be introduced after 1990, it is impossible to know whether these late reforms could have had real impact within socialism.

Within the state-owned enterprise, the director would formally receive the production targets from the VHJ, and devise internal plans for their attainment. These plans would include ensuring that adequate supplies were forthcoming from the designated partners at agreed delivery times. The duty of line management was to realize the production plans by setting up production systems and schedules, and to control the resources that would permit the production process to proceed smoothly. Non-line middle managers were mainly collectors, recorders and transmitters of information regarding the fulfilment of the plan. The performance of the enterprise was judged according to a mixture of financial and physical criteria, the exact nature of which changed periodically, and according to whether the system was in a centralizing or a decentralizing phase. The workforce was expected to meet the schedules by working to norms. Reward systems for managers were linked to the successful meeting of production targets, and capital investment in the enterprise, which was an external central planning decision, was related in part to the enterprise's track record. It was in the interests of managers at all levels to do all they could to ensure the visible attainment of production targets. Those managers of units which demonstrably failed to realize plans were liable to be demoted, moved or otherwise to lose status and access to associated 'privileges' (e.g. cars, foreign travel, special accommodation). It was thus normal in some enterprises for management personnel to change quite frequently.

The state-owned enterprise performed both economic, productive activities and social, welfare roles within strong political and institutional contexts that led to general similarities in enterprise structures and activities (Tsoukas, 1994). Each enterprise functioned within the strictures of the planning hierarchy, which placed powerful constraints on the structuring and management of industrial enterprises. The enterprise was formally organized in a strict hierarchical form, with its own internal institutions to ensure conformity with downward commands and to produce an adequate supply of upward flowing information. The organization chart was invariably based upon an approved 'blueprint', which was largely a simple functional arrangement of support services around a direct line structure (see Figure 3.2). The staff

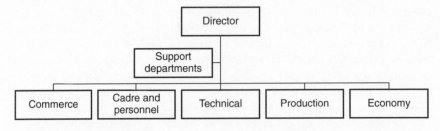

Figure 3.2 The basic functional structure

structures provided basic administrative support, as well as the security and 'defence' activities that typified the state socialist mentality. The production department within the mechanical engineering enterprise was paramount, and the head of the function was the most important deputy director. Under the production director were the various subordinated plants, factories and workshops. The larger plants themselves were big enough to be considered a production unit. The production facility was given strong support by the technical department, which provided design, research and development, organized and implemented investments and offered other engineering services. In the mechanical engineering sectors, the technical function was regarded as the most important structure after production, and was staffed by highly qualified, very professional engineers.

The mechanical engineering state enterprise had a trade or commercial department which could best be described as sales administration. It co-operated with the technical and production functions to arrange specifications, supplies and delivery times for products whose destination had normally been determined by higher authorities in the planning structures. The VHJ, for example, had varying degrees of decision-making power over trading exchanges, dependent on the significance of the project or the historical phase; but the basic relations of trade were decided under the overall direction of the state plan. In terms of foreign trade, it was the branch FTO that performed the active side of the selling, sometimes developing skills that in many ways resembled 'marketing', although in the ČSSR for most of the communist era it was inadvisable to use the term 'market'. Where the enterprise's overall target actually exceeded the deliveries specified in its plan, as set by state-agreed contracts with partner enterprises at home or abroad, the commercial department might have had to be more proactive in finding clients.

In addition to administrative controls, the enterprise was essentially economically monitored from the outside, with financial responsibility lying mostly with the VHJ, which accumulated the surpluses of its member enterprises, paid state taxes and distributed funds (from depreciation) for materials purchasing, research and development and long-term investments in accordance with the priorities set by its part of the state plan. The economy department within the enterprise was therefore predominantly a bookkeeping function, with duties to collect, analyse and supply internal information to the VHJ. Except for short historical periods, the economy department in the subordinate enterprise was not a location for financial decision-making, though, as performance targets became more based on financial rather than simple output figures, the internal economists would collect quite sophisticated information about costs, wages, prices, revenues, output and depreciation as well as various measures of 'profit'.

Perhaps the most controversial department in the enterprise structure was the cadre and personnel (*kádrové a personální*) department, whose tasks not only covered the activities of maintaining staff records and overseeing wages, but also involved the creation and supervision of political records, especially about prospective or aspiring managers. Whereas most of the management functions within the organization structure were rational elements to be found in any business activity, the cadre and personnel department was the most visible sign of the underlying communist control within enterprise management. At the local level, it was the cadre section of the personnel department that enabled the functioning of the *nomenklatura* system (see Brewster, 1992, p. 571; Koubek and Brewster, 1995, p. 225).

However, the cadre and personnel department was not the only mechanism for reinforcing the socialist goals of the local enterprise. First, parallel to the management structures, each enterprise had political structures which oversaw and scrutinized management decisions. The enterprise had a CP committee, whose membership and functions served to link enterprise activities with the local and district party organs; and each section or department within the enterprise would normally have a nominated representative of the party. Second, the trade union was an institution responsible to the CP rather than its 'members', and served particularly to administer and supervise the enterprise's social policy. Trade unions were subordinate to the CP both nationally and at plant level, and had little authority with either the workforce or management (Wolchik, 1991, p. 220). Strikes were illegal, and trade unions had little power to exercise on behalf of workers. However, they were part of the 'bargaining' machinery to decide the exact sums of money to be put aside from the wage fund and other sources for social welfare services (in the cultural and social fund), and were signatories to the annual 'collective agreement'.

The party was also represented through other political and ideological organs, such as the Youth League, the society for Friendship with the Soviet Union and the enterprise militia (*milice*), but this triumvirate of senior management, CP committee and trade union were the main forces of power in the enterprise. Together they were expected to ensure that state priorities as well as working-class opinion was represented in enterprise decision-making. The operation of the *nomenklatura* system, the institutional ties between party and trade union and the ultimate power of the Communist Party at all levels led to an overlapping of the three elements in the enterprise power structure, and a dependency in decision-making that, to people on the outside, looked more conspiratorial than representative.

Summary

The economic system of state socialism was designed to operate strictly hierarchically, ensuring that the priorities decided at state level through the dual structures of Central Committee of the Communist Party and state government were driven through intermediate levels of the command economy and the party system to be represented in each and every enterprise by the dual and overlapping structures of the party committee and enterprise management. Despite various attempts at reforming the highly centralized planning mechanisms introduced from the Soviet Union in the late 1940s, the basic institutional principles remained more or less intact, and the macro and micro structures of the command-economic system retained an interlocked functional coherence. These neo-Stalinist systems and structures continued to constitute the essential features of the economic-administrative environment of state enterprise management right up to the end of the 1980s.

In the next chapter, we explain how, within concrete state enterprises, there arose significant divergences between these formal economic institutions of state socialism and the institutionalized practices of those charged with realizing state socialist production. Unlike many researchers who have been interested in the malfunctioning of the command economy, we are able to draw directly upon the experiences and memories of enterprise managers whose work involved making the system work. We argue that the divergent everyday management practices that our respondents recall can be understood as normal social responses to the formal institutions, given the economic realities of state socialism. In Chapter 5, in recapitulating the nature of pre-1989 management and organization, we explore institutional explanations of these findings, and begin to examine their implications for the post-communist transition.

Notes

1 The complexities and ambiguities of the *nomenklatura* status emerge at various stages of the argument during the book.
2 Hasager (1986, p. 170) cites an example of such a VHJ–FTO arrangement between Tesla and Kovo, which gave Tesla more direct contact with its clients overseas, changed its accounting methods and fed a profit item straight into its budget. The earlier mechanism had meant that Tesla only dealt with Kovo, through whose transactions 'profits' would slip back into the state budget.

4 State enterprises and their management in Czechoslovakia

In Chapter 1, we outlined some of the general characteristics of the four enterprises (see Table 1.2 as a summary), and recounted how they had fared within the institutional structures of the Czechoslovak command economy described in Chapter 3. The enterprises grew and adapted in the light of the political and economic processes of state socialism, and each enterprise was a product of its industrial branch – the economically strategic engineering sectors. On the other hand, they were also shaped by the ways in which their managers attempted to make sense of the planning system imposed on them, and manoeuvred to satisfy the institutional and technical demands of important stakeholders such as the state, the central planning machinery, various partner enterprises, the workforce and the community in which they were located. The managers were able to utilize their discretion openly while the command economy was in a liberal, decentralizing phase; during more conservative, recentralizing periods they were under greater economic or political pressure to enact practices that toed the institutional line. The state-owned enterprise was not just an economic production unit, but also an instrument of national and local social policy, and, relatedly, a political mechanism for ensuring that the economic institutions operated in the material interests of the Communist Party and, by extension, of the people. These diverse functions were represented in both the structures of the enterprises and the activities of their managements.

In this chapter, we report our managerial respondents' direct experiences of state socialism, how its institutions and priorities impacted upon their lives and work within the enterprises. We have drawn heavily upon the research materials that were assembled from the interviews in the four enterprises, but make links with the findings of related research conducted in Czechoslovakia and the wider region.

The socio-economic reality of state enterprise management

In Chapter 3 we explained some of the key features of the institutional landscape of the typical state enterprise in the ČSSR in the late 1980s. This picture of the command economy was captured by many economic observers of the state socialist system from a distance, by examining formal and legislative records and newspaper items. In fact, at a micro level of enterprise behaviour, the system sometimes worked in ways very different from its institutional formalities. In order to understand the economics of 'really existing socialism',[1] it is necessary to examine the everyday experiences and practices of enterprise managers – an objective that was very difficult to realize at the time.

When the rational principles for central economic planning were applied within the institutional structures and ideological context of state socialism, their effects on human motivation and action built up tendencies towards the well-documented vicious circle of macroeconomic inefficiency. As elsewhere in the former Soviet bloc, Czechoslovak state enterprises suffered persistently from low productivity, low morale, lack of shopfloor discipline, inadequate investment and chronically ageing technology, poor quality products, overproduction of waste, hoarding of labour power, overstaffing and so on (Kornai, 1980; Dyker, 1981; Seeger, 1981; Lane, 1987; Arnot, 1988; Wolchik, 1991, p. 224; Burawoy and Lukács, 1992). The sources of these problems of economic performance lay in the operational relationships between the central planning institutions, the management of state enterprises and the dynamics of the labour process. In the 1980s, Czechoslovak enterprises had to address the irrationalities of a centralized, neo-Stalinist economic system more than anywhere else in Central Europe. The institutional structures of Czechoslovak state planning created major problems for enterprise managers, who had to cultivate locally rational business strategies and recipes[2] in order to fulfil their duties within the planned economy – notably the visible attainment of the production targets set within the planning hierarchy.

But the problems and subsequent practices of Czechoslovak enterprise management in the 1980s were influenced not just by the technical aspects of assuring production activities in the autocratically managed, shortage economy of state socialism, but also by the socio-political context of enterprise life during the years of normalization which followed the Warsaw Pact invasion of 1968. According to Jeffries (1993, p. 253), normalization was like a 'heavy mantle descending on the country', in which, in the words of Myant (1989, p. 182), the 'principal weapon . . . was carefully controlled repression'. Before examining the development of management as institutionalized practices, we need to explore in more depth the ways in which normalization impacted upon everyday life in the enterprise, and the subsequent problems that arose from the need for managers to deal with their own legitimacy.

Normalization and the management of managerial legitimacy

The normalization process had profound effects that went beyond the political subservience of Prague to Moscow, the rigidifying of its economic institutions and the stultification of the economy, which we considered in Chapter 3. The autocratic enforcement of the neo-Stalinist political reality and its social consequences defined critical dimensions of Czechoslovak society, in which context the management of industrial enterprises had to take place between 1970 and 1989. Normalization placed a wedge between the Czechoslovak state and its people that was to diminish the standard of civil life in a society proud of its democratic past. The acquiescence of the Dubček government, the purging of the Communist Party of nearly half a million members and the reassertion of the party in renewed Stalinist form undermined the relationship between the political elite and the citizens. This had major implications for the social support of state socialism, diminishing the degree of normative consent and creating a system dependent on passive support bolstered by the continuing threat of coercion. The ensuing crisis of legitimacy was reflected in all spheres of society (Pelikan, 1976, pp. 29ff; Kusin, 1978; Paul, 1979, p. 39; Renner, 1989, pp. 86ff), which suffered from overwhelming disillusionment. According to one observer, the 'gap between the ruled and the rulers (whose tenure is solely dependent on Soviet patronage) is greater than that to be found in any other society in Eastern Europe' (Ulč, 1978, p. 422).

From this state of political and social illegitimacy, there emerged an implicit social contract, where

> the rulers rule and the citizenry, for not meddling into public affairs, is rewarded with an opportunity to attend to its private affairs. Preoccupation with the pleasures of a consumer society . . . is the order of the day . . . The citizens are immune to ideology, but their passivity within the political realm is also reflected in the economic sphere where minimum exertion is the norm followed by the working force.
>
> (Ulč, 1978, p. 430; compare Šimečka, 1984, pp. 142ff)

Normalization exacted a moral price, in that normal citizens renounced political activity and withdrew from the public and civic spheres of society. But in economic terms, the price was possibly much higher and more far-reaching (see Paul, 1979, pp. 27ff). The socio-political repercussions of the events of 1968 had major consequences for enterprise managers both as individuals and as a group of *nomenklatura* associated with the widely despised political regime; and for management as an activity, the aim of which was to control and motivate employees in a troubled economic system.

First, the widespread purges of reformist communists that followed the normalization policy led to the loss of a whole generation of talented managers. Many managers or potential managers had their careers truncated because their conduct and attachments during the Prague Spring were deemed contrary to the priorities of the CP, and their names were not approved in connection with *nomenklatura* posts (Wolchik, 1991, pp. 36–7). There were several people in our sample whose careers were caught up in the consequences of normalization. In 1970, one aspiring manager in Vols was told that his managerial career was finished, and was prevented by the party from writing a technical book on cutting technologies, so he decided to opt out of creative work in his department and joined the enterprise basketball club in order to express his potential. A Jesenické Strojírny production manager had to resign his party membership in 1976, and returned to manual work until the changes in 1989. One engineer in the same enterprise submitted a technical paper to be given at an engineering conference in Cannes (France), and duly applied for leave. His request was turned down, because some 'sleepy party worker' had recorded the applicant as a member of KAN (*Klub angažovaných nestraníků*; see Brisch and Volgyes, 1979, pp. 217–19), the banned movement of non-party members. He was not allowed to travel again, and received no promotion.

A group of Jesenické Strojírny managers just below directorate level had in August 1968 jointly signed a letter on enterprise notepaper protesting about the Soviet invasion, only to be demoted to technical or labouring positions. Such explicit opposition was inevitably punished, in this case the minimum sanction being banishment to the shopfloor. Another respondent who received such treatment after 1968 spoke of being 'angry but powerless'. By 1989, many of these 'men of '68', who were around forty years of age at the time of the Prague Spring, were too old to realize their abilities.

Second, and as significantly, those who filled the senior managerial positions in state-owned enterprises after normalization were thereafter more closely identified with the discredited Communist Party. In order to hold any such position, managers had had to sign documents approving of the 1968 invasion. According to one interviewee, after 1968 many of these managers were purely political appointments and were often regarded by employees as 'stupid', because, following the Warsaw Pact invasion, no sane Czech or Slovak could believe any more in the political propriety of Soviet-style communism. The purely political nature of post-invasion appointments led to a managerial cadre which lacked professional credibility or competence. Other expedient and ambitious aspirants attached themselves to the Communist Party and its subsidiary organs in order to progress their managerial careers. For example, junior managers in Jesenické Strojírny joined the enterprise *milice*, understanding that those in the party structures would perceive this act as a sign of ideological commitment. Some of these enterprise managers were technically qualified and capable of fulfilling their duties, and their connections with the party were, as argued below, crucial to making the irrationalities of the economic system work to the enterprise's benefit. However, at the same time, their participation in the *nomenklatura* system, with its rewards and privileges, eroded their social status, their personal credibility and their managerial legitimacy in the eyes of employees, employees' families and the community at large.

Third, and relatedly, normalization and the public revelation of the 'real meaning' of communism had a major impact on employee attitudes, and the nature of community and social life in the former Czechoslovakia. Individuals withdrew psychologically and in spirit, and could 'submerge themselves deeply in their private lives' (Šimečka, 1984, p. 143; see also Ulč, 1978, p. 430; Wolchik, 1991, pp. 37–8; Wheaton and Kavan, 1992, p. 9). They continued to attend work in order to make a living, but working hard was seen to be an act of support for the regime. Under pressure, they turned up for the ritual social manifestations of socialist achievement, such as May Day and celebrations of the October Revolution,[3] but these were poor indicators of their enthusiasm or commitment.

> There were no conflicts before the revolution because of fear. Non-communists had to attend meetings and play along by reading prepared speeches saying how wonderful communism, the situation and work were.
>
> (Vols department head)

The 1970s and 1980s became a period when people would spend their spare time building their private houses or weekend cottages, or tending their allotments (Paul, 1979, pp. 33–4). This flight into privacy, or 'internal migration', was a way of seeking peace of mind and social sanctuary.

> There were lots of stories; people resorted to stories because they were unable to live their personal lives . . . most stories in Jesenické Strojírny are negative, the worst symbol being that the name of the plant was originally [that of a famous Stalinist leader].

This legacy of illegitimacy and mistrust was a special feature of Czechoslovak enterprise relations. When asked about enterprise 'heroes', one of our respondents in Jesenické Strojírny suggested: 'The real heroes [of the enterprise] were heroes in a negative sense, in that they resisted the regime, the local situation and management.' Or again, in the same enterprise: 'the heroes were those who would speak out, because they would often have to leave'.

These social features of the normalized Czechoslovakia made the tasks of management especially difficult. The government tried to find methods to improve labour productivity – for example, by building up the incentive element of the monetary wage in the 1970s and 1980s – but it proved ineffective. Czechoslovakia probably had the smallest wage differentials between occupational groups in the industrialized world, but central efforts to increase motivation tended to reinforce existing, narrow differentials as the norm (Altmann, 1987; Teichová, 1988, pp. 110–11; Večerník, 1992).

Employees' attitudes and responses to the structure of monetary and social rewards were a major influence within the enterprise on the poor efficiency of labour, the underutilization of working time and weak labour discipline. Apart from East German workers, the Czechs and Slovaks were the most 'pampered' workforce, with one of the highest standards of living in the

Soviet bloc (Renner, 1989, p. 146; Dawisha, 1990, p. 189; Glenny, 1993, p. 31; Lewis, 1994, p. 167).[4] Enterprise managers struggled to exert real control in the workplace and to find ways to improve performance, because economically, politically and morally there was very little reason for the workers to cooperate beyond conceding surface-level compliance.

These social processes were not unique to Czechoslovakia, but took on an exaggerated form as a direct result of the 1968 experience and its socio-political consequences. They exacerbated the enormous problems of enterprise management. The difficulties of managing the shopfloor and the failure of managers to create high enterprise performance were partly the consequence of macroeconomic systemic dysfunctions, as described in many economic analyses since Kornai (1980); but, at the level of the enterprise itself, economic failure was a *social accomplishment*. Despite their relative successes in 'achieving the plan' through the development of micro-institutional practices (see below), many enterprise managers were disabled by the low popular esteem of the regime, and their own related social illegitimacy.

Enterprise managers strove to overcome their own lack of esteem and credibility and to acquire social legitimacy for both personal and enterprise reasons. One way in which they could improve their social status was by increasing enterprise involvement in their local communities. Most managers and employees of Vols and Jesenické Strojírny, which had been sited in the late 1940s and early 1950s with little economic justification in village and small rural town environments respectively, saw the fate of their enterprises as being inevitably tied up with the development of the community – a view encouraged by dominant communist rhetoric. As we have seen, they directly built, or indirectly attracted money to build, blocks of apartments, supplied hot water and energy directly to the community as a free by-product, invested copiously in the recreation facilities of the growing town and subsidized local activities. Such social participation took on an even stronger symbolic value during the 1970s and 1980s.

By building up the cultural and social fund and developing agreements on social projects with the trade union, the local district councils and party committees, it was possible for enterprise managers to undertake the role of benefactor within the community. Managers in all four enterprises offered substantial financial and material support for the construction of social and sports facilities through the channelling of legally accumulated funds into community projects. But directors were also often able to utilize their position and power to exploit the practice of soft budgeting and to develop informal, even illegal, methods of financial support.[5] Such methods could be highly confidential and risky if discovered, and involved a transfer to social usage of capital monies formally allocated to the development of production assets and activities. For example, the enterprise might seek central permission and resources to build facilities for business use, but later, as intended all along, the new facilities would be converted to social ends.

Such seems to be the case for Jesenické Strojírny's interest in sports. The enterprise director of Jesenické Strojírny was a devoted supporter of tennis, and became a major benefactor and patron of the sport. In his capacity as enterprise director, he committed a lot of the enterprise's cultural and social fund to the development of dedicated facilities in Jesenice. However, this fund did not cover the real costs of the enterprise's social activities, so he financed sports activities and the building of recreation facilities by illegally transferring capital funds. The interests and power of Jesenické Strojírny's senior directors led to its much greater involvement in sports and recreation than the neighbouring enterprises, and the enterprise and its senior managers had a strong and positive image. According to one long-standing employee, Jesenické Strojírny 'was one of the best enterprises in the past . . . The wages were the highest in the region, and people could spend their leisure time with the help of the enterprise.' Or again: 'It was a thing of honour to work for Jesenické Strojírny because it built up sporting facilities and funded sporting activities' (former basketball 'amateur', working for Jesenické Strojírny). The last respondent thought that the enterprise's director 'affected life in Jesenické Strojírny and the whole region. He exploited his abilities to the full, for the benefit of the region, social activities and the community.'

All managers were keen to impress the community, to improve the respect for enterprise management and to enhance the reputation of the enterprise as an employer. The directors of Jesenické Strojírny enjoyed a good reputation in the community for the building of the tennis complex, an extravagant swimming pool, grass-roots basketball facilities etc. The methods used suggest that insinuating the enterprise into community affairs was motivated by more than obedience to party policy. Directors were aware of the benefits of a closer enterprise–community relationship in their attempts to retrieve the goodwill of increasingly withdrawn employees and their families. Their success was limited, and the problem of the social legitimacy of enterprise management following normalization continued to plague individual managers and their management performance right up to 1989 – and, as we shall see, remained a critical problem for post-communist management.

The technical problems of central planning

State enterprise management in Czechoslovakia was formally defined in accordance with the socio-economic structures of late state socialism, but had to be socially enacted by managers at enterprise level against the background of the real, everyday production and distribution problems created by the malfunctioning of the central planning system (see McDermott, 1993, pp. 10ff; Soulsby and Clark, 1996b). In order to overcome the microeconomic problems created by really existing socialism, senior managers often had to resort to quasi-legal, 'uninstitutional' or deviant practices. Where such conduct became the normal, accepted methods of management, part of the social organization and normative practices of state enterprise management, it effectively became institutionalized in social behaviour. In the next chapter, we shall argue that these socially produced, institutionalized practices of management gradually overrode and amended the formal institutions of the command economy. In what follows, we shall focus on the experiences of the managers in Vols, Agstroj, Jesenické Strojírny and Montáže Jesenice, and the approaches, strategies and practices they developed in order to overcome the critical operational problems that dominated their working lives as state socialist managers. The key problems fall into four interrelated areas of management: managing hierarchical relations with the VHJ and the central institutions; managing lateral relations with supplier and client partners; managing the labour force; and managing production and capital investment needs.

Being at the end of a hierarchical chain of decision-making, state-owned enterprises had little formal input into their own operational conduct, so one of the major potential sources of problems was the external authoritative structure of which it was a subordinate part. From the perspective of the managers, the central planning authorities always handed down to the enterprise production plans that were 'impossible'. One senior manager in Montáže Jesenice spoke of the pressures of central planning:

> Then the enterprise received the [VHJ]-stamped targets, and the directors on receipt responded by 'no, it's not possible', and tried to resist the plan or tried to change it to something realizable . . . The plan was not connected with reality.

This lack of realism was also associated with inflexibility. In Vols, a manager commented:

> the targets were exact, but the figures were inexact. Everyone [the centre] requested more and the figures were high and unrealistic . . . plans were rigid, because everything was planned well in advance. Sudden adjustments to production were difficult.

The rigid, unreal plans led to internal disputes within the enterprises, as each plant or section struggled to minimize its difficulties. Jesenické Strojírny's VHJ would divide the plan between the various factories of Jesenické Strojírny:

> It was often impossible to fulfil the plans so each [section] looked for ways to blame the others. They fought over being left with 'Black Peter' [the most difficult or least desirable part of the plan[6]], that's why there were lots of sackings of deputies; it was dangerous not to meet the production plan.

For most enterprises, the plan came in two parts: the specific targets, which demanded particular products linked to particular client enterprises; and the general targets, which were often defined in financial terms and required the enterprise to look for unspecified partners. Each type of target had its own difficulties, and, as we shall see, called for different types of response. Central planners were often seen as detached bureaucrats with little idea about the reality of the mechanical engineering industry, with its supply shortages and low technology (see below), and became the butt of enterprise managers.

> The relationship [of Jesenické Strojírny] with VVV [its VHJ] was not good, because if they could not fulfil the plan Jesenické Strojírny had to indicate why, whether because of lack of productive capacity or lack of materials – management had to spend a lot of time considering how to deal with the problem.

The funding arrangements, reward and punishment systems put enterprise managers under continuous pressure to meet production plans. Managerial careers blossomed or died according to whether the plan was accomplished or not.

Once the plans were in place, problems shifted to the more operational level of creating conditions for their delivery. Yet in the prevailing economic conditions there were a variety of difficulties, chief among which concerned the supply of raw materials and semi-products. There were not only shortages and haphazard deliveries, but also worries about their quality and reliability. This had significant implications for all those in the enterprise, especially when taken alongside the problems arising from the main resource of the production enterprise – labour.

The state's commitment to full employment led to acute labour shortages, especially in the skilled jobs that were typical of the mechanical engineering sector, but the central planning of labour resources (with only fringe labour markets) kept money wages tightly regulated at low levels. In a society committed to social equality and flat wage differentials, it was really difficult for enterprises to attract and retain 'sufficient' workers of the right calibre, and to motivate them to work hard. These problems were particularly critical for enterprises built in rural locations like Volna, and to a degree Jesenice, and during periods of rapid enterprise expansion, such as for Vols from 1955 to 1965 and for Jesenické Strojírny in the following decade.

Poor labour productivity was a chronic feature of state enterprises. The ageing technology (see below) and the poor supply and quality of materials and components became perpetual and increasing characteristics of the mechanical engineering industry. As we shall see later, the management was driven by state employment policy and these economic circumstances to hoard labour power beyond economically efficient numbers in order to meet the sudden demands of rush jobs and to perform the enterprises' wider social role as distributer of welfare and provider of 'voluntary labour' to various community and agricultural schemes (Kornai, 1980, p. 256). These responses had clear implications for the management of the labour process. Agstroj managers spoke of the 'hidden unemployment' that resulted from the hoarding, and since 'work and social welfare were guaranteed, it was not possible to shed labour'. A worker in Vols's metallurgy plant spoke of 'the negative attitude on the shopfloor. There were so many workers that people could refuse to do things.'

Another Vols worker from the press shop spoke of the bad working practices, such as extending break times from twenty to ninety minutes. Such practices were related to the poor discipline that resulted from the power of labour, the dependence of managers on their goodwill and the overemployment. An Agstroj manager complained: 'it was not possible to reward people if they were not in the party, so people would say "I am only paid for being here" [i.e. not for doing work]. There was a sense of apathy.' So employees suffered from low motivation. A Vols manager explained: 'Culture was not good because the employees did not care; for example, they did not keep the workplace clean. Everybody had to be forced to do things because they were not interested.' It was a similar story in Jesenické Strojírny: 'In former times . . . the motivation of workers was at a low level – people were not expected to be effective.'

Managers recognized that underlying many of the economic problems of engineering enterprises under Czechoslovak state socialism were the poor state of production technology and the related matter of under-investment. This had a major impact on the productivity of enterprises, and posed important questions for managers who were under pressure to meet production plans. The enterprises had little control over any surplus revenues from business activities: '[Our machines] were exported to earn hard currency, but Agstroj never had enough money; it was creamed off by the ministry for other reasons.' In Vols, according to a director, 'Before, Vols had no ability to spend. Management had to pass profits back to the ministry, and then claim it back, and start to fight to increase [productive] capacity.' A former technical director at Jesenické Strojírny expressed the same frustrations: 'If Jesenické Strojírny wanted to invest in some capital equipment, it had to get in the queue for central money . . . but the ministry allocated it between enterprises to do certain projects.'

Accumulated centrally or in the VHJs, surpluses were redistributed to enterprises in accordance with national production and investment priorities. According to one senior manager in Agstroj: 'VHJs organized both good and poor enterprises, but made them all average' [through their investment and planning activities]. This tendency towards industrial mediocrity was directly linked to the declining productivity of the enterprises. In Vols, for example, the outdated production technology led to quality problems, machine breakdowns, uncompetitive production, the missing of delivery deadlines and non-fulfilment of plans. In Jesenické Strojírny, they functioned with assembly equipment such as mobile cranes that were twenty-five years old, and were liable to break down and delay work. Inadequate capital investment further increased management's dependence upon the flexibility and skill of the workforce and increased overstaffing, as special workshops (compare Dyker, 1981, pp. 64–5; Arnot, 1988, p. 58) and maintenance teams were required to keep production turning over.

Research funds also resided at central and VHJ levels, and access to them depended on hierarchically determined rules. Sound investment and research and development decisions were barely possible at levels above the enterprise, because even at the point of production, according to an Agstroj manager with twenty years of state socialist experience, 'at that time no one really knew the cost of a machine. Economic calculations were done at ministry level [and] prices were calculated to suit political ends.' Former VHJ managers saw costing and pricing of products as more rational, based on enterprise costing methods; but even then, as one said, local management only knew the real costs 'to some extent'.

The premises of enterprise management: Hierarchy, fear and conformity

The command economy routinely presented everyday enterprise management with economic and technical problems, arising from the subordinate position of the enterprise in the planning hierarchy. Managerial responses to these problems were of course variable, and depended to some extent on managerial experience, competence and imagination; however, they were not random or idiosyncratic. Evidence across the three enterprises and the plant suggests that over the period of state socialism, and within the constraints of the centralized institutional system, managers developed a shared repertoire of practices and recipes that helped in alleviating the symptoms of the problems, while not tackling their causes, which were beyond their sphere of influence. Underlying this repertoire was a set of socially accepted, well-understood precepts and expectations which defined the limits to and the possibilities of their responses. Chief among these precepts were the inevitable facticity of an authoritarian hierarchy, the Communist Party as the supporting principle of managerial power, the centrality of production values and the normality of middle management conformity and passivity.

Managers at all levels of the enterprises accepted and acknowledged the inviolability of the hierarchical principle of the economy. In all they said, the central planning institutions were acknowledged as an unavoidable feature of their lives. Respondents at Agstroj expressed it thus:

> [Agstroj] was governed by the general direction [i.e. the VHJ], which got its basic direction from the government . . . Managers were trained to fulfil the plan or be criticized.

[Managers] worked under a centrally directed system and could not work independently.

One senior manager in Jesenické Strojírny understood plan fulfilment as the 'first law of enterprise management', which managers had to pursue irrespective of other factors such as cost. Everyone got used to this system, and humorous stories were circulated that underlined the absoluteness of the 'law'. One story, told by a director at Agstroj, concerned Tesla, the famous manufacturer of radios and televisions across the region. 'Tesla, in Slovakia, made lots of radios for stock. Every barn in Slovakia was full of Tesla radios; there were five trainloads of Tesla TVs forever travelling around Slovakia. But they fulfilled their plan!' In another story, recounted by a manager at Jesenické Strojírny, plan fulfilment remains the central theme, but from the opposite angle. 'In 1988 a planner at the National Planning Committee made a [clerical] error in leaving off six zeros from the order for sanitary towels. Two factories were closed and there was a national shortage!' We can only hope that the stories were apocryphal.

The importance of the plan and of the centralized norms supporting it was also impressed within the enterprise. The state enterprise itself was accepted as naturally hierarchical, a direct reflection of the external institutional world, and there developed a distinctive management style. In Agstroj, the main management building was known as the *hrad*, or castle; the enterprise directors in the enterprises were seen as 'autocratic', 'imperial, hard and strong', 'the king of everything . . . demanding obedience', 'centralized style', 'always had to win', 'mostly formal'. Although these descriptors sometimes carried a value judgement – for example, coupled with words like 'arrogant' and 'meddling' – they were accepted very matter-of-factly, as a necessary aspect of the system at that time. A department head in Jesenické Strojírny spoke of a former enterprise director: 'Mr P was director from 1962 to 1968; a centralized man, a real socialist manager. He had a primitive method of managing the factory, despatching orders from the top to the bottom, unable to delegate anything, he had to know everything.'

A common and related part of managerial life was the fear of punishment that characterized the enforcement of hierarchical rule. Underlying the authority of the executive management was the power of the communist establishment, which oversaw all or most aspects of enterprise life. Each enterprise had its parallel communist structures, each department had its party representative, each career manager was a *nomenklatura* or aspiring *nomenklatura* member, and the enterprise cadre policy was assiduously administered by the personnel department. 'Most decisions were made by the ruling party . . . the party came first, and people joined it in order to have a chance' (Director at Jesenické Strojírny).

The Communist Party appeared to be especially strong in Vols, possibly because of its involvement with military engineering:

The most powerful department before the changes was cadre and personnel because of its party security role . . . Everyone had personal files held on them, saying what they could do, whom they could know and what they could have access to. Managers could get information on anyone to see if they could be promoted, transferred etc. . . . . People were afraid of relations with party members. (An assembly worker)

Vols again, this time from two directors:

The situation before the revolution depended on the Communist Party, because the [enterprise] director was also a member of the party. Vols was an important communist factory . . . Most important management decisions were taken at the very centre of the party, in Brno and Prague; top management just accepted them.

Every important decision was made by the Communist Party, or by the individuals put in place by the party . . . The enterprise director had a formal responsibility to the party.

A number of managers and workers spoke of the fear of always being under scrutiny. The presumptions of hierarchical rule were complemented by the knowledge that the authority of the executive was founded on the ubiquitous power of the party.

The hierarchical nature of economic management permeated the political processes and structures of enterprise life and reinforced the bases of internal managerial power. However, the content of the planning process – the specific focus on production and output targets for each enterprise – ensured that the state enterprises had strong production and quantity orientations. The production department was the most important function, alongside technical, and the production and technical directors were the most important deputies, who often succeeded to the top position. This functional importance was also reflected in enterprise values. For example, most of the 'heroes' identified from state socialist days were remembered because of their technical expertise, and their political or managerial skills tended to be less memorable. The inventor of a machine or process, the founder of a workshop or product line, the technical genius or research engineer, even the star production worker – such were the 'heroic' employees recalled by most respondents. The following are typical:

My hero is Engineer X, who was technical director between 1975 and 1985, and went on to be enterprise director. He spent his whole career in Vols, was skilled, experienced and had a wide knowledge . . .

There are heroes in Agstroj's past. Engineer Y started his research in Vojenská Stroměstská, but moved to Agstroj. In the early days he was a real pioneer, the father of a whole family of machines. Engineer Z was enterprise director in the 1960s, and pioneered production . . .

Mr S is an example of a hero. He was an assembly worker [assembly supervisor] abroad. Such workers could work for ten or fifteen years abroad, a heroic commitment to the enterprise. (Montáže Jesenice director; Mr S was also cited by respondents at Jesenické Strojírny)

The consistency with which such people were identified suggests a shared set of values about the importance of production under socialism. The quality manager in Jesenické Strojírny highlighted the implications of the emphasis on the production plan. His training in 'metrology' was based on the principles of physics, which was then applied to the issues of quality control under central management. According to him, the focus of central plans on the quantitative aspects of production meant that it was less like quality, and more like quantity, control.

The centralized planning of outputs supported by external and internal hierarchical political processes had major implications for the nature of middle management. Line managers were caught in the direct demands associated with achieving the plan, and those in staff or support functions were snowed under with the administrative paperwork controlling and checking the process. Comments from three Vols managers identify the nature of such work:

There was big administration, with useless things to do, lots of reports to the state and to the authorities. (Sales manager)

In the past, commercial work was very easy, because of known five-year contracts with the USSR and East European countries. (Director)

Sales in the old regime was just getting rid of the products. Central planning led to order books being filled five years ahead; the main job was often to say 'no' politely to new customers.

This was echoed in the other enterprises, such as in Jesenické Strojírny: 'The sales department did not sell, it only handled formal orders prepared for domestic and eastern markets. Contracts were done via the plan . . . one signed and the other did.' This reactivity was also present in other departments. In Vols, for example, a former 'economic information' manager recalled that the accounting function was known as the 'almost dead department'.

Such middle managerial work called for passivity and conformity, and this was well understood. One Agstroj manager spoke of his frustration at not being able to be creative: 'at this time it was difficult to introduce [new methods] . . . because management was far from innovative . . . It was a time when people sat in their jobs but were afraid to adopt solutions that did not conform to party policy.' The general director at Montáže Jesenice – a former director of Jesenické Strojírny – described middle managerial behaviour in two words: passivity and laziness. Because the superordinate decided everything and a manager's future career depended on not crossing the superordinate, the natural behaviour was to be conformist, to 'play along' and to pass all problems up the line. People were just 'not given the chance to shine'.

The inexorable structural tendency towards passivity was reflected in the attitudes and behaviour of line managers. At the point of production, as we have seen, the workforce, developed extensive autonomy as a response to the uncertain quality of materials and the haphazard deliveries, which called for the 'spontaneous' loyalty and goodwill of workers if targets were to be met (compare the accounts of 'storming' in Dyker, 1981, p. 64; Seeger, 1981, pp. 84–5; Linz, 1988, pp. 186–7). The heavy dependence of managers on the skill and creativity of workers reinforced their insulation from the formal authority of the enterprise. Line managers conceded ground to the workforce and were unable or unwilling to exercise control or discipline that might jeopardize the career-enhancing attainment of production targets.

Management strategies: Discretion, networks and fiddles

Senior managers, middle managers and ordinary workers shared fairly common values and expectations of the state-owned enterprise, based on an awareness of the essentially hierarchical nature of economic management, the centres and bases of enterprise power and authority, the enterprise as a production unit and the strains towards passivity and conformity. Yet given the inherent technical and economic problems described above, it is unlikely that the command economy could have survived for forty years under these conditions. What is particularly interesting is how the shared assumptions about enterprise and enterprise management allowed the development of managerial practices quite different from these formalistic, bureaucratic and centralistic precepts.

The key to the paradox lies in the functioning of the relationship between enterprise management and the communist apparatus. The connection was in part formally instituted to oversee local enterprise behaviour and ensure the conformity of local decision-making with national policies. In practice, the party's authority underpinned and boosted the nature of the executive managerial role: it first, under certain circumstances, enhanced managerial influence and allowed senior managers opportunities to develop their own discretion to act beyond formal managerial responsibilities; second, the party provided a ready-made network of interrelated contacts with common political and economic interests in circumventing the dysfunctions of the command economy.

We have already shown how the power of enterprise management derived from and was supported by the Communist Party, and how the dominant autocratic and paternalistic style was assumed by respondents to be the natural and appropriate approach to managing state enterprises. But it is also crucial to understand how these patterns influenced the ways in which managers went about resolving the problems their enterprises faced in the command economy. The connections between the senior managers and the party, and the latter's endorsement of the activities of its trusted members, created a scope for decision-making and action far in excess of the formal authority of the managerial position.

Enterprise directors realized the importance of gaining support from the party, and some were in a better position to cultivate contacts in the central planning institutions as a result of their connections. The better connected the director, the more likely were both the enterprise and the community to benefit. Vols and Volna were strongly influenced, for example, by the national achievements of Engineer S, who, a technical expert, rose during the 1970s to being the enterprise director. His success in the regional party structures led to his elevation in the 1980s to the Central Committee of the KSČ, and promotion out of Vols to the industrial ministry and eventually to a position abroad as ambassador in an important socialist country. Engineer S was understood to have been a good communist, but one who always used his power to back Vols. While he was director at Vols, his contacts in Prague were seen as important in attracting resources to the region and enterprise; when he moved to Prague he continued to use his influence to profit both Vols and Volna. The Communist Party gave Engineer S power and influence beyond his formal position in the enterprise, and he was able to use this discretion to bias the allocation of resources to overcome some of Vols's economic problems.

Engineer J of Jesenické Strojírny remained in the enterprise until 1990, but was also known to be exceptionally well connected in the central organs of the party. It was argued that he acquired the position of enterprise director in 1968 from a close party contact, Mr K, who was at the time both general director of VVV, Jesenické Strojírny's VHJ, and a member of the inner circle of the Central Committee of the party in Prague. Mr K survived the Warsaw Pact invasion, and became a leading 'normalizer', and so remained a powerful ally for most of Engineer J's twenty-two year career as enterprise director. The evidence suggests that Engineer J was able to run Jesenické Strojírny with a lot more freedom than his formal position alone would have permitted. In the words of one man of '68, Engineer J 'had unlimited power, supported by the communist organization of the enterprise'.

A former *nomenklatura* argued that formal and informal power were concentrated in him, and agreed with a contemporary director who likened him to Napoleon and said: 'I can say negative things about him, though he was intelligent and would probably be all right today.' Others tended to agree, identifying the paradox in his managerial regime: 'Engineer J [was a] bit of a hero. In some ways he was traditional, in keeping with the previous regime. But in other ways he was progressive.' It is likely that this 'progressiveness' was only possible because of the support he got from his important party allies. The extra discretion he was able to develop allowed him to do what in retrospect seem extraordinary things. For example, he supported some managers with known ability in spite of their expulsion from the party or their refusal to approve the 1968 invasion; he allowed greater discussion among senior managers over policy; at a time of normalization fervour in the early 1970s, he personally went to Prague to argue with the ministry in support of decentralizing structural experiments that had been instigated in Jesenické Strojírny (see Chapter 8); he insisted on his commercial managers getting direct experience of foreign clients. These acts were virtually anathema, and would only have been possible with reliable endorsement in high places, and certainly led to the reputation of Jesenické Strojírny as a progressive enterprise.

Engineers S and J might have been exceptional or extreme examples of the level and extent of patronage that enterprise directors were able to foster in the communist structures. However, most enterprise directors, given their *nomenklatura* clearing and the nature of the local or regional role the job entailed, would have benefited in some degree from the political resources with which the party endowed the trusted guardians of the economy.

Beyond the backing provided to individual, autocratic enterprise directors, perhaps the most significant contribution of the party to the conduct of business was its social structure: a web which connected members within and between enterprises, locally, regionally, nationally and, ultimately, internationally. The members in principle shared social and political values about national progress and policy; in practice, following normalization, they shared common *interests* in preserving the institutions and structures which had provided them with career opportunities and with social, political and material privileges that were denied the non-party citizen. Our evidence suggests that the socio-economic networks of managerial contacts, enabled and motivated by the common interests of their participants, were crucial to the everyday management of industrial enterprises.

The nature of such a network, at enterprise level, was graphically described by a young department manager at Agstroj:

> The enterprise was like a big jug of wine with a small hole – that is, it was hard to get in, but there was lots of nourishment once you were in. The big problem was how to get in. After getting in, all was well because you had a job and you had your friends. Your party friends were a mafia, a network in which each depended on and defended the others . . . If you did something wrong, ranks would close.

It will be remembered that the main technical problems of management originated from outside the enterprise, in the hierarchial relations with the central planning authorities, and in the lateral relations with supplier and client partners. The creation and active manipulation of contacts – the process of socio-economic networking – were at the heart of most managerial strategies and practices for coping with these enterprise problems. The main aim of these activities was to *informalize* external relations in order to short-circuit the hierarchical, authoritarian nature of economic management, a process which reinforced the essentially politicized nature of problem-solving in enterprises. Gifted enterprise managers constructed a network of personal contacts at the ministry and/or in the VHJ, and some even developed their later careers within the planning apparatus, and therefore made it more possible to get a sympathetic voice into the apparatus. Engineer S, whose nickname was 'little Napoleon', was the ultimate example of the latter, but our respondents also identified less dramatic promotions to directorate positions in the VHJ, such as an admired commercial director of Jesenické Strojírny who was promoted to VVV in Prague.

With contacts in place, enterprise directors were able to plead more successfully for an 'improvement' in the plan's realizability (compare Linz, 1988, pp. 183ff; Burawoy and Lukács, 1992, p. 90; Burawoy and Krotov, 1992, pp. 28ff), or to exert greater control over the enterprise's production plans. For example, in Jesenické Strojírny, which had both specific and general plans (see above), there was always anxiety about finding enough work to satisfy the unspecified parts of the general plan, by securing safe contracts:

> personal contacts with state bureaucrats were very important . . . because bureaucrats, given a project and several enterprises to choose from, narrowed the field of choice down by selecting enterprises they were familiar with. (Former Jesenické Strojírny director)

> To do the general work, we would look to [our FTO] . . . we looked abroad . . . The commercial and technical people would call contacts in [the FTO] to hunt for appropriate clients. Or [the FTO] would come to Jesenické Strojírny with known contacts, for example in South America. It was a tight, total network between [the VHJ's] planning departments, Jesenické Strojírny and [the FTO]. (Current Jesenické Strojírny director)

Concerning Agstroj and Agrov, its VHJ

> Formally the economic directors would meet every fourteen days to check the plan, but would meet informally to solve any outstanding problems; and through this process managers became friends. (Former Agrov director, now Agstroj manager)

This was very important, because, in the words of another manager, 'In order to buy spare parts and components, I had to ask Agrov; revenue also had to be passed to Agrov, which dispersed money among its member enterprises.'

Hierarchical contacts were also important in attempts to increase capital investment and update technologies. Senior managers negotiated and bargained with their contacts in the planning hierarchy, and used other contacts in the Communist Party to plead the case of their own enterprise in the allocation process. Success in securing investment in its industrial sector, or in the sub-sector governed by a particular VHJ, was related to how well an enterprise's directors could marshal support from their socio-economic networks. While Agstroj's machines lacked competitive technological sophistication in advanced countries, the enterprise's ability to earn hard currency in less developed nations because of the basic reliability and ruggedness of the products, and its very close relationship with the industry VHJ, gave its senior managers strong leverage in investment discussions within the planning institutions. In the period from 1978 to 1988, Agstroj was extremely successful in expanding its production capacity with the use of German and Italian technology. Substantial capital investment in Jesenické Strojírny followed its success in getting a sizable part of the CMEA-organized SOVREP project; respondents felt that the international political significance of its VHJ – with its own offices in Moscow – was instrumental in winning the contract for Jesenické Strojírny, and the personal closeness of Jesenické Strojírny's and its VHJ's directorate connections cemented the deal.

In addition to the adjustment of targets, the seeking of new clients and the acquisition of money for additional supplies or for capital investment, the personal contacts in the VHJ, the FTO or higher up were crucial for building up the enterprise's social and welfare capacity. The most common reason given by interviewees of all statuses for joining Vols, Agstroj or Jesenické Strojírny was to gain an apartment for their families in the conditions of inadequate accommodation that prevailed throughout the ČSSR at virtually all times. Enterprises which cultivated a good reputation for accommodation and welfare provision were more likely to be able to attract and keep workers during times of industrial expansion but continuing labour shortage. Having contacts in the ministry or in the Central Committee was almost a political guarantee of being able to attract social investments, such as apartment block building, to the enterprise or its local district. It is clear that Vols had particularly strong influence in this respect, and was more than averagely successful.

While use of networking practices was important in managing relationships with the planning hierarchy, senior managers also entered into *lateral* discussions with contacts in partner organizations in order to facilitate the achievement of the plan. The development and use of personal contacts with suppliers and clients were prevalent even in enterprises like Agstroj, where central control seemed more exacting. One Agstroj manager remembered:

'There was never any official contact between Agstroj and its foreign clients [which were handled by its FTO]. Unofficially, clients would come straight to Agstroj for repairs and spare parts.' However, in Jesenické Strojírny, the use of contacts was more relaxed, because of the way the enterprise director ran the organization and what he could get away with. Exploiting the degree of discretion he had generated, he not only expanded his own influential network of foreign contacts, but insisted that his trusted commercial managers also be allowed to meet and negotiate with clients. As a result, 'Plenty of people in Jesenické Strojírny had [personal] contacts around the world. These contacts enabled us to find new customers and to export other products such as [Xs]' (Montáže Jesenice section head).

It was in the nature of Vols's and Jesenické Strojírny's work that unpredictable difficulties often arose because of the long-term, technical nature of their contracts. Bureaucrats were unable to appreciate the finer engineering points of such large-scale projects, and the resulting plans were too inflexible. Making the right sort of agreement with client partners over product specifications which recognized the technical complications of making the product not only gave the client a more realistic delivery time, but also allowed suppliers to renegotiate the details of the plan more strongly with the external hierarchy. A former project manager in Vols explained the enterprise's response:

> Targets were always high, specified by year of delivery and by quantity. Receiving its part of the project, Vols would prepare its plan . . . It then met representatives of the concrete partners [suppliers and clients] and negotiated realistic targets – the difference between the set and the real targets would be fed back up to the authorities.

Senior managers would thus draw upon personal contacts in socio-economic networks that they had cultivated over the years, within the hierarchical institutions, which themselves could be well-integrated into international business networks across a variety of partner enterprises, including foreign clients. Such practices could provide the basis for easing problems of plan fulfilment, assurance of supplies, labour shortage and capital investment.

Enterprise managers understood planning as having the characteristics of an economic ritual. The planners would automatically expect a 5 to 10 per cent per annum improvement in performance, independent of whether of not there were clients or adequate production facilities. The irrationalities of such planning were directly reflected in the managerial responses to such expectations, which included a range of techniques, some legal, but many not so. Managers developed ways of fiddling the numbers in order to improve their 'performance' in the eyes of the authorities. One Jesenické Strojírny production director recalled a number of ways in which output volume could be 'increased' and the plan 'fulfilled'. One method was to attempt to intensify the labour process by speeding up work norms – but this not only alienated an already apathetic workforce, but also encouraged cutting corners and diminishing product quality.

Another practice was to improve the productivity by utilizing more capital equipment, an approach favoured by technical managers who were keen to demonstrate their technical expertise. The production managers only wanted to achieve the plan, but also tended to see problems in the higher expectations of future productivity that new equipment would set up among planners.

> The technical people usually won because they sang the song the ministry wanted to hear – increased productivity, reduced labour costs. New machines would only be bought and paid for by the ministry if production [managers] agreed to sign to say that productivity would increase two-fold. The paperwork would need fixing later to make it so.

Invariably the machines could not realize the technical claims, so the enterprise over time developed a formal production capacity – and hence higher production targets from the centre – beyond its real capability. Such behaviour placed even greater strain on plan fulfilment, in a vicious circle. This called for further fiddling and fixing, as enterprise managers sought ways to make the output *look* as if it met the plan.

One response was to bring into play the socio-economic networks. The same Jesenické Strojírny production director continued:

> as the plans increased, Jesenické Strojírny would bring in half complete machines from other mechanical engineering enterprises, perform some simple work and send the machines back again. Then both enterprises claimed the whole machines as part of their output [contributing] to their plans.

The spiral of increased ministry expectations and a real production capacity that simply could not meet the plan became a nightmare that senior enterprise managers, with their jobs on the line, were unable to confront.

Another response was to increase output of those products which were simpler and cheaper to make at the expense of those that were actually planned. The shift of production to simpler products minimized the costs of production and maximized the throughput, but there were obviously limits to the extent to which this method could be used. It was, however, quite normal to manufacture machinery directly for stock, knowing that the centralized soft budgets ensured that costs would be met, while the output approximated the quantitative targets. A former Jesenické Strojírny technician, now employed at Montáže Jesenice, spoke of the inefficiency of some central targets which made sub-optimal use of resources, e.g. requiring one machine where it was economically more efficient to make a small batch: 'Often we made two or three machines for every one ordered by the state, because it was more efficient, and we knew that the state would order more in the future . . . We knew the money would be there.'

Whether through internal practices of fiddling information or fixing paperwork, or through inter-enterprise collusion to overcome mutually impossible targets, enterprise managers developed a range of methods for protecting their own careers in the face of the irrationalities of central planning.

Conclusions

The Czechoslovak state socialist mechanical engineering industry operated through the networks of long-term business contacts, which were created and sustained in the everyday managerial work of negotiating and assuring the fulfilment of contracts.

> External supply relations grew increasingly unreliable, and the firms narrowed the assortment of production. Hence the tightly integrated production lines and the shortage uncertainties reinforced the interdependence between customers and suppliers, managers and workers, and managers and local Party officials. Within the VHJ or locality constituent actors forged informal compacts to bargain with the center and to compensate supply failures and facilitate the flow of goods . . . Informal cooperation agreements evolved from being stop-gap measures to institutionalized features of the firm.
>
> (McDermott, 1993, p. 12)

Although the formality of central planning procedures left enterprise managers with very little discretion in decision-making, the reality of the situation called upon top management to manage the enterprise's relationships actively, so that its continued performance in the command economy could be secured. In dealing with the demands of meeting production plans, senior managers needed to be active networkers, bringing into play their personal, political and business contacts in order to solve supply, investment and delivery problems. Networking and bargaining both hierarchically and horizontally became accepted as natural management practices, as did the invention of strategies to create and sustain at least the illusion of plan fulfilment. Such was the importance of solving external dilemmas and the tendencies towards shopfloor autonomy that the efforts and energies of senior managers were inevitably focused upwards, outwards and sideways. Since the management cadre was to a greater or lesser degree based on the *nomenklatura* system, and given the political-administrative nature of economic decisions, the socio-economic networks through whose conduits enterprise management exercised its influence were directly or indirectly connected to the Communist Party.

The relative autonomy of the shopfloor, a structural consequence of external labour market conditions as well as of operational enterprise problems, left middle line and functional managers virtually stranded in the hierarchy, despite the formal command hierarchy.[7] Line management was reduced to basic administration and passing commands downwards and information upwards, having little recourse to the expression of initiative[8] or responsibility. The only way out for ambitious middle managers was to join the Communist Party and its sub-organs, to make appropriate contacts in management and to wait for the call to take on a senior role.

In summary, the reality of enterprise management was at variance with its formal administrative principles, not only because of variable human commitments, but also because the system created practical and motivational conditions which necessitated divergent, informal responses from both management and workers for the visible realization of production plans. Paradoxically, the party offered enterprise managers both the political resources and the social structures which could, under the right conditions, be used to circumvent the worst excesses of central planning, at the expense of undermining or sidelining the authority and credibility of formal economic institutions. The accumulated effect of managers' institutionalized practices to fulfil the plan was a vicious circle of operational inefficiency. The economic and social institutions, when perceived and enacted at the point of production, assured that economic inefficiency was the inevitable outcome of the 'rational' behaviour of managers and workers under pressure to meet enterprise planning targets.

Notes

1 'The Czechoslovak political system as it exists in Husák's era of "normalization" is officially called *reálný socialismus*. The exact meaning of this awkward term is not clear either in English translation or in its Czech original, for that matter. *Reálný socialismus* – real, realistic, fatalistic, given once and for all, in resigned acquiescence to the facts of life' (Ulč, 1979, p. 201).

2 Kornai (1980), for example, characterizes the management motives towards production as a quantity drive, towards resources as a hoarding tendency and towards investment as an expansion drive.

3 In Volna, for example, in the square there were well-attended rallies to celebrate the October Revolution and Czechoslovak–Soviet relations. It was normal for people to attend the rally, but express their opposition through humour, such as well-directed graffiti. For example, to the typical socialist slogan 'Friendship with the Soviet Union Forever', some wag appended the afterthought '. . . and not a minute longer'.

4 A joke, told to us by a number of Czechs, makes the point. There were two dogs, one Polish and the other Czechoslovakian. They meet at the border, each heading to the other's country. The Czechoslovak dog asks why the Polish dog is going to Czechoslovakia, and the Polish dog says: 'I'm going to find food to eat. But why are you going to Poland?' The Czechoslovak dog replies, 'To be free to bark.'

5 On the surface, it would appear that any direct financial involvement in sport by the enterprise was illegal. The state budget directly financed sporting activities through an institution called *Tělovýchovná jednota* (TJ), with the minority balance of funds

supposedly coming from the community. However, local enterprises became involved in various ways, including 'voluntary' schemes such as *Akce Z̆*.

6 The reference is to a children's card game, rather like the British 'Black Maria', in which players must avoid winning a certain card, such as the Queen of Spades.

7 In the case of both Vols and Montáže Jesenice, it is important to distinguish the position of technocrats from the line managers. In Vols, for example, the technical designers were an elite group, able to develop their careers virtually independently of the influence of the Communist Party. They were highly trained and in relatively short supply, and the reputation of the enterprise was dependent on the quality of their highly skilled work. Only at times of severe crisis (as in the time of 'normalization' post-1968) were non-conforming designers victimized for their views; however, movement into senior management still demanded their participation in the *nomenklatura* system.

8 Though the fear engendered in the autocratic enterprise system encouraged middle managers to join in the occupational ritual of dressing up or biasing information to improve their apparent performance in the eyes of superiors.

5 Czechoslovak management and organization

The historical inheritance

In this chapter, we build on the previous arguments in order to come to some conclusions about management and organization under state socialism, and hence draw forward some lessons for examining the changes introduced during the early years of the socio-economic transition. The main aim is to act as a bridge between Part Two, in which we have examined the historical processes and experiences of organization and management under Czechoslovak state socialism, and Part Three, in which we investigate the changes in organization and management that have taken place during the initial transition period of 1990 to 1995. To accomplish this objective, we sketch the general macroeconomic state of Czechoslovakia in the late 1980s, and summarize from our earlier work the key aspects of Czechoslovak state enterprise and enterprise management. This summary provides both the starting point of the socio-economic transition and the historical legacy of state socialism; it forms, first, a significant descriptive baseline for understanding the post-1989 changes, and, second, a critical theoretical resource for explaining the processes of transformation in the emerging post-communist economy.

The second task is to evaluate the processes outlined in Chapters 3 and 4 in the context of the theoretical perspective developed in Chapter 2. By constructing a conceptual and theoretical synopsis, we offer an interpretation of the underlying social, economic and political processes which first held state socialism in place, and then threatened the communist status quo. We show that these processes of inertia and change operated at and between the levels of formal institutional structure and micro institutionalized practices. We complete the chapter by considering the implications of these state socialist legacies for the emergence of market-economic characteristics at the level of enterprise and management over the early post-communist period.

Economic and managerial legacies of state socialism

The state of the economy

In terms of the formal institutional system, the Czechoslovak command economy of the late 1980s was closer to the orthodox Stalinist model outlined in

Chapter 3 than the other Visegrád[1] countries, and probably more so than many of the regimes within the Soviet sphere of influence. The economic consequences of this state of affairs were mixed, being both a blessing and a problem. On the one hand, the country was more than self-sufficient in food; it had a relatively highly qualified and skilled workforce, which is often identified as the most important legacy favouring an effective industrial transition; people experienced low inflation and relatively high living standards; the economy probably showed some annual growth; and, significantly, it enjoyed a relatively low level of gross foreign debt (Myant, 1993, p. 155; Svejnar, 1995b, pp. 2ff). Paradoxically, these characteristics were all the beneficial results of the orthodox, conservative, politically centralized and oppressive regime, which, unlike Hungary and Poland, had resisted effective economic and political reform during the 1980s (Svejnar, 1995b, p. 3).

However, the Czechoslovak state had traded off industrial investment, which declined dramatically over the 1980s, for buying political acquiescence, and preferred the degradation of its technological base to borrowing from capitalist countries. The very low levels of labour productivity and the continuing decline in the international competitiveness of Czechoslovak industry were among the prices that had to be paid (Šuhan and Šuhanová, 1995). Capital starvation in the 1980s had limited the ability of Czechoslovak industry to perform efficiently on a domestic or global stage. Exports were mainly oriented to less developed and CMEA countries whose own industries were less demanding of product quality, and whose imports were financed by trade credits or transferable rubles, rather than hard currencies that might have permitted purchase of Western know-how. Even within the socialist world, Czechoslovakia had a regional reputation for technological obsolescence, operating with machines which were on average twenty years old (Šik, 1993; Bohatá *et al.*, 1995, p. 256).

Between 97 and 98 per cent of Czechoslovak production came from the state sector, in which assets were concentrated in national enterprises that were gigantic even by state socialist standards. Over the decades, with one or two short periods of reversal, industrial activities had become grouped under the system of VHJ trusts, so that, even after their official dissolution in 1989, there were about 700 industrial enterprises,[2] many with multiple plants and an average staff of 3000 or more (see Jeffries, 1993, p. 248; Mejstřik, 1993, p. 125; Myant, 1993, p. 158). Of these, the largest fifty accounted for 42 per cent of manufacturing output, and more than a quarter of industrial employment (Zemplinerová and Stíbal, 1995, p. 235). Enterprise managers felt some loosening of the reins in the late 1980s, but the decentralizing reforms had mostly been planned to take effect from 1991 (Adam, 1993, p. 629), and there was strong resistance from many of the VHJ directors (McDermott, 1993; also Myant, 1993, p. 158).

The domination of each industrial branch by one or two huge enterprise associations gave rise to monopolistic conditions, but, as Lavigne (1995, pp. 33–4) notes, it is doubtful whether the term 'monopoly' is very useful, since it is predicated upon some notion of 'market power structure', rather than mandatory plans. Such power structures and the structures of vertically and horizontally linked enterprises could not be associated with any *market logic*, such as that which arises from theories of strategic alliance, merger and take-over, since they were formed through 'political-administrative decision' (Lavigne, 1995, p. 34). The integration of Jesenické Strojírny under the aegis of VVV's highly diversified industrial structure had been an act of almost political whim, and its persistence right up to 1988 illustrates the lack of any market-economic rationality in such organizational arrangements. Evidently, their unravelling would involve more than the application of received, anti-trust, market-competitive reasoning (see McDermott, 1993).

Within these industrial structures, there was an acute lack of small and medium-size enterprises (SMEs) in the manufacturing branches, and all work conventionally associated with small business that would normally be put out or subcontracted in advanced capitalist economies was conducted in-house, in small workshops, by special brigades or units. The factory sites of the enterprises under view were scattered with such small workshops, which before 1989 had undertaken correction work, pallet building, machine mending etc. Only 4.2 per cent of manufacturing enterprises employed fewer than 200 workers (Zemplinerová and Stíbal, 1995, p. 237); only 1 per cent of industrial employment was in enterprises employing under 500 (Myant, 1993, p. 16). The absence of SMEs created a very undynamic, inflexible economy, making rapid adjustment to new conditions highly problematic (Bohatá, 1996b, p. 6).

But over forty years, various economic policies had encouraged the development of a 'grossly obsolete' industrial base (Sobell, 1988, p. 47) with a strong bias towards mechanical engineering and steel sectors. The military–industrial complex was especially represented in Slovakia, while, in the Czech lands, the traditional strength of light engineering had been undermined. By 1989, the accumulation of state socialist priorities had been concretized in the extreme 'deformation of the industrial structure' (Šuhan and Šuhanová, 1995, p. 121). State enterprises like Vols and Jesenické Strojírny, which typified the heavy and mechanical engineering branch, enjoyed an important, at times even privileged, status within the central planning process, because of their economic and political significance as manufacturing and exporting units (Lavigne, 1995, p. 33). These enterprises and their communities often benefited directly and indirectly from this status in terms of security, investment and prestige, and their managers and workers were apparently given preferential rewards. However, heavy industry made enormous, inefficient demands on energy and raw materials which had been imported from the Soviet Union at what had been unrealistic, highly subsidized prices (see, for example, Adam, 1993, pp. 627–9; Myant, 1993, pp. 10–11; Wolchik, 1995, p. 158); and it typically exported its products in large degree to the Soviet Union, usually in return for credits.

Alongside this overemphasis on heavy engineering and metallurgy went the underdevelopment of service industries. In particular, the financial and banking institutions played a passive role in the command economy, and their role and position effectively isolated their management and operations from financial developments in Western societies. Being state owned and functioning as a mere conduit for industrial and commercial finances and credits, the monobank had little experience of evaluating risk for loans, and played no financial role in the governance of individual enterprises. Like every other late 1980s reform, the separation of the central bank's functions by the creation of new commercial and investment banks came as too little and too late to allow bankers any effective experience of more market-oriented banking (Brom and Orenstein, 1994, p. 894).

These industrial, market and economic structures of late Czechoslovak state socialism constituted contextual legacies which any transformation strategy had to tackle at a macro, institutional level in order to prepare its command economy for the economic transition (Volgyes, 1995, pp. 48–50). As we have seen in Part Two, the neo-Stalinist economics of the normalized Czechoslovakia resulted in the existence of these features and legacies in more extreme form than elsewhere in the region, creating potentially greater than average obstacles to the transition process.

The state enterprise as organization

The structure and process of the subordinated state enterprise, operating under the institutional conditions of central planning, provides the typical environment within which managers and employees have developed their career and work expectations. Their routine memories and experiences of the work organization are not just 'interesting', but constitute critical everyday *resources* for making sense of the post-communist world of the 1990s. Large state enterprises like Vols, Agstroj and Jesenické Strojírny were 'multifaceted': 'They were not just production and management units. They had political, administrative and social functions' (Lavigne, 1995, p. 35).

Vols, Jesenické Strojírny, Agstroj and Montáže Jesenice were subordinated elements of the hierarchical command-economic system, and each adopted, as a matter of political necessity, the standardized, rigid, functional, centralized bureaucratic form that was the organizational blueprint of the Czechoslovak state enterprise. This general organizational form mirrored the external formal economic and political institutions. Internal structural units locked the enterprise's activities into the normative demands of its institutional environment; and, in a command economy strongly shaped by centrally given values and priorities, the enterprise structure developed an internal technical coherence in terms of serving its business-economic goals. Each state enterprise was designed with dual, parallel structures: one revealed the executive, managerial control of productive activities, with functional departments or sections familiar enough to Western observers; the other, based on local Communist Party organs, supported the enterprise's socio-political role and provided ideological control and monitoring functions. The two structures overlapped in regard to membership, and acted to join the internal concerns of the business to the social community of the region or town.

The internal coherence of the organization's structural components rendered this organizational form very unresponsive to external change, but changes on any significant scale happened rarely in the highly controlled economic and industrial environment. Coherence of organizational form not only produced a strain towards structural inertia, as a result of the repercussive implications of changing any one part, but also led to vested interests that were socially and politically resistant to economic reforms and new technical and managerial ideas (Clark and Soulsby, 1995).

Holding subordinate positions in the planning hierarchy as the production units for their VHJs, and having objectives governed by the overarching concern to meet the plan, the three pre-1989 state enterprises and the plant developed a dominant production orientation and a structural balance of power favouring those functions at the organization's technical core. The obsession with meeting quantitative production and financial targets overwhelmed all other enterprise activities, and kept any interest in quality and cost control issues to the periphery of the enterprise.

The nature of the state enterprise was profoundly affected by its legal role in the overall social and welfare policies and practices of the communist state, which allocated funds to the local enterprise as an instrument for delivering social provision. In many cases, state enterprises were consciously established with social purposes in mind; so Vols was intended to bring industrial employment to a remote rural area, and the material, human and financial resources necessary for building or expanding communities to serve the enterprise followed such decisions. Enterprises grew because of the state policy preference for achieving rational economies of scale through economic cooperation and an associated predilection for gigantism; but also, with unemployment illegal and labour resources, especially skilled workers, in short supply, enterprise managers had both a strategic and an operational interest in being overstaffed.

The nature of enterprise management

The processes and structures implicit in the Czechoslovak central planning institutions had fundamental ramifications for the reality and experience of enterprise management. Managers generally had high technical engineering qualifications, which were sometimes acquired on a part-time basis, and tended to spend their whole career within the same enterprise, though not necessarily through personal choice. Despite their often formal technical expertise, individuals' moves into enterprise management were ultimately based on political credentials. The power, influence and career development of senior management and various middle management positions were founded on their *nomenklatura* status, formally underwritten by the Communist Party, and actually accomplished through membership of and participation in its organs. Lavigne (1995, p. 52) argues that the managers in the heavy engineering, military–industrial complex were particularly powerful among the *nomenklatura* economic leaders.

Managerial authority derived its formal legitimacy from the clearly defined and delimited role of enterprise management in the external institutional hierarchy described in Chapter 3. Formally, management was tightly constrained by bureaucracy and the directive rule of the plan. However, the typical enterprise director was 'appointed by political authority on the basis of "one-man rule"' (Lavigne, 1995, p. 35), was severely autocratic in management style and operated in a highly authoritarian, even arrogant manner, albeit with a paternalistic streak. We have seen that our respondents described the pre-1989 directors as having a tendency towards personalized, arbitrary, despotic decision-making, and thus their 'strong' leadership very much set the tone of management.

Enterprise directors were able to create varying degrees of independence and distance from the formalities of central planning, apparently deriving leverage from their political bases in the enterprises' dual structures and in the district party apparatus in order to expand their managerial discretion and, within certain bounds, to express their own priorities. While this emergent autonomy could be used to augment their sphere of personal influence, privilege and credibility, it could also be drawn on as a resource to manage the technical problems of the state enterprise in the command economy. Senior enterprise management normally operated through the development of competent managerial practices which deviated from the formal prescriptions of rule- and plan-driven constraints. In order to resolve everyday problems of management – especially linked to resource acquisition and flow – key managers honed informal, quasi-legitimate but organizationally necessary skills. In particular, they built socio-economic networks of contacts, based on party structures and penetrating all levels of economic institutions. The combination of informally generated discretion and socially reproduced networks gave senior managers some room to undertake flexible and creative problem-solving.

In contrast, middle managers in both line and staff functions had only a narrow experience, and their jobs could best be described as administration. At this level, management was a passive activity, with little experience of decision-making responsibility. Production and plant managers were in the worst of positions, because they were trapped between autocratic, centralized decisions of the directorate, and informal bottom-up power of the shopfloor, able to exert enormous influence because of their skills, their iconic role as socialist workers, the dependence of plant managers on their goodwill and flexible practices, and the exacting discipline of the labour shortage.

The formal enterprise roles of the staff-function managers were quite clear, in that they offered only marginal opportunities to develop expertise and experience of responsibilities beyond passive obedience. Indeed, functional departments operated as little more than gatherers of information for the use of superordinates at higher levels of the command economy structures, and clerks in the administration of the technical needs of the plan. Strategic planning, by definition, was a higher level function, taking place in the VHJ or in the branch ministry. Commerce or trade managers were formally involved in administering purchases and sales effected as a consequence of the higher plan, and to the extent that more proactive selling or domestic and foreign marketing existed, it lay with the VHJs or FTOs. Managers of the economy department were collectors and analysts of basic accounting information, mostly for use outside the enterprise, leaving investment and financing decisions at the centre or VHJ; while personnel was the most politically tainted organizational activity by virtue of its association with the political records of staff, and hence the most disliked management function of all. From our evidence, it should be said that the reality of most middle managers appeared to be very much like the institutional formality. There was little room for creativity or experimentation, but at the same time, the overall incentive system and the general state of social motivation, in terms of developing a managerial career or simply securing your family, encouraged conformity to what existed and keeping your head low. Managerial initiative was not only rarely called for, but when it was expressed it was likely to be seen as a deviance and liable to sanction.

While the fairly rich experiences of management were limited mostly to those in senior director and deputy director positions, it has to be recognized that some enterprises had informal reputations for being quite progressive, even experimental, according to how the senior enterprise directors decided to use the autonomy they were able to generate. When economic and political circumstances allowed – but particularly in the late 1960s and even the early 1970s – some state enterprises, like Jesenické Strojírny, attempted to spread more flexible, responsible decision-making practices further down the line. Since the enterprise director of Jesenické Strojírny was particularly strong, with powerful friends in high positions in the CP in Prague, he was able to run a more flexible, decentralized internal regime into the early 1970s, and these experiences continued to exist at the margins of the enterprise's culture until the Velvet Revolution. This director retained a reputation for being arrogant and tyrannical, at one level, but also a progressive manager whose strength of will allowed generations of trusted commercial managers to gain direct experience of exports, foreign markets and Western management.

In order to grasp the state of Czechoslovak management in 1989, it is important to understand its involvement in the local community, which was expressed in the social and welfare functions of the enterprise. We have seen how enterprise managers realized these obligations by building up social assets and facilities through which to provide concrete services (e.g. housing, cultural events, recreation, holidays) to their employees and their families. But the complementary aspect is that, particularly in the smaller towns of Volna and Jesenice, these managers were also members of their communities, shared the enterprise- or state-built subsidized facilities, and identified strongly with their communities. The sense of social responsibility, emphasized through the official communist creed, but concretized in managers' physical location in the community, has been a fundamental management-cultural legacy which cannot be underestimated.

While the *nomenklatura* managers became important local figures – economically, socially and politically – and some went on to feature significantly in national (even international) politics, their association with the process of normalization in the 1970s and 1980s constituted the Achilles' heel of their social and managerial status. Right up to the Velvet Revolution, state enterprise management as an occupation, and *nomenklatura* managers both as a group and as individuals, had to tolerate the low esteem which they received from individual employees and the public at large. These problems of professional credibility, social legitimacy and personal identity became crises which were inherited into the post-communist world of 1990. The processes of privatization and of transformation have been fundamentally influenced by the ways in which post-communist managers have tried to deal with these issues of managerial legitimacy.

We have been able to identify the typical features of enterprise management, in terms of style, knowledge, competence, experience, values and legitimacy, that were present in the four enterprises under study at the start of the post-communist transition. The picture is not simple and unambiguous. The real managerial practices that had to develop in order to make the command economy work at the micro level of the enterprise became increasingly divorced from the formalities of the institutional framework of Czechoslovak central planning. This led to a surprising wealth of managerial expertise and experience, some of which has direct relevance for the problems of managing for profit within an internationally competitive market economy. On the other hand, key aspects and elements of 'normal' Western management, such as marketing, human resource, quality and strategic management, were largely absent from the available and accessible managerial repertoire at enterprise level, or had taken on a rather different form.

Czechoslovak state socialism: The widening institutional gap

Economic institutions: The hierarchy of hierarchies

The Soviet command-economic structures which had been imported wholesale in the early years of Czechoslovak communism had been under waves of internal and external pressure for change up to 1989; but they had survived in an adapted yet recognizable *neo*-Stalinist form to a greater extent than in most comparable countries in the region. The two decades following the Warsaw Pact invasion were a period of sustained centralization in the central planning institutions, during which any tendencies to decentralize or open up the economic system – one of the enduring motifs of the mid-1960s and the Prague Spring – were resisted, retarded and even sabotaged by those whose political and economic interests lay in the status quo, and who feared the consequences of unravelling the internal coherence of the economic institutions.

In this centralized, hierarchical process,

> lower rank objectives become the means for attaining higher level ones, and the criteria for rational behaviour of the sub-systems (sectors, branches, enterprises) are subordinated to those of the system as a whole.
> (Brus and Laski, cited in Tsoukas, 1994, p. 26)

State-owned enterprises like Vols, Jesenické Strojírny and Agstroj were situated at the lowest level of the hierarchy, at the subordinate end of the chain of objective setting, where formal compliance was at its maximum and decision-making initiative and responsibility at their minimum. The economic structures were governed by formal rules and procedures for allocating tasks, resources, people and rewards. Central planning was formally institutionalized as a hierarchy of hierarchies, with strong political and ideological pressures for each level to conform in structure and procedure to the levels above it. In principle, the allegiance to the superior goals of socialism was reflected in institutional expressions at all levels of society and economy, and the general interests, as defined and decided by the authorities at the centre, came to take precedence over the sectionalist interests of economic sub-groups, such as those which existed in the subordinate enterprises. It is in these respects that Child (1993, p. 207) speaks of the centralized locus of state socialist economies (see Table 5.1, p. 106).

In formal institutional terms, economic management was defined as the enactment of economic and social policies and priorities which emanated from on high, and access to managerial roles was mediated by the institution of the *nomenklatura*. It was the political duty of *nomenklatura* managers to ensure that enterprises and social spheres under their control reflected the supreme goals of the CP and the state, and their economic task was to comply with the production and distribution needs of the plan. Given these institutional expressions, there arose 'isomorphic relationships between enterprises and the state caused by the structural and political-ideological dependence of the former upon the latter' (Tsoukas, 1994, p. 23).

State enterprises adopted internal structures which were not only isomorphic with external shapes, as copies of the blueprints legally defined by the state, but which also represented a task-contingent fit with the essential stability of enterprises' state-controlled economic environment. During the decades of normalization, for example, the central power of the state and its guiding political-ideological principles were paramount, making external institutional or normative processes a virtually irresistible influence on individual enterprises. Enterprises and their managers had a strong, coercively felt incentive to copy institutionalized components, systems and rules directly from the wider central planning system into their internal structures, and, given the core official ideology that was already embedded in the enterprise, such formal components fitted well into the existing organizational form (Clark and Soulsby, 1995). Hence, 'The organization becomes a political-cum-ideological miniature of the state' (Tsoukas, 1994, p. 34; cf. Child, 1993). Under these circumstances, sporadic organizational experiments (e.g. during the late 1960s) to develop decentralized structures could easily be drawn back within the dominant institutional paradigm of neo-Stalinism – indeed, lack of commitment to reforms virtually guaranteed such relapses.

The robust tendency towards institutional coherence, both within the central planning system and within individual enterprises, revealed the near-complete domination of normative over technical criteria of structural design. It is clear that attempted reforms (e.g. in the early and late 1980s) were never radical enough to disturb this cosy state of coherence, and they were never powerful enough to upset and divert the established interests of the political and economic elite from the status quo. Much of the success of the command-economic system in being resistant to change, despite its widely recognized technical inefficiencies, was paradoxically related to the ability of economic managers to 'make it work' by behaving outside the formal institutional requirements. It was not until the period leading up to 1989 that these important economic actors decided that the credibility gap between their formal work and their actual managerial experience was no longer bridgeable.

Managerial behaviour in state enterprises

It is therefore our contention that a *full* understanding of the durability of the normalized economic status quo after 1968, as well as of its eventual destruction in 1989, must take into account the complex processes of state socialist management at the lower levels of the command economy. The deterioration of the state-planned economy was recognized as an inbuilt tendency from very early times, though the massive industrialization drives based upon more extensive use of labour resources disguised the limits of growth for some time. By the early 1960s, the performance problems of the Czechoslovak command economy, and those of other communist countries, were well known (e.g. Kornai, 1980). The miracle, so to speak, of Czechoslovak state socialism was that the enterprises continued to make it look as if its economic state was not so bad.

The creation of this miracle was the work of, among others, the managers of state enterprises, whose job was to disguise the practical economic shortcomings and to make it look as if enterprises were meeting their parts of the overall state plan. In doing so, with the presentational collaboration of politicians, they put a gloss on economic performance and, to the extent that this cover-up was persuasive, acted to sustain the ailing economy. When the performance inadequacies became transparent, it was economic management which tended to get the blame (e.g. for being too independent of the centre) and, in the political dynamics of the hierarchical system, official censure tended to focus on the lower echelons, with concrete enterprise managers (Myant, 1989). This social reality simply reinforced managers' interests in making the system *look as if it were working*: for example, by exploiting state socialist processes like soft budgeting to renegotiate targets, or by distorting the production information to create the appearance of plan fulfilment.

As we have seen, enterprise managers frequently behaved in deviant or 'uninstitutional' ways in order to secure the necessary fiction of achieving enterprise targets, in particular drawing upon socio-economic networks. It was therefore a paradoxical feature of Czechoslovak state socialism that the functioning of the economic system called for 'the systematic decoupling of the formal organizational system from actual organizational practices' (Tsoukas, 1994, p. 23). The frequent decoupling of management practices from the conduct prescribed in the formal hierarchical institutions led to a distinctive, yet socially accepted, managerial culture, in which the best managers were known for their ability to draw on networks of social contacts as resources for facilitating the survival and development of state enterprises and the communities in which they were located. The main irony is that while such managerial behaviour on the one hand subverted the formal processes of hierarchical rule, its known and conscious consequence – for the managers' careers were bound to this outcome – was to bolster the existing, formally institutionalized system.

To the extent that such real management practices became commonplace rituals for satisfying the technical and institutional demands of the command economy, there arose new, socially sanctioned patterns of management. These emergent institutionalized practices coexisted with the institutionalized forms that were expressed in the central planning hierarchy, and, while serving the status quo in the short term, became the focus of an ever-widening institutional gap. Unlike in other countries, this gap could not be reduced because politicians in the former ČSSR, implicated as they had been in the Warsaw Pact invasion and in the subsequent crackdown of the normalized 1970s and 1980s, failed to reform the formal institutions to keep up with reality. Citizens and workers withdrew social legitimacy from the system, and were never persuaded by the communist-ideological apparatus to resubscribe. Czechoslovak communism came to suffer from interrelated system and social crises, and politicians resorted to coercion as a means of resolving these crisis tendencies in both the political economy and civil society.

The withdrawal of legitimacy from the formal institutions of state socialism resulted from both economic and socio-political underperformance, and became a recurrent feature of everyday social arenas, as illustrated by the social and psychological retreat referred to in Chapter 4. Managers found it increasingly difficult to carry out their tasks. First, the command-economic system created technical-economic challenges to their effectiveness as enterprise managers. Second, employees passed judgement on them about their social and professional credibility as local flag-bearers of a blemished social system, and withheld goodwill and motivation from the workplace (see Arato, 1982). The social and personal identity of managers, and the very nature of managerial work, were being contested by the critical conditions of both formal systems and social reality.

The institutional gap and the end of state socialism

The institutional gap between the formal, legal structures of the command economy and the socially accepted and normatively reproduced practices of economic behaviour grew wider and wider during normalization, and the failure of traditional socialist-ideological appeals reinforced the centralizing and coercive trends in all social spheres. This further enlarged the gap between the formal institutional system and emergent institutionalized practices of the social world, as well as detaching national and local elites representing the communist system from any base of social legitimacy.

Late attempts to reform Czechoslovak state socialism following the rise of Gorbachev in the Soviet Union were widely perceived as reluctant concessions by the communist leadership under Husák, whose former commitment to normalization reinforced their antipathy to and mistrust of decentralization. The replacement of Husák by Jakeš at the end of 1987 was, according to Rothschild (1993, p. 211) 'at best, enigmatic', because the latter's involvement in the post-1968 purges made it equally difficult for him to be sufficiently change-minded. The economic reforms that did emerge in the later 1980s were also resisted at lower levels. For example, Vols's VHJ was very slow to disband itself, and even at the fall of communism its management was still trying hard to keep Vols within its operational structures. In 1989, then, the centralized economic and organizational forms which had been re-established since 1970 were still more or less intact, but precarious. Over time, Czechoslovak state socialism continued to generate greater problems and incipient crises at both system and social levels, forcing those responsible for managing it to indulge in increasing levels of (self-) deception. By 1989, not even the elite cadres of the Communist Party believed the intricate deceits upon which state socialism was based, and the local economic elites, represented by enterprise managers, had to endure a combination of top-down and bottom-up pressures which had become intolerable. While it cannot be demonstrated, it could be argued that the mortal wound to the system that had, in retrospect, been faltering for many years was the decision of the *nomenklatura* political and economic elites to withdraw their normative and passive support for communism.

> The existing ruling classes in order to maintain the core of their power shifted their ground, accommodated to the popular mood, sacrificed their most hated representatives and recomposed themselves so as to be better able to maintain themselves in the future.
>
> (Haynes, 1992, p. 46)

The transformation as institutional change

The sudden changes following the Velvet Revolution in November 1989, like those that repercussed throughout the region, were to involve a transformation in social, economic and political structures with little historical precedent. Underlying our arguments is the view that the first step in formulating any credible explanation of the socio-economic transformation is an understanding of the institutional legacies of Czechoslovak state socialism. These legacies, conceptualized as formal institutions and as institutionalized practices which each operate at both macro and micro levels, include the business recipes and strategies that were the basis of state enterprise management as technical work and as a legitimate profession. By exposing the historical realities of state enterprise management, we have identified the experiential bedrock on which basis post-communist managers have constructed their approach to the organizational changes associated with the transition to a market economy. These experiences, methods and practices of state enterprise management have constituted critical *resources* for those managers facing the problems of enterprise survival and change in the post command-economic world.

The essence of the transition period is its very ambiguity and uncertainty. The purpose of transition economists and politicians has been to dismantle the established formal institutions and eliminate the socially sanctioned institutionalized micro practices which were the well-known social and economic conditions of Czechoslovak state socialism, and to replace them with an 'alternative' set. The future alternative was based on a broad consensus to abolish the political structures of totalitarian control and restore the democratic pluralism which Czechoslovakia had enjoyed before the Second World War; and to dissolve the centralized, autarkic command-economic system by reintroducing the principles of an open market economy. In institutional terms, the enterprise and its management, located as they were in a 'hierarchy of hierarchies', were self-evidently inappropriate to the needs of any economy purporting to leave supply and demand decisions at the lowest rung of the economic ladder – in firms and in households. But the move from a system of tight, centralized, authoritarian structure to one comprising decentralized, liberalized organizations loosely connected in market relations was not just a logical and logistical set of macro system problems; it was a fundamental

Table 5.1 The transformation requirements of Czech post-communism

Characteristics	Command-economic	Market-economic
Macro-institutional	*1 Centralized*	*1 Decentralized*
Property	State monopoly	Dispersed private rights
Politics	Totalitarian control	Pluralistic control
	2 Undifferentiated	*2 Differentiated*
Coordination of parts	Bureaucratic coordination	Emergent coordination
Institutional separation	Convergence of institutional power	Division of institutional powers
	3 Concentration of information	*3 Diffusion of information*
Sources	Information impactedness	Multiple sources
Accessibility	Closed, secretive	Open, transparent
Enterprise		
Ownership	State	Private
Control	Political-administrative	Shareholder management
Goals	Central production plan and social policies	Profit, market-oriented
Basic structural features	Simple functional hierarchy	Decentralized, divisionalized
Financial control	Weak, soft	Strong, hard
Key functions	Production, technical	Marketing, strategy
Management	*Nomenklatura*	
Selection criterion		Competitive, technical qualification
Basic problem	Supply constraints	Demand constraints
Primary strategy	Networking, external bargaining	Seek competitive advantage
Top management	External focus, autocratic style	External, devolved style
Middle management	Routine administrators, passive conformists	Devolved, responsible decision-makers
Key values	Social, ideological	Utilitarian, materialist
Attitude to labour	Hoard as valuable resource	Intensify use, cost of production
Attitudes to work	Low motivation, risk avoidance, develop informal adjustment practices	Involved, intrapreneurial, continual learning

Source: partly adapted from Child, 1993, p. 206.

transformation in the human, social and cultural patterns which had been the established, if disputed, heart of the working life of millions of managers and employees in state-owned enterprises.

Table 5.1 summarizes many of the arguments that have been developed in this book, and portrays at the same time the dilemmas implicit in the dominant conception of a post-communist transition. The table presents a conceptualized view of the Czechoslovak command economy, abstracted from the discussions of state socialist institutionalized forms and practices at the various levels of the command economy. The same three levels are presented for a notional 'market economy', which approximates more to the Anglo-American variant than to a 'social market' or Asian economic system. The Anglo-American model highlights the transformational requirements and difficulties of the transition path chosen and preferred by the dominant political players in Czechoslovakia (1990 to 1992) and the Czech Republic (1993 to 1995), where neo-liberalism has been the prevailing economic ideology. Table 5.1 lists twenty criteria, grouped by three levels of analysis, against which the full challenge of the socio-economic transformation can be judged.

The first level draws from the work of John Child (1993) and suggests the broad directions of macro-institutional changes. State socialist society is built upon a centralized, hierarchical state, which is coordinated through bureaucratically administered structures. Political, economic and other forms of institutional power derive from the same source and operate uni-directionally, providing for strong control and concentration of information. These institutional principles are in turn concretely expressed at the levels of organization and management: both directly as institutionally isomorphic reflections, such as in the hierarchical, plan-led production orientation, managed through an autocratic director and passive administration; and through decoupled, institutionalized practices like external networking, bargaining and hoarding resources.

In juxtaposition, Child describes the institutional features of the market-economic system to which Czech politicians have aspired, which exposes the transformational requirements of post-communism in terms of the three Ds: increased decentralization of economic and political decision-making; the differentiation of political, economic and other forms of institutional power, in turn requiring societal coordination to be an emergent property of relatively autonomous micro relations, rather than directives from above; and greater diffusion of information, with a plurality of sources and more transparency. At the levels of organization and management, these changes in institutional principle presage economic organizations becoming more loosely coordinated in their independent, bottom-up responses to market signals and information. In order to function efficiently, management authority similarly has to be delegated, and decision-making located near the sources of problems and information. The dynamism of decentralized market systems requires quick, adaptive managerial learning and simple economic criteria (profit, cost) to guide decisions.

This analysis demonstrates the profoundly institutional nature of the post-communist transformation, affecting as it does the established forms of structure and behaviour at all levels of society. The scale of the changes required to effect the move from the hierarchical, centrally planned economy to some form of decentralized market economy demands the resolution of three generic problems. First, the historical structures and institutions of state socialism need to be dissolved in order to remove the legal and formal supports for continuing patterns of economic behaviour. In Chapter 2, we referred to this process as *deinstitutionalization*. Second, new structures and institutions necessary to support and encourage behaviour appropriate to a market-economic system need to be designed, agreed and implemented, a process we have called *reinstitutionalization*. Third, and critical to the success of the transition period, these phasing-out and phasing-in processes, what Kouba (1994, p. 384) has called an 'institutional vacuum', have to be simultaneously controlled by what we could call *transition management*.

In Chapter 6, we apply this framework to the processes of formal institutional change in Czechoslovakia and the Czech Republic. In Chapters 7, 8 and 9 we draw evidence directly from our four enterprises to examine the ways in which managers have coped with the transitional problems they have faced. The aim is to comprehend how in general, at enterprise and management levels, the three processes of deinstitutionalization, reinstitutionalization and transitional management have been controlled and experienced, and how in particular the various interested parties have gone about defining, assembling and constructing the new institutional forms and practices from the cultural and material resources available to them from their historical and contemporary experiences. It is from these processes of institutional (re)production that the new post-communist Czech economy will emerge.

Notes

1 The three Central European states of Hungary, Poland and Czechoslovakia met at Visegrád in Hungary in February 1991 in order to coordinate their approach to the European Community. Although they do not themselves like the term, they have become known as the 'Visegrád group'. Following the split of the Czech and Slovak Republics in 1993, the name now extends to the four nations.
2 The actual numbers of enterprises cited in different sources varies enormously, creating a problem in describing the process of restructuring in the Czech(oslovak) economy. The differences almost certainly arise from the legacy of the VHJs: whether they are counted as the main industrial units, or whether the enterprises under their control are recognized. Authors often do not make the basis of their calculations clear.

Part III

The emergence of post-communist management

6 The post-communist context of organizational transformation

The institutional structure of the Czechoslovak economy, within the logic of the communist world, was characterized by highly centralized, autocratic elements which served to distort the industrial and market structures of the economy. Strong price regulation, central control of domestic and foreign trade, and enterprise targets poorly related to actual demand created a distinctive pattern of economic relations among enterprises, and between enterprises and the command-economic centre. Yet, in the words of two Czech economists:

> By 1992, most prices were liberalized, state monopolization of foreign trade was abolished, and internal convertibility of currency was achieved. By the end of 1992, almost all manufacturing enterprises entered the privatization process and by the end of 1994 the process was virtually finished . . . The Czech Republic thus represents an interesting case for studying the adjustment of the market structure in transition.
>
> (Zemplinerová and Stíbal, 1995, p. 234)

With the exception of the former East Germany in its special conditions of political and economic reunification, the Czech Republic has transferred more state assets to private hands than any other country, creating within a matter of four years a privatized sector of enormous size. In order to achieve this transformation, the Czech economy underwent substantial changes in its institutional structures and management, and individual citizens and communities endured various hardships.

At the level of the enterprise itself, these massive social, political and economic changes provide the historical context of the organizational and managerial upheavals that conditioned the transformational experiences of privatization. In this chapter, we will explore the institutional and economic landscape that constituted the environment in which organizational changes in our four enterprises were managed. These external contexts provide a backcloth for organizational transformation, but also furnish the incentives and motives that lay behind the management behaviour that itself guided and drove privatization and enterprise restructuring.

The chapter has two purposes. First, it outlines the social and political events that constituted the Velvet Revolution of November 1989, and examines the initial political context in which debates over the transition process took place. Second, using the categories of institutional change defined in Chapters 2 and 5, it explores the major socio-economic and institutional changes that have taken place during the early transition period, in as much as they impacted upon the transformational experiences of managers and enterprises in Czechoslovakia and the later Czech Republic.

The Velvet Revolution and the politics of the transition

The events of 1989

Against the stable background of two decades of normalization, the events of late 1989 came as a surprise to most Czechoslovaks (Adam, 1993, p. 627). The main preconditions of the Velvet Revolution appear to have originated mainly from the outside, as the prevailing public response to decades of Czechoslovak state socialism, even at its harshest, had been one of toleration and restraint in the face of political adversity but relative economic well-being. The rise of Gorbachev and *perestroika* from 1985; the democratizing processes in neighbouring Poland and Hungary in the early 1988–9 period; the flight of the East Germans over the summer of 1989, leading to large-scale demonstrations and the eventual opening of the Berlin Wall on 9 November 1989 (Batt, 1991, pp. 22ff; Rothschild, 1993, pp. 226ff; Lewis, 1994, pp. 229ff; Oberschall, 1994) – these were all external events of considerable importance for understanding what happened in November 1989 in Czechoslovakia.

The Czechoslovak communist leadership, bereft of a reform-communist faction after the purges of normalization, had found it hard to respond positively to these external trends.

> Gorbachev and *perestroika* changed the situation in a fundamental way. It accelerated the erosion of the system in all Eastern European countries. The Czechoslovak leadership, however, which took its legitimacy from the Brezhnevite occupation, became increasingly isolated and derided, not least for its attempts to talk about *Přestavba* – our *Perestroika*. It answered in the only way it knew – with increased repression.
>
> (Urban, 1990, p. 113)

The demonstrations on 21 August 1988 to remember the twentieth anniversary of the Warsaw Pact invasion elicited a large response, especially from young people, and the authorities reacted with pre-emptive arrests of known (e.g. Charter 77) leaders, and with tear gas and batons. This pattern continued at further demonstrations in October and December 1988, at which demonstrators had begun to invoke old national (non-communist) symbols, such as allusions to Masaryk and the First Republic, and there emerged clearer signs of committed opposition (Wheaton and Kavan, 1992, pp. 25ff). The arrest of Václav Havel and other dissidents in January 1989, at the commemoration of the twentieth anniversary of Jan Palach's self-immolation, and the subsequent imprisonment of Havel provoked outrage at home and abroad, and led to open letters and petitions of protest.

Further demonstrations in 1989 continued to be met with repressive policing methods, and the political events of the late summer and early autumn in East Germany, Poland and Hungary were felt in Prague, where the West German embassy was besieged by East German refugees. Popular dissatisfaction grew in Czechoslovakia as the ultimate frailty of the other communist regimes, especially the hard-line East German one, was revealed. Soon after the fall of the Berlin Wall, there was an officially sanctioned student march to commemorate the Nazi crushing of the Czech student movement (Urban, 1990, p. 116; Wheaton and Kavan, 1992, p. 41), and this became a natural focus of the new spirit of freedom. The march continued unofficially and led to confrontation and violence, the possible result, some commentators have alleged, of the work of *agents provocateurs*.

This was the catalyst for the changes in Czechoslovakia, arousing intense discussion among intellectuals and students (see Garton Ash, 1990; Glenny, 1993), and resulting in a General Strike which was called for 27 November and was well supported by the workers at even the large Prague factories that had been the traditional bastions of the communist working class. With the preceding and continuing events in the other Central European communist states, the Czechoslovak communist leaders began to become aware of their weakening bargaining position and of the increasing organization of the previously powerless opposition, led by former dissidents organized under the banner of Civic Forum (*Občanské forum*). In response to the gathering support for the strike, Miloš Jakeš, the General Secretary of the Party, had resigned on 24 November, to be replaced by Karel Urbánek. In the face of the success of the strike, Prime Minister Ladislav Adamec tried to salvage the situation by forming a new coalition government, but underestimated the weakness of his position by naming fifteen communists in the twenty-one person body.

Threats of further strike action led to Adamec's resignation, and he was replaced by another communist, Marian Čalfa, who formed a twenty-strong interim 'Government of National Understanding', with a minority of communists, most of whom were soon to resign their party membership. Under instruction, the communist-controlled Federal Assembly voted to delete the constitutional clause that defined the leading role of the party and to acknowledge the interim government, which Gustav Husák swore in on 10 December as his last presidential deed. The final symbolic act was the election to the Presidency by the Federal Assembly on 29 December of Václav Havel, who had been a political prisoner only eight months earlier (Wheaton and Kavan, 1992; also Batt, 1991; Mason, 1992; Lewis, 1994). These social and political events served as the backcloth against which one of the most dramatic of societal transformations was to be played out.

The politics of the economic transition

The collapse of the communist states immediately attracted the attention of many Western economists, but especially those whose political and economic predilections reflected neo-liberal monetarist thinking. Such economists had been involved or interested in the various free-market initiatives in Western capitalist societies, of which Thatcherite privatization fervour in Britain was held to be the model. The breakdown of state socialism, the ideological arch-enemy of such economists, was the ideal opportunity for American and British neo-liberals to disseminate their ideas and policies to a very receptive audience. According to Šik (1993), the leading reform economist of the mid-1960s, there was no serious debate over the aims of the post-communist transition, since the command economy was condemned by experience, and 'third way' experiments were discredited by the failure of pre-1989 attempted reforms. Czech economists and politicians also agreed in principle on the main features of transitional economics (see Table 6.1). Any disagreement that existed was over the speed of institutional change, and the sequencing of these restructuring efforts in relation to broad economic management (e.g. Rybczynski, 1991; Clague, 1992; Murrell, 1992).

Table 6.1 The main policy characteristics of economic transformation

Policy objective	Main policy instruments
Economic stabilization	Monetary instruments: restrictive monetary policy using interest rate increases and direct credit controls. Fiscal instruments: balancing the state budget, increasing taxes to control monetary overhang, control domestic demand and wage increases.
Price and trade liberalization	Free price controls and subsidies to create more open competitive environment; allow prices to serve as the basis of value and economic exchange, and of business decision-making; devalue the crown substantially and introduce limited convertibility; remove restrictions on domestic and foreign trade.
Transfer of state assets to private hands	Define private property rights; encourage new small business; restitution of property; small and large privatization schemes; municipalize state property.
Reform of the social security net	Redefine employment rights, unemployment and other safety net benefits and obligations.

See, for example, Clague, 1992, p. 5; Adam, 1993, pp. 629ff; Parker, 1993, pp. 393–4; Šik, 1993, p. 193; Crocioni, 1995, pp. 79–80; Drábek, 1995, p. 239; Lavigne, 1995, pp. 114ff.

The interim government, which included some of the most trenchant economic critics of the former regime, proposed that full democratic elections should take place in June 1990, and in April 1990 embarked upon devising and enacting policies aimed at macroeconomic stabilization and basic institutional reform to reorient the economy away from command-planning principles. For those involved, the political goal was to make a return to communism and central planning as difficult as possible (Wheaton and Kavan, 1992, pp. 127ff; Mejstřik and Hlávaček, 1993, p. 61; Kotrba, 1995, p. 161).

The politics of the economic transition were played out between three former academic economists in the new government elected in June 1990: Václav Klaus, Vladimír Dlouhý and Valtr Komárek (both Dlouhý and Komárek had resigned their CP memberships soon after the Velvet Revolution). Klaus and Dlouhý had become respectively Ministers of Finance and for Planning, were soon closely identified with the monetarist schools of Western economics and advocated a radical economic transformation. This involved the rapid dismantling of central regulations and structures, and privatizing state assets in a short time in order to leave economic and industrial restructuring effectively in the hands of private owners, who would then act freely in the interests of capital, and independently of the former *nomenklatura* interests entrenched in the existing state and enterprise structures (see Sacks, 1993; Meaney, 1995, pp. 276ff). Klaus sought, in the words of a famous speech, a market economy with 'no adjectives' (Šik, 1993, p. 202).

Komárek had been the head of the Institute for Economic Forecasting and thus senior to both Klaus and Dlouhý. He had been made deputy prime minister and led a group which favoured a more prolonged, gradualist path to a market economy. This approach revisited some of the themes of his 1980s work (see Myant, 1989), and emphasized the necessarily slow building of economic and institutional preconditions. By allowing, for example, a commercialized state sector to develop internal competition between smaller organizational units, it would be possible to reshape the disadvantageous industrial structure away from heavy industry. He argued for the encouragement of foreign investment, and the protection of living standards by the gradual removal of central regulations. In this way, the economy could stabilize and grow, before embarking on sales of public assets on a big scale (Adam, 1993; Frydman *et al.*, 1993, p. 71; Myant, 1993; Pick, 1993). This debate and the ensuing conflicts foreshadowed the fragmentation of Civic Forum into multiple parties scattered around the centre (Meaney, 1995, p. 295). As history now records, Klaus's liberal economic, monetarist views became the main ideology of the Civic Democratic Party (*Občanská demokratická strana*, or ODS). The economic policies of the ODS, supported by smaller right-of-centre parties, have in turn come to dominate the transition strategy of the Czech Republic.

Institutional change and the economic transition

We shall examine the institutional changes involved in the early transition period by discussing them in terms of the three processes outlined in Chapters 2 and 5: namely deinstitutionalization, transition management and reinstitutionalization. It is important to recognize that the actual changes introduced do not so neatly fall into any one category. However, the general approach of the government has been based on rapid economic deregulation to undermine past institutions, cautious fiscal and monetary control in order to stabilize an economy in transition and radical privatization to establish new patterns of economic behaviour.

Deinstitutionalization

The first stage in the transformational process has been the process of breaking from the past, and the main formal steps have involved the elimination of the state socialist institutional environment, including the derecognition of the legal role and status of communist organizations and the deregulation of the command-economic structures and practices, which enabled the sustained reproduction of state socialism. It was deemed crucial that the structural and institutional reforms should disable the institutionalized practices of economic actors (industries, enterprises and managers) in order to clear the way for the development of new patterns of market economic behaviour: 'the institutional structure of the reforming economy will reflect the characteristics of the communist era that are carried into the transition by the organizations shaped by that era' (Murrell and Wang, 1993, p. 389).

Czechoslovaks in particular recognized the urgency of getting on with the process of eliminating institutional supports for socialistic behaviour: 'Whereas in Hungary and Poland the collapse of socialism was a gradual process lasting several years, in the former Czechoslovakia . . . it occurred in a matter of weeks' (Adam, 1993, p. 627). Although this is an exaggeration when looking at the economic system, the sharp, dramatic and radical nature of the changes in Czechoslovakia was quite different from that of most other countries in the region because of the more orthodox starting point, which we have explored in detail in Part Two. With regard to the political changes, however, the break from the past was virtually immediate.

As we have seen above, the notorious Article 4 of the constitution, which proclaimed the leading role of the Communist Party of Czechoslovakia, was formally renunciated on 29 November 1989 by the Federal Assembly, and this was rapidly followed by the other mainstays of Communist Party power: the dissolution of the party basic organizations at factory level; and the abolition of Marxism-Leninism as the official state ideology and as the basis of cultural and educational policy (Wheaton and Kavan, 1992, pp. 98–9). These formal acts were mirrored in other social acts that took place at the grass-roots, such as the participation of communists in the general strike, or their resignation from the party or the militia. The undermining of these institutional structures and practices started the larger process of deinstitutionalization rolling. The simultaneous rebuilding of democratic procedures, such as the development of Civic Forum branches in the enterprises, served to underline the determination of ordinary Czechoslovak citizens to make the political changes stick.

There were some notable changes in personnel at the very top of state structures. But many people noticed, and were angered by, the facility with which the former *nomenklatura* in the state machinery or in enterprise management, who had benefited at others' personal cost from the communist regime, had been able to move into post-communist positions which were equally politically or economically rewarding (see Reed, 1995). This popular frustration was openly expressed in public debates about how to purge the emerging democratic state of those people whose conduct as senior communists had demonstrated patently undemocratic proclivities. In October 1991 (effective 1 January 1992), Parliament passed the controversial *lustrace* law.

This legislation, also known as the Screening Act, prevented certain categories of former communists from holding positions in state administration and other state organizations for five years.[1] The legislation covered members of the secret police, registered agents and collaborators with the secret police, senior party cadres from district level up, members of the people's militia and those communists who sat on normalizing committees which conducted the post-1948 and post-1968 purges. Within industry, directors, deputy directors and senior managers of former state enterprises were affected, but not middle management staff, even when their *nomenklatura* status provided them with lifestyle benefits. The legislation had many critics: on grounds of principle that these 'rules' for public office simply replaced one system of discrimination with another; and on practical grounds that many senior communists who had benefited as *nomenklatura* acted quickly enough to escape the net, such as by moving to positions outside the state apparatus (Wheaton and Kavan, 1992, pp. 179ff; Janyska, 1992; Kavan, 1992).

With the whole economic system coherently structured around the principles and practices of central planning, its legal end was brought about more cautiously, the command-economic institutions being phased out mostly during 1990. In July 1990, the State Planning Commission was replaced by the Ministry of the Economy, and the rule of the central plan was eliminated for most enterprises (Wolchik, 1991, p. 222). At the same time, the State Prices Board was abolished (Jeffries, 1993, p. 386), and in January 1991, 85 per cent of prices were liberated from central control as state subsidies were dramatically reduced – declining from 16.5 per cent of GDP in 1990 to a mere 4.5 per cent of GDP in 1992. The foreign trade monopoly was dismantled in stages over 1990, the former FTOs losing the last vestiges of control in February 1991, when the need for special export and import licences was restricted to only a small range of products (Frydman *et al.*, 1993, p. 49; Jeffries, 1993, p. 390; Mejstřik and Hlávaček, 1993, p. 68). In 1988, only fifty FTOs had been legally permitted to engage in foreign trade, a figure which, corresponding to the number of formally registered companies, increased to over 26,000 by May 1995 (Bohatá, 1996a, p. 23). At the same time that prices were freed from central control, the government made the Czechoslovak crown internally convertible, thereby allowing businesses to conduct foreign trade more freely. The liberalization of prices and of domestic and foreign trade were critical steps along the path to a market economy, but they had repercussions throughout the whole economy, with prices taking on the role of market signals rather than mere units of account.

In April 1990, the 1988 Law on State Enterprises was amended in order to reflect the greater strategic and operational independence required of enterprises working in more deregulated environments. This law, and its companion on joint stock companies, created a transitional framework for the corporatization of state enterprises, moving ownership from the all-encompassing state to a concrete founding organ (usually a ministry), while leaving effective management in the local hands. The strategic management of corporatized or marketized enterprises was to be conducted by an executive board of directors (*představenstvo*), and overseen by a supervisory board (*dozorčí rada*) whose structure and membership was approved by the founding organ. Until the end of 1990, when the transitional debate on state enterprises shifted track to the agenda of privatization, the founding organ could transform its state enterprises into 'state-owned joint stock companies', in which the new legal entity had full control of profits and financial independence in decision-making (Rychetnik, 1992, p. 121; Frydman *et al.*, 1993, pp. 52–4; Mejstik, 1993, p. 135).

The increased decentralization of economic decision-making to individual enterprises was partly created by these legal moves, but the very atmosphere and expectation, not to mention the chaos, of the early transition period was sufficient to effect real changes in the giganticist structure of the economy. Lízal *et al.* (1995, pp. 211ff) identify the tendency for the large monopolistic state enterprises to break up without policy or legislation being put in place. They identified some 700 industrial enterprises which employed more than twenty-five people at the start of 1990, but by mid-1992, mostly through break-ups, some 2000 enterprises had been created. Furthermore, the institutional vacuum left room for enterprise managers to search for and strike deals with foreign investors (Mann, 1993, p. 963).

Further processes of formal deinstitutionalization are important in understanding the changing context of state enterprises in the early transition period. First, the collapse of the CMEA structures had major consequences for Czechoslovak industry, especially in the heavy engineering sectors. It was decided in January 1990 that, as of 1 January 1991, all CMEA trade would be conducted on the basis of world prices, and transactions would be settled in hard currencies. This instantly disadvantaged the Czechoslovak economy by increasing the prices of energy and raw materials, mainly imported from the Soviet Union, which were used for the manufacture of machinery and metallurgical products which, in turn, dominated its export structures. This made these already uncompetitive products more expensive and more diffi-cult to sell either to former clients in the East or to new Western markets. In fact, on this basis, the Soviet Union found it difficult to repay its net debts to virtually every CMEA nation, leading to the collapse of many existing CMEA contracts inherited from the 1980s. Because their exports had made leading contributions to CMEA projects, Czechoslovak enterprises in the heavy engineering branches were especially hard hit by the impact of bad loans and withdrawn credits when, in July 1991, the structures of the CMEA were formally dissolved (Hrnčíř, 1993, p. 307). The early 1990s therefore saw an enormous reorientation of trade away from the Soviet Union and the transitional economies as enterprises sought new markets for their products, especially those that had accumulated as unsold stock, and the safe haven of hard currency trade (Havlik, 1995; Lavigne, 1995, pp. 102ff; Mitov, 1995; Bohatá, 1996a).

Second, as a consequence of new political priorities, and reinforced by the economic reality of the wider post-communist world, there was a dramatic shrinkage of the military/arms industry of Czechoslovakia. Czechoslovak military expenditure had accounted for 3.7 per cent of GDP in 1989, when over 75 per cent of military output, worth kčs22.7 billion, had been exported, making Czechoslovakia the world's seventh largest exporter of such products. The defence agenda of the new government had massive effects on the mechanical engineering industry of post-communist Czechoslovakia, with 60 per cent of the 'damage' occurring in Slovak industry (Jeffries, 1993, p. 390; Kiss, 1993).

Third, it has been argued that the command economies differed most from their market counterparts in the nature of their financial systems (e.g. Székely, 1995, p. 200), because of the simplicity of their role in central plan-ning. In that the development of a capital market as a efficient conduit for channelling savings into investment is a prerequisite for the operation of a market economy (Hrnčíř, 1993), it was critical at an early stage to deinstitu-tionalize the monobank system. Early in 1990, a two-tier system on a Western model was created from the State Bank, some of its property being divided between seven new operating banks. These banks inherited the portfolios of the former monobank, which included both non-performing loans and low-interest bearing credits, some of which were the bad loan legacies of pre-1989 foreign trade. As such, the process of deregulating and demonopolizing the former financial system reproduced in the new banking institutions a tech-nical insolvency and consequent operating fragility (Hrnčíř, 1993, p. 307; Drábek, 1995, pp. 259–60).

Finally, the new government needed to tackle issues arising from the legacy of state socialist social policy, whereby the state, directly or through its local representatives, channelled social and welfare support, often through highly subsidized pricing regimes, to the population (McAuley, 1991, pp. 100ff).

The Czechoslovak route to the market economy, supported by the international financial institutions (e.g. International Monetary Fund, World
Bank, European Bank for Reconstruction and Development), would not be
able to bear high deficit financing (e.g. Drábek, 1995, p. 240), and the new,
anticipated private sector could not be expected to continue to fund social
and welfare activities. Therefore, the old structures of social welfare and provision, which planned, organized and subsidized, for example, the building,
management and maintenance of the housing stock, or physical culture
(swimming pools, winter stadia etc.), were disbanded as the state reduced its
role. Centrally owned and managed facilities such as these were legally decentralized to more local agents, such as municipalities, voluntary clubs, housing
cooperatives and associations. At the same time, rents were deregulated in
stages (e.g. 100 per cent increase in 1992, and a further 70 per cent in 1994)
and legislation was put in place to allow municipalities to sell their newly
acquired properties (Musil, 1995, p. 1680).

Transition management

Many of the important measures to deregulate and destatize the economy
were in place and effective by early 1991. Their consequences were far-
reaching, affecting the everyday lives of citizens and consumers, of workers
and enterprises. In 1991, retail prices rose by 56.7 per cent, while in January
alone consumer prices increased by 26 per cent (higher for foodstuffs) and
producer prices by 24 per cent; real wages over the year declined by 25.5 per
cent, and industrial employment diminished by nearly 12 per cent (e.g.
Frydman *et al.*, 1993, pp. 43ff; Jeffries, 1993, pp. 385ff; Drábek, 1995,
pp. 241–3). These negative socio-economic impacts continued through 1992,
at a decreasing rate, affecting Slovaks far more dramatically than Czechs
because of the divergent industrial structures of the republics. According to
Drábek (1995) the real purchasing power of wages at the start of 1994 was
still only 80 per cent of its 1989 value.

Deinstitutionalization affected industry and business by exacerbating the
shocks caused by the collapse of communism:

> Although . . . [state trading organizations and the central planning
> mechanism] had been defective, they had provided a framework for
> economic transactions. Their swift abolition produced management
> confusion and a collapse in investment, especially in the large-scale
> industries.
>
> (Parker, 1993, p. 392)

Klaus's economic stabilization programme imposed a radical austerity package on the Czechoslovaks while there existed a high degree of popular support
for change, and was designed to ameliorate the extreme effects of such large-

scale economic dislocation. He set about controlling the key macroeconomic processes, thereby holding the transitional economy in financial check while it moved away from centrally administered economic planning. Chief among his objectives was the mastery of inflation, which he pursued through operating a tight financial regime, including the control of interest rates and bank credits, the restraint of government expenditure and reduction of the tax burden, the balancing of the national budget and the control of incomes via tax penalties (see Frydman *et al.*, 1993; Jeffries, 1993; Drábek, 1995).

In addition to stabilizing the economy at a time when the government was releasing it from many administratively imposed restrictions of central planning, the purpose of transitional macroeconomic changes was to 'create a competitive economic environment where price signals would guide the decision making of enterprise managers and thus make them look for ways to increase economic efficiency in their enterprises' (Adam, 1993, p. 629). In other words, the destatization supported by economic stabilization was intended to have major microeconomic effects, supportive of new patterns of market-economic business behaviour. This combination strategy of proceeding simultaneously and with conviction at both macro and micro levels and in institutional and stabilization directions was felt to overcome the risk of failure to which pre-1989 reform attempts had succumbed (see Mejstřik and Hlávaček, 1993, pp. 58ff).

Economists consider the stabilization programme to have been fairly successful. Table 6.2 indicates that the key variable, inflation, has been brought back under control after the high of 1991, and the rate of unemployment has remained remarkably low throughout the whole period. Furthermore, this has been achieved with little recourse to external borrowing (Drábek, 1995, p. 237). The reality behind the data is, of course, more complex than it appears, and this success owes much to rather less explicit government policies, such as the tacit government support for inefficient enterprises during the transition.

Tight credit control and high interest rates, as well as poor development of the financial sector and its lending practices, have resulted in one of the major problems to face enterprises during the early period of transition, namely the difficulty in gaining access to credit. The micro, managerial reaction has been to delay the payment of debts as a means of 'borrowing' money to restructure, invest etc. The consequence of such behaviour on a macro scale has been to seize up debt settlement processes and create a massive problem of inter-enterprise debt. One researcher estimates that inter-enterprise debt in Czechoslovakia escalated from kčs6.6 billion in December 1989 to kčs154.6 billion in September 1992 (Hrnčíř, 1993, p. 309; but compare Čapek, 1994; Takla, 1994, p. 168), and continued to plague the Czech Republic in 1993 and 1994 (Dyba and Svejnar, 1995). State-sponsored schemes to encourage multilateral settlement had barely any effect on the scale of the problem (Brom and Orenstein, 1994, p. 902).

Table 6.2 Key economic indicators of the Czech transition

	1990	1991	1992	1993	1994	1995
Inflation* (%)	9.7	56.7	11.1	20.8	10.0	9.0
Unemployment (%)	0.8	4.1	2.6	3.4	3.2	2.9
Real wages (%)	−5.7	−25.5	9.8	3.5	17.6	13.4
GDP (%)	−1.2	−14.2	−6.6	−0.9	2.6	5.2
Industrial production (%)	−3.3	−22.3	−13.8	−5.3	2.3	9.5
Accumulated FDI ($ billion)	0.36	1.07	1.68	2.22	3.2	5.8
Inter-enterprise debt (kč(s) billion)	39.3	113.2	94.4	150.0	132.0	n.a.

* 1990–2 inflation figures for Czechoslovakia; others for the Czech Republic.
All percentage change unless stated.
Sources: Trade Links, 1993, 1994; Drábek, 1995; Dyba and Svejnar, 1995; Lavigne, 1995; Business Central Europe, various editions.

Reinstitutionalization

At the same time as eliminating the formal institutional restraints on the development of the market economy, and attempting to maintain the stability of the transitional economy using the central authority of the state, it was important to start building the 'microfoundations of a market economy' and those systems that would allow the new rules to be enforced (Hrnčíř, 1993, p. 306). Parker (1993, p. 394) summarizes the range of formal institutions necessary to support a successful market economy, virtually all of which were absent during the first years of the transition. These included a freely operational capital market with rights of legal foreclosure, a fully functioning financial sector with an independent national bank, employment, industrial relations and welfare legislation, the adoption of market-appropriate accounting conventions and laws to ensure ownership and property rights. In order to implement such institutional restructuring in the short period envisaged by the Czechoslovak government, legal structures had to be invented or imported on a massive scale.

The creation of a market-economic environment required the filling of the institutional spaces deregulated by the unravelling of state socialism. The legal machinery for the economic transition included the establishment of two kinds of structure, procedure or rule system. The first of these may be called *transitional structures*, which were designed to have only a temporary life-span, and whose role was to guide the transition process towards the market economy. For example, in the sphere of privatization, which was the centre of Klaus's economic transition plans, many such structures had to be established: the Ministries of Privatization, city and district privatization committees, the Centre for Voucher Privatization, founding organs, the National Property Funds, the Consolidation Bank (*Konsolidační banka*) and so on. Such structures were expected to self-destruct when their contribution to the transition was deemed complete. The existence of such structures highlights the differences with privatization in Western capitalist economies such as the United Kingdom, for in the Czech Republic there was no private sector to which state enterprises could be transferred, and no relevant institutions were in place that could manage and control the 'transfer' (Kenway, 1993, p. 60). At the same time, paradoxically, this ensured that the state had to play a key role in privatizing state assets, and this has had implications beyond Klaus's formal plans for the emerging (institutionalizing) patterns of ownership and control, e.g. regarding the critical question of corporate governance that has so exercized Czech and Western economists since privatization (e.g. Mládek and Hashi, 1993; Parker, 1993; Brom and Orenstein, 1994; Dlouhý and Mládek, 1994; Laštovička *et al.*, 1995; see below).

Beyond these temporary, instrumental structures of reinstitutionalization, the legal changes have had the goal of creating more enduring *market-economic institutions*. The early economic legislation was directly aimed at the micro-foundations of business, a new commercial code being adopted as soon as April 1990 (amended in 1991). This, and another law on private enterprise, defined the nature, scope and legal forms of possible business activities, from individual trade licences, unlimited and limited partnerships, limited liability (*společnost s ručením omezeným*, or s.r.o.) and joint stock companies (*akciová společnost*, or a.s.) and cooperatives. A business register was established. Other legislation liberalized the rules on foreign capital participation, defined the rights of debtors and established the rules for bankruptcy proceedings. In the field of large-scale privatization, legislation provided for specialized private financial enterprises – the investment privatization funds – which were founded in accordance with the commercial code to participate specifically in voucher privatization. This hive of legislative activity in 1990 and 1991 established the new ground-rules of domestic business and market behaviour, but the ways in which they have taken hold in everyday business practice have at times been rather different from the intent.

Before attending to the processes of privatization in greater detail, we need to explore some other major developments in the institutional environment which have important consequences for the transformation of enterprises and management. First, we consider the emergence of the financial sector that has followed the collapse of the monobanking system, and the characteristics of the financial environment that faced the privatizing and privatized enterprises. Second, we turn to the changing face of foreign trade following the demise of the CMEA.

The large commercial banks that were established as the two tiers of the post-communist banking system have become the institutional backbone of the banking services sector, but they suffered from major handicaps inherited with their property from the planning system. Not only did they have 'inadequate governance, insufficient capital, weak loan portfolios and a weak system of supervision' (Schwartz *et al.*, 1994, p. 298), but they had little experience of lending on commercial conditions, and little incentive to develop new lending practices. In early 1991, the Czech government established the Consolidation Bank in order to 'prevent a chain of bankruptcies in the economy by relieving the commercial banks and enterprises of the legacy of the former system of enterprise finance' (Brom and Orenstein, 1994, p. 900).

The newly created banks had inherited a portfolio of bad debts and 'permanently revolving credits' from the Central Bank, and these had been serviced at ridiculously low pre-1989 interest rates. In the liberalized world of 1991, the banks could not afford to support business of this sort, but cancelling credits would have threatened a spiral of bankruptcies throughout the Czechoslovak economy. The government made available kčs50 billion, plus a share in the early proceeds of privatization, for the Consolidation Bank to buy from the large banks some proportion of the inherited perpetual credits, amounting to some 20 per cent of all bank credits at the time (Hrnčíř, 1993, p. 313; Čapek, 1994, p. 63; Takla, 1994, p. 169). Through this process of restructuring loan repayments, 6000 enterprises, or 80 per cent of all medium and large firms, became obligated to this new 'state' institution (Brom and Orenstein, 1994, p. 901), but made a direct contribution to 'cleaning up' bank and enterprise balance sheets in advance of privatization.

The new banks realized that loans to small businesses in the transition period bore a high risk, so they 'played safe' and continued to lend to enterprises or managers with whom they had dealt in the past (Čapek, 1994, p. 64; Perotti, 1994, p. 62), consequently adding more non-performing loans to those that had remained in their portfolios.

> In the given environment, the 'old' bad loans and debt contract failures inherited from the past interacted with the 'new' ones arising in the course of transition itself . . . [Hence] bad loans and debt contract failures in EMEs [emerging market economies], unlike in market economies, became a widespread, mass phenomenon and acquired a persistent and structural character, not only a cyclical one.
>
> (Hrnčíř, 1993, pp. 306–7)

As we have seen, in the climate of tight credit control and with the effects of poor lending practices, many enterprises found it not only convenient but also necessary to 'borrow' money unofficially by delaying payment of bills to suppliers (Takla, 1994, p. 167). As this became a normal business practice, and amid the process of spiralling inter-enterprise debt, each enterprise also suffered from acute 'payment inability', and struggled to find enough liquidity to meet everyday expenses such as wages. The situation became too chronic for the financial restructuring of any one enterprise to be a feasible answer.

In the process of reinstitutionalization, the financial enterprises were to be treated like other former state enterprise structures. Rather than complete dismantlement and replacement, these banks, with their strong state socialist legacies, were to be privatized as ongoing entities, and restructured according to the decisions of real private owners, and in response to the competitive pressures of foreign and new domestic banks. Furthermore, like various state industrial enterprises, many banks were technically insolvent during the period of transition, and could only be saved during the pre-privatization period of 1990 to 1992 by the liberal interpretation of the bankruptcy rules.

A bankruptcy law had in fact been put into place in October 1991 (Frydman *et al.*, 1993, pp. 62–3), but its use was postponed twice until April 1993, and even then has been used to little effect (Brom and Orenstein, 1994, p. 899; Stark and Bruszt, 1995, p. 19). Given the scale of inter-enterprise debt, illiquidity and longer-term insolvency of many major enterprises, it appears to have been a conscious policy on behalf of the government that the financial restructuring of enterprises should proceed on other grounds. Under the 1991 law, the founding ministry of the state enterprise had to initiate bankruptcy proceedings, and only a small number of smaller enterprises were liquidated in this way. The enactment in April 1993, following the first wave of privatization, allowed creditors to file for bankruptcy proceedings, but with safeguards to prevent the threat of a domino collapse (Hrnčíř, 1993, p. 306; Schwartz *et al.*, 1994, p. 295). The consequence was only a small flow of insignificant cases (Čapek, 1994, p. 67). This effective anti-bankruptcy policy therefore preserved many inefficient enterprises for the two waves of large privatization.

The rundown and ultimate collapse of trade with the Soviet Union and CMEA led to far-reaching economic problems. For enterprises whose longer-term production schedules had in 1989 been confidently projected on the assurance of state socialist plans and low-cost credits, there was an urgent need to find new clients who would accept their products, often from stock accumulated through failed Eastern contracts (Dobrinsky, 1995), and to seek business which paid hard currency to sustain solvency. For the economy as a whole, whose performance, albeit declining, had been guaranteed by trade with the 'East', there was the wish to trade more with Western nations in order to encourage the importation of more modern technologies. The early transition period saw a radical reorientation of trade away from the former CMEA to the Western developed countries. During most of the 1980s, Czechoslovakia had shown itself, more than most of its neighbours, to be dependent on CMEA or CMEA-related trade, which accounted consistently for about three-quarters of its exports and imports (Wolchik, 1991, p. 260; Jeffries, 1993, p. 252; Kouba, 1994, p. 386; Bohatá, 1996a). Over 1990–1, there was a dramatic shift, so that by 1993 only 20 per cent of trade was with the former communist states (Dyba and Svejnar, 1995, p. 42), while trade with the European Union increased from 20 to 25 per cent in 1989 to nearly 50 per cent by 1993 (Graziani, 1995, p. 169; Havlik, 1995, p. 141; Lavigne, 1995, p. 192; Wolchik, 1995, pp. 161–2).

In the context of these processes, there has emerged new international institutional frameworks aimed at regulating the trading forces unleashed by the post-communist economies' search for alternative, hard currency trade.

Western commentators have feared the importation of East European goods, which were understood to have an anti-competitive advantage resulting from low labour costs and even indirect state subsidies. Further, their low technological content and sometimes poor product quality might lead to something tantamount to social and environmental dumping. Foremost among these new arrangements were the Europe Agreements (EAs), completed between the then Economic Community (EC) and, independently, the transitional nations. The EA with Czechoslovakia was signed in 1991, and came into force in March 1992. It drew up a timetable for opening up free trading conditions between the (now) European Union (EU) and Czechoslovakia, later extended to the new Czech Republic. The arrangements were asymmetrical, affording the Czech Republic nine years to remove all barriers, while the EU applied quotas, at a reducing rate, only to a specified set of 'sensitive' products, i.e. agricultural products, textile products and steel products (Lavigne, 1995, p. 215; Bohatá, 1996a, pp. 11–12). The longer-term consequences of the EA will be favourable when quotas are removed and following the gradual readjustment of export structures and product qualities to meet foreign demands (see Dobrinsky, 1995; Landesmann, 1995). However, industrial production during the transition period has been affected, because the EU definition of sensitive goods has included products that had been the traditional strength of Czech exporting, notably steel products, which were also influenced by some anti-dumping procedures (Cekota, 1995, p. 36; Bohatá, 1996a, pp. 11–12).

The process of Czech(oslovak) privatization

The most direct way in which the broader societal changes have influenced the organization and management of the former state enterprises has been through the policies adopted and measures introduced to shift productive assets from the state sector into private hands, as part of the programme to marketize the economy. The scale and speed of the privatization programme are without parallel, with the exception of the former East Germany, whose transition via reintegration was entirely different. In 1989, the socialized state sector, including cooperatives, accounted for 97 per cent of Czechoslovak output, and 98.8 per cent of employment (Mejstřik and Hlávaček, 1993, p. 50; Bohatá, 1996b, p. 6); by the end of 1993, following the first wave of large-scale privatization, restitution (or 'reprivatization') and small privatization processes, the Czech Republic's state sector had declined to 46 per cent of output and 49 per cent of employment, while private enterprises then accounted for over 30 per cent of output and of employment (Bohatá *et al.*, 1995, p. 274). According to Lavigne (1995, p. 176), by the end of 1994 the private sector was producing 46 per cent of Czech GDP, and employing over 60 per cent of the occupied population.

In 1991, the Ministry of Privatization established the National Property Funds (NPF) in each republic with the specific aim of managing existing state assets, and an ultimate objective of selling, allocating or otherwise disposing of the assets of enterprises awaiting privatization. The NPF was to collect the money arising from sales of state property, which could then be used in various ways to assist the privatization process (*Trade Links*, 1993, pp. 66ff; Kotrba, 1995, p. 167). In this section, we overview the three main processes of privatization in the Czech Republic, but focus on those aspects that are particularly relevant to understanding the enterprises under examination. We therefore consider in greater detail the attributes of so-called 'large privatization' and of the 'voucher scheme' which has been characteristic of the speedy privatization of the huge enterprises that constituted the Czechoslovak economy in 1989. We start by looking at the two processes that started off the development of a private sector: restitution and small-scale privatization.

During the 1950s in particular, many large enterprises were assembled from small private firms or built on land which had been expropriated from private individuals. Such people not only lost their property and their jobs, but were often retrained in manual skills more appropriate to the socialist task, and then relocated to growing enterprises like Vols and Jesenické Strojírny. There were also political confiscations that had deprived dissidents and other victims of the regime of their property. Despite many politicians' preferences for avoiding issues of restitution for fear of opening up a can of worms over property and thereby delaying the larger privatization process, public opinion in 1990 forced restitution on to the agenda. In addition to restitution of Church land, five major acts or amendments were passed in 1990 and 1991 aimed at returning land and buildings to private individuals, whose property had been nationalized or otherwise appropriated by the communists between 25 February 1948 and 1 January 1990 (Frydman *et al.*, 1993, pp. 50–1; Kupka, 1993, pp. 99–101; Dlouhý and Mládek, 1994, pp. 158–60). Since 82 per cent of productive capital assets had been nationalized before the seizure of power by the communists, restitution affected industrial enterprises in a relatively small way. The emphasis was on returning the actual property expropriated to resident Czechoslovak citizens, and there was a strict timetable for making and processing claims which had the effect of expediting the process. In cases where the return of real property was not feasible, e.g. where it had been integrated into a larger enterprise, or land had been used for building apartment blocks, claimants had the favourable opportunity of bidding for the whole consolidated property under other privatization schemes, such as submitting a competing project proposal under large privatization. It was otherwise possible to receive financial or equivalent recompense, available from the Restitution Fund set up under NPF and financed by a mandatory contribution of 3 per cent of shares from privatizing state enterprises (Kotrba, 1995, p. 161). It is claimed that over 100,000 properties were restituted by the end of 1993, and of these some 20,000 were business units, mostly shops, restaurants, hotels and so on. Restitution claims were the basis of 742 successful large-scale privatization projects (Dlouhý and Mládek, 1994, p. 160; Kotrba, 1995, p. 160; Bohatá, 1996b, p. 7).

The process of small privatization, which took place between 1990 and 1993, also had substantial impact upon the development of the private sector, with an estimated number of business units (predominantly shops and restaurants) in excess of 22,000 expanding the small business sector (Kupka, 1993, p. 103; Bohatá, 1996b, p. 9). Legislation for the transfer of state-owned 'movable and unmovable properties' to private individuals or legal entities was passed in October 1990, to be effected primarily by public auction. Local privatization committees, set up by the Ministry of Privatization, were responsible for organizing and conducting the auctions, and the money raised from the successful bidders, totalling kč30.2 billion in the Czech Republic, was paid to the NPF. The first public auction took place in January 1991, and small privatization was virtually complete by the end of 1993. Together with restitution, and the general burgeoning of small trades – by the end of 1991, some 1.15 to 1.4 million individuals had registered as private entrepreneurs (Frydman *et al.*, 1993, p. 66; Bohatá, 1996b) – small scale privatization had major social consequences for the expansion of retail services and the emergence of a new business class (Dlouhý and Mládek, 1994, pp. 160–1; Kotrba and Svejnar, 1994, pp. 155–60).

The third process, or phase, of privatization was the main plank of Klaus's aim to transform the economy once and for all (Adam, 1994, p. 90). The large-scale privatization process was based upon the Act on the Conditions of Transfer of State-owned Property to Other Persons (February 1991), and it foresaw a massive movement of those state assets 'for which state enterprises, state financial institutions and other state organizations . . . have the right of management' into the private sector (Large Privatization Act, translated in *Trade Links*, 1993). The Act defined five privatization methods: direct sale, public auction, public tender, free transfer to municipalities or other social institutions and, most daring and innovative, the voucher system (*kuponová privatizace*). In fact, any one project to privatize state assets (an enterprise or part of an enterprise) could nominate any of the five methods in any combination, though it had to allocate 3 per cent of its book value to the special Restitution Fund, whose function was described above. However, the government expressed clear expectations about the importance of the voucher scheme as a means of spreading capital ownership across the nation – seen as having economic, political and moral benefits – so it was virtually guaranteed that those designing the projects for certain enterprises would recommend a substantial allocation to this method.

There has been some debate as to how much restructuring of the large state enterprises occurred outside the framework of privatization. Owing to the tighter degree of central control and absence of a legal framework propitious to destatization, it is generally agreed that there was little spontaneous (or *nomenklatura*) privatization of the kind that pre-empted the transition in Hungary and Poland (Adam, 1994, p. 88; Brom and Orenstein, 1994, p. 894;

Lavigne, 1995, pp. 168–9). However, after the revolution gigantic state-owned industrial associations and enterprises underwent a lot of spontaneous restructuring (see Chapters 8 and 9). Those *nomenklatura* managers who survived the immediate impact of the revolution were often able to exploit the early transition period (1990–1), because they experienced an expansion of operating autonomy while the state withdrew from exercising active control. They frequently decided to break up and/or restructure their enterprises, and thereby established effective control over microeconomic changes before legal regulations were introduced (e.g. Mann, 1993, p. 963).

In 1991, the Czechoslovakian government estimated that there were about 5500 state-owned enterprises, of which over 4000 were deemed eligible for privatization; about 2900 of these were located in the Czech lands. Some 1000 enterprises were considered in some way strategic (e.g. utilities) and were to be held back from privatization for at least five years; another one hundred would be earmarked for liquidation[2] (Mládek, 1993, p. 132; Dlouhý and Mládek, 1994, p. 162; compare Kenway, 1993, p. 63). Eligible enterprises were to participate in two privatization waves: one was to involve 1630 Czech and 626 Slovak enterprises, starting in October 1991 and ending in July 1993 with the distribution of shares (Mládek and Hashi, 1993, p. 78); the second was to comprise 1248 Czech and 573 Slovak enterprises, start in October 1993 and end at the beginning of 1995 (Kotrba, 1995, p. 172). The list of state-owned enterprises allocated to each wave was selected and published by the government, and, in keeping with the dominant political values, the role of the state was thereafter to be minimized by devolving the detailed aspects of privatization (in contrast with, for example, Hungary).

The 1990 Laws on State Enterprises and Joint Stock Companies had provided the framework for the 'corporatization' or 'marketization' of the enterprises, as an intermediary stage between state-owned enterprise and privatized company, and each enterprise had been attached to a concrete 'founding organ', such as a ministry. The founder's formal responsibility under the large privatization legislation was to design a 'basic privatization project' for each enterprise under its aegis, but the expectation was that the task of writing such a project would be delegated to the enterprise's management, with a deadline for submission. Anyone else, enterprise managers or outsiders, could submit 'competing projects', which would be evaluated alongside the basic project, first by the founding organ and then by the Ministry of Privatization, which had the final say in approving a project.

The basic projects for the first wave had to be submitted to the founding organ by 31 October 1991, and competing projects were given an extension to 20 January 1992. Approval was given at the end of April 1992. In fact, as first wave analyses show, basic projects were far more likely to succeed than competing ones, and internal competing projects were more likely to succeed that external ones (Kupka, 1993; Coffee, 1994, p. 14; Kotrba and Svejnar, 1994; Kotrba, 1995). Following approval of one project by the Ministry of Privatization, the founding organ formally dissolved the enterprise without financially liquidating it, and its property was transferred to the National Property Fund. The enterprise would then normally take on the corporatized status of a 'state-owned joint stock company'.

Some 2200 Czech enterprises eventually entered the first wave of privatization, for which over 11,000 projects were submitted. Where the ministry deemed that an enterprise had not been the subject of a satisfactory project, it was placed on the list for the second wave. The successful projects of 988 Czech enterprises included some allocation to the voucher system, each offering an average of 62 per cent of its shares in this way (Kotrba, 1995, p. 178). Some 660 of these enterprises gave over 75 per cent of their book value to vouchers, and 392 were to be privatized 100 per cent through the voucher scheme (Kotrba and Svejnar, 1994, p. 173).

In all, 8,562,421 Czechoslovak citizens (75 per cent of the eligible population), and 5,977,466 (77 per cent) of adult Czechs – twice as many as estimated by the government – participated in voucher privatization. They purchased books of vouchers, worth a nominal 1000 points, for kčs1035, the equivalent of about one week's average salary. The take-up rate was very slow until one or two investment privatization funds (*Investiční privatizacní fond*, or IPF) began to make apparently astonishing offers to citizens who placed their voucher points with them, in return for a share certificate with regard to the fund's assets. The IPFs had been legally founded by investment companies (ICs), and their purpose was precisely to collect voucher points and invest them in the mass privatization scheme. Some of the large ICs, mostly subsidiaries of the biggest banking and insurance institutions, operated multiple funds, specializing, for example, in particular industrial branches. In fact IPFs promised a payback in 12 months time of kčs10,350 or more (i.e. ten or more times the original price[3]), and this excited so much popular interest in the scheme that in 'round zero' of the bidding process in March 1992, 430 registered IPFs collected 72 per cent of all voucher points in order to enter the bidding process proper.

Surprised by the rise of IPFs and their success in attracting voucher points, the government hastily passed new legislative amendments in 1992, limiting any IPF to 20 per cent ownership of any one enterprise, and any IC, through multiple IPFs, to 40 per cent of one enterprise. Further, neither IC nor IPF could invest more than 10 per cent of its total points in any one enterprise. The voucher points were none the less heavily concentrated in a few ICs and IPFs, the top three ICs controlling 27 per cent of all points, the top ten more than 50 per cent, and the smallest 300 or so only 4 per cent (Brom and Orenstein, 1994, pp. 907–8). With the exception of the notorious Harvard Capital and Consulting IC, the top thirteen were all large financial institutions, many of which had – and continued to have – significant proportions of their assets held by the NPF.

The process of voucher privatization took the form of price-adjusting rounds of bidding by voucher holders, dominated, of course, by the strategies of the large IPFs. In the first round, the price of shares was the same for all enterprises, independent of performance, valued by a simple mechanism of dividing the total book value of the assets offered to the scheme by the total number of points available. This gave a first round price of thirty shares per voucher book. In the first wave, there were five time-bound rounds of auctions, and shares were distributed, or held back to the next round, according to demand and supply conditions (see, for example, Kotrba, 1995, p. 174). Shares were sold as long as demand was below, equal to or less than 25 per cent in excess of supply (in the latter case, IPFs had their demands reduced in preference to individuals). Oversubscription by more than 25 per cent led to the withdrawal of the shares, which were repriced for the next round. By the end of five rounds, 93.2 per cent of the total shares on offer were sold and 99 per cent of the points allocated (Mládek and Hashi, 1993, pp. 80–1; Rutland, 1993/4, pp. 113ff; Dlouhý and Mládek, 1994, p. 165; Svejnar and Singer, 1994; Centre for Voucher Privatization, 1995; Shafik, 1995).

The second wave of privatization was based on primarily the same principles. Originally, about 1300 Czech enterprises had been put on the second wave list, and 861 enterprises had projects accepted that included some proportion committed to vouchers, amounting to 44 per cent of the total property available in the wave (Dlouhý and Mládek, 1994, p. 157). Of these 861, 185 enterprises had been delayed from the first wave, and 676 were newly privatized. 79 per cent of the eligible Czech population bought voucher books, and a lower proportion than the first round (63.5 per cent) of points were committed to the IPFs. A total of 354 investment agencies were registered by ICs, of which 133 were IPFs which had participated in the first wave, 63 were new IPFs and 158 were mutual funds made possible with legal changes since 1992. Concentration of points was less pronounced, but still the largest fifteen ICs accumulated some 41 per cent of the 6.16 billion points. The sixth and final round of bidding took place in December 1994, completing the sale of 96.3 per cent of shares on offer, exhausting 99 per cent of all voucher points (Coffee, 1994, pp. 27ff; Centre for Voucher Privatization, 1995) and moving another kč150 billion of productive assets out of the state sector.

Over the two waves, voucher privatization accounted for over 50 per cent of the transfer of joint stock company assets into private hands, and its role in realizing the speed of this turnaround is unquestionable. As a result of the various privatization programmes, and the mass privatization scheme in particular, the Czech Republic in the five years since the Velvet Revolution successfully changed the balance of its economy to one in which over 65 per cent of economic activity took place in the private sector (Coffee, 1994, p. 1). The post-privatization economy has developed a number of microeconomic characteristics as a result of the approach taken towards the macroeconomic transformation, especially related issues regarding corporate governance, the efficient operation of capital markets (including open, transparent information sources and bankruptcy rules) and access to adequate capital investment funds.

Česká spořitelna, Investiční banka and Komerční banka are three large successor banks of the monobank system, in which the state, via the NPF, has retained a substantial ownership interest (respectively 40, 45 and 44 per cent in 1993). They established three of the most successful ICs (Dlouhý and Mládek, 1994, pp. 168–9), and in the first wave their 'grandchildren', the IPFs, accumulated 25 per cent of voucher points, which they turned into 17 per cent of shares distributed in the scheme. Although their success diminished in the second wave, these banks have ended up with substantial indirect holdings of manufacturing industry, and, via interlocking share ownership, of each other. Their investment company subsidiaries, the IPFs, have built up a substantial portfolio of privatized companies which includes many of their grandparents' clients. The latter in turn had substantial outstanding bank loans, some of which were non-performing (McDermott, 1993, pp. 22–3). In terms of corporate governance, these banks have had little or no incentive to use the provisions of the revised 1993 bankruptcy legislation to foreclose on the insolvent clients, partly because this revealed publicly their poor lending practices, and partly because it was counter-productive to bankrupt firms in which its subsidiaries were major shareholders. Some researchers have further commented on the potential fragility of the ownership structures in an economy in which the various large financial institutions, as owners of and lenders to private industry, are heavily intertwined through mutual ownership (see Brom and Orenstein, 1994, pp. 908ff; Coffee, 1994, pp. 39ff for graphic examples; also Takla, 1994, pp. 164–5; Laštovička *et al.*, 1995, pp. 203–4).

In April 1993, the Prague Stock Exchange commenced trading shares of a small number of privatized enterprises. By April 1995, there were forty-three listed companies, capitalized at kč161 billion, and 1661 unlisted companies, with a lot of trading being done informally or through a computerized retail system, which had originally formed the basis of the voucher-bidding mechanism (*Trade Links*, 1993, p. 27; *Business Central Europe*, June 1995, p. 54). The stock market continues to have many problems, not least of which are doubts about the openness and transparency of the information necessary to trade freely, and the limited ability of the market to raise new capital for its participating companies (see also *Central European Business Weekly*, 1996, no. 195).

The problem of bad debts, inherited from state socialism and reproduced through the early transition period, has remained a feature of the post-privatization period and of the emerging market economy, tying up much needed domestic capital in enterprises that may not be best able to invest in new products and technologies, and having the further impact of inhibiting the modernization and elaboration of the traditional industrial structures. The most important way of filling the gap between the investment needs of the modernizing economy and the paucity of domestic capital[4] is by encouraging the influx of foreign direct investment (FDI) (Stern, 1995). The legislative changes in early 1990 improved the conditions imposed by the late

1980s reforms and had the desired effect of attracting capital from overseas, but the predisposition of the government towards the voucher system and the exclusion of foreign bidders in small privatization have limited the overall impact of foreign participation in the privatization process. Much of the FDI has come through a few high profile deals, in which the government sold famous elements of Czechoslovak industry: e.g. the arrangements for Volkswagen to purchase a substantial share in Škoda Mlada Boleslav; Proctor and Gamble and Rakona; K-Mart and Raj. In 1993, around 63 per cent of FDI had been brought by just five large investments (*Business Central Europe*, April 1994). This policy of selling off the 'crown jewels' (Radice, 1995b, p. 120) of Czech industry has led to a lot of internal criticism.

FDI has also been particularly attracted to certain industrial sectors, especially the fast-moving consumer goods industry (Dubey-Villinger, 1996). Over a third of all FDI had been drawn into consumer goods, tobacco and retailing, with firms like Nestlé and Philip Morris buying into traditional Czech producers (Čokolodovny and Tabák) in order to enter the domestic market, or set up exporting opportunities into the former East European markets where there was existing awareness of Czech brands. Germany and the USA have been the dominant investing nations (*Business Central Europe*, April 1994, p. 38). With the exception of Hungary, the Czech Republic has been the most successful of the former communist states in drawing in FDI, which reached the level of US$5.8 billion by the end of 1995 (see Table 6.2, p. 122), as a result of its high international credit rating and a reputation for being politically the most stable of the post-communist countries. While foreign capital has flowed in, it is still minuscule in comparison with the global extent of FDI, and is by no means of the size that can renew or update the technological base of industry which was in such a poor state in 1989 (Stern, 1995). By 1994, only 6.4 per cent of enterprises, accounting for 10 per cent of output and 5.7 per cent of employment, had any form or degree of foreign capital participation (Bohatá, 1996a, p. 28). The above pattern of foreign investment by sector and activity reflects the primary effects of the marketing strategies of the multinational donors, rather than the strategic developmental and exporting needs of Czech industry.

Despite the destatizing, neo-liberal rhetoric of Czech politicians like Václav Klaus, the state has played a significant role in the planning, management and decision-making processes associated with privatization and continues to be a critical actor in the operation of the emergent economy. 'The Czech experience provides the first example of the difficulties a mass privatized sector may have in wrenching itself free of a long legacy of state control' (Brom and Orenstein, 1994, p. 893).

The effective anti-bankruptcy policies of the government, which have operated through the Consolidation Bank to reduce the effects of bad debts, have minimized enterprise closures and hence reduced the probability of the spiralling unemployment which affected the neighbouring post-communist economies. Economists have noted the continuing presence of the state in the guise of the NPF, which after the two waves of large privatization remains the largest single owner of industry. Laštovička *et al.* (1995, p. 203) report that following the first wave, the NPF had more than a 50 per cent stake in twenty-three of the enterprises 'privatized', and more than a 20 per cent shareholding in 118 enterprises. We have commented above on the shape of the NPF's minority ownership of the large banks, whose ICs run IPFs which in turn own significant chunks of major enterprises, including other banks. Anti-statist rhetoric, combined with a continuing real role, is part of the environment of the privatized Czech economy (Kenway, 1993, p. 69).

Conclusions

We have analysed the early economic transition period as three sub-processes, which together have created the unique character of the Czech post-communist transformation. The deregulation of the centralized command economy took place fairly steadily during 1990, leading to the big bang of price and trade liberalization at the beginning of 1991. High inflation, rising unemployment, increased material costs and the demise of traditional trading structures and partners had critical impacts upon the business environment while the government was inventing ways of restructuring the economy on more market-oriented principles. The formal use of strict fiscal and monetary measures in accordance with the prevailing economic ideology in Prague was supported by effective if tacit anti-bankruptcy practices to sustain the large enterprises during the institutional vacuum. This held the micro-economies in balance, while re-establishing control of the macroeconomic indicators of prices, employment and national output.

The foundations of a competitive market economy were chiefly laid between 1990 and 1992, and were the formal institutional precursors to the privatization processes aimed at transferring productive state property to the private or privatized sector. Central to this programme were the mass privatization waves, in which the voucher scheme held pride of place. In the three phases of privatization – restitution, small privatization and two waves of large privatization – the ownership structure of the Czech Republic was radically transformed, and the structure of the economy developed new characteristics. Small-scale capitalism – the basis of the new 'private sector' – flourishes in sectors which provide labour-intensive, low-capital services. On the other hand, sophisticated industrial and consumer needs are served by the medium and large businesses, dominated by the former state enterprises, which make up the 'privatized sector', possessing its own distinctive features of corporate governance. Among these large companies, industrial leadership, innovation and investment tend to be in the hands of a few firms with foreign participation (Murrell and Wang, 1993).

The privatized former state enterprises and their managements existed within this uncertain, still evolving economic and institutional environment, in which there has been not only the uncertainty of radical change in structures, but also the acute ambiguity that arose from the lack of institutionalized framework within which radical change could be anchored and referenced. Enterprises such as Vols, Jesenické Strojírny, Montáže Jesenice and Agstroj belonged to the traditional engineering sectors which had underpinned the economic efforts of state socialism, and have suffered more than most others. The CMEA had provided cheap raw materials and energy to supply their inefficient, resource-hungry appetite, and in turn guaranteed purchase of quite low-technology machine products. Its collapse foreshadowed a major reorientation of trade to the West, with its more sophisticated competitors and more demanding clients (Bohatá *et al.*, 1995). This created specific challenges for their undercapitalized enterprises and their managements. But, given the social and economic legacies of state socialism and the emergent characteristics of the market capitalism, there are more general questions about the ability of the large privatized industrial enterprises to become truly 'private' and to behave in a purely market-oriented way.

In the following chapters we trace the changes in managerial behaviour that have become visible in the four privatized enterprises over the first five years of the Czech economic transition, and show how these developments at enterprise level reflect the historical and contemporary institutional contexts of Czech post-communism.

Notes

1 As the five-year span of the 1991 Act was about to elapse, there arose a strong public debate about extending the Act for another five years.
2 As a result of the restructuring and fragmentation of state enterprises during 1990 and 1991, the estimates of numbers of enterprises vary between researchers.
3 Simple calculations based on the total book value offered to vouchers (kčs299.4 billion) and the total number of points finally registered in the first wave (kčs8.56 billion) make it clear that these offers, however dramatic, were always conservative in the long run. Each voucher book was nominally worth about kčs 235,000 (see Kupka, 1993, p. 97).
4 Šik (1993, p. 194) estimated that domestic savings were able to purchase only 13.9 per cent of industrial assets in the state sector.

7 Management, enterprises and institutional change

In Part Two, we examined the development of the state-owned enterprise within the context of the ebbs and flows of the post-war Czechoslovak state socialist command economy. By considering the experiences of four such enterprises, we showed not only how they were strongly influenced by the institutional features of the wider political economy, but also how, at the level of local economic decision-making, managers developed their own distinctive recipes and practices for coping with the exigencies and vicissitudes of the system. In Chapter 5, we summarized the state of the Czechoslovak enterprise in the 1980s, and projected some of the generally agreed changes that would be the inevitable requirements of enterprise and management if they were to emerge from the transitional post-communist period in a 'market-economic' condition.

Since 1989, as we have seen in Chapter 6, there have been substantial changes to the social, economic, political and institutional environment of Czechoslovakia and, since January 1993, the new Czech Republic. At a macro level, we have analysed these changes using the terminology of institutional change: deinstitutionalization, transition management and reinstitutionalization. We shall show in the next two chapters that these macro external processes are not only reflected within the enterprises in that evidently their managers have to take cognizance of and respond to the wider processes; but also, and significantly, that enterprises and their managements – *qua* institutions and institutionalized practices – themselves went through processes of change in order to adjust to the circumstances of the post-communist environment. Just as the path and nature of Czechoslovak communism were influenced by the micro level behaviour in the enterprises, the practices adopted by the post-communist managers in their attempts to assure enterprise survival and to pursue their own managerial careers have begun to have implications for the larger development of the post-1989 Czech economy and society. As we have argued in Chapter 2, the macro institutional order and micro institutional practices are thus inextricably linked, and both levels need to be explored if the dynamics of socio-economic life are to be understood.

The emergence of post-communist organization and management can be understood as processes of institutional change. It is obvious from our analysis in Chapter 5 – and it was equally and blindingly clear to the enterprise managers themselves – that the management practices that had served enterprises so well in the problematic conditions of the command economy would not in themselves be suitable – that is, neither technically proficient nor normatively acceptable – for the much lauded market circumstances. Our managers saw as a prerequisite of the survival of both their enterprises and themselves the distancing of their own identities and patterns of behaviour from the managers 'they used to be'. This deinstitutionalization was a priority, and those who were unable, or unwilling, to undertake this process of 'self' and professional disconnection from the past were unlikely to weather the first winter months that followed the Velvet Revolution. However, we will also show that, in the transition environment, it was not in itself rational to abandon entirely those practices that represented good state socialist management. For technical as well as normative reasons, managers continued to draw upon their old ways because the enterprise environment still contained many characteristics of the former command economy, e.g. supply constraints. However, the most important element of institutional change was the process of reinstitutionalization of enterprise and management. The process of managerial and organizational redefinition has both technical and normative aspects. On the one hand, it is crucial for post-communist managers to take on the techniques, practices and language that are technically compatible with the demands of the new market-economic concept; on the other hand, management as a function, managers as a group and managers as individuals must adopt and be identified with definitions that are socially acceptable to the new economic order. This latter normative process is inherently tied to the first redefinition process – in that social acceptability in the case of 'capitalist' management is tied up with technically rational competence. Further, 'managerial redefinition', both technically and normatively, is invariably and inextricably involved with 'organizational redefinition', because it is at least in part, in the decentralized, independent world of market economics, the bona fide task of management and managers to restructure, redesign and reform the enterprise – its culture, structures and systems (see Clark and Soulsby, 1995).

In the next three chapters we shall be exploring these processes of institutional change within the four former state-owned enterprises. In this chapter, we shall first look at the general changes that took place in the enterprises and their managements; then we shall look at the processes of deinstitutionalization. In Chapter 8, we shall continue by looking in detail at the tendencies to institutional inertia, whereby the features of state socialist management have continued in the face of external change. In Chapter 9, we consider the efforts to redefine management, managers and the organization. It should be noted that much of the reality of these processes is simultaneous rather than consecutive in order, so that there will be some inevitable overlap in the discussion.

The post-communist managers

Before we go any further, we should consider the nature of the managements which were in control of the enterprises during the post-1989 period, when the significant processes of internal change and restructuring took place. We wish in particular to focus on the constitution of the enterprise managements and the managers' backgrounds in state socialism, for these are indicative of the interests and stakes which managers had in the redefinition of management and organization (see Clark and Soulsby, 1996).

Within the four enterprises there were varying degrees of change in the composition of senior and middle management. Only in the case of Vols has the general director before November 1989 continued in post during the years until 1996, though he was appointed only two months before the Revolution as result of the party's dissatisfaction with his predecessor. In each of the three other cases, the new general director had been appointed through competitive interview, but had very solid former *nomenklatura* credentials. The story is similar when we look at the formation of the new directorates, i.e. the heads in the new or emergent divisional structures who, with the general director, made up the senior management team – the team which was responsible for making the key restructuring, financial and strategic decisions during the initial phases of the transition. The stories are slightly different for each enterprise, as one would expect, but the outcomes show a pattern of continuity of personnel at this level. Thus, the new directorate of Vols was eight strong, but three of the pre-1989 directors stayed in position, and only two were non-*nomenklatura* appointments. The directorate of Jesenické Strojírny, on the other hand, was entirely new in 1990; however, all but two – one, notably, the new director of human resources – had been *nomenklatura* middle managers with aspirations to director status under the old regime. Agstroj showed a similar pattern to Vols, while Montáže Jesenice was similar to its former parent, Jesenické Strojírny.

Whether the composition of the new senior management team emerged through 'evolution' or 'revolution', the continuing relevance of pre-1989 communist associations is clear. Our overall sample of managers reflects this picture of continuity at this level of management, though the reader is reminded that the sample is not statistically representative either of the enterprises in question or of Czech management in general. In addition to the eighteen managers of director status whom we interviewed, we also have very high-quality information on nine directors whom we did not interview, yet who featured strongly in our case research. Table 7.1 presents a summary of these findings.

The table confirms that 100 per cent of the general directors had *nomenkla-tura* status, while 74 per cent of the new directors had also been members of

Table 7.1 Post-communist directors and *nomenklatura* origins

	Vols	*MJ*	*JS*	*Agstroj*	*Totals*
General directors	1	1	1	1	4
of whom former					
nomenklatura	1	1	1	1	4
Directors	7	5	8	3	23
or whom former					
nomenklatura	5	3	6	3	17
Total directorate	8	6	9	4	27

the CP. The overall figure for directorates in the sample is 78 per cent. One obvious conclusion from this analysis is that the vast majority of the new senior post-communist managers were those who had been, or were being, groomed for such positions under the former regime. The irony here is that the Velvet Revolution, far from being a managerial revolution, actually acted as a catalyst for these managers' careers.

The picture is rather different if we look at post-1989 middle managers – most of whom in our sample are department managers who report to the directors. Only 40 per cent (see Table 7.2) of these department managers were former *nomenklatura*, revealing a strong pattern of upward mobility from positions in which party affiliation and approval were not necessary. In the sample as a whole, then, some 56 per cent of the post-communist managers were previously in CP approved positions, and had been, through ideological commitment or desire to improve their managerial careers, members of the party and/or its organs. The proportion of former *nomenklatura* managers diminishes as you descend the enterprise hierarchies, but it is clear that the major decisions about the redefinition of management and organization in these four enterprises were being taken by people who used to be in the CP.

The *nomenklatura* backgrounds of the new senior managers were well known, both across the enterprises and within the communities, despite any technical or managerial competence they may have had, many employees and their families had expected changes in the distribution of power and reward to follow the revolution. In the words of one former *nomenklatura* manager in Jesenické Strojírny, 'In 1990, people wanted change, any change.' The

Table 7.2 Department managers and pre-1989 *nomenklatura* status

	Vols	*MJ*	*JS*	*Agstroj*	*Totals*
Department managers	8	9	11	7	35
of whom former					
nomenklatura	3	3	4	4	14

senior managers knew that their future status as bona fide managers required more than technical ability if they were to gain the respect of employees. As the general director of Montáže Jesenice (former technical director of Jesenické Strojírny) explained: 'I hope to persuade people of the quality of my ideas. But I am in a difficult position [as general director] – because I was a director in the previous regime I carry the mark of Cain.'

This lack of professional, personal and social legitimacy was profoundly felt by other directors with party backgrounds, but also attributed to each other and recognized as a problem for their current managerial status and future managerial careers. The general director of Vols, appointed before the revolution, was seen as having problems of credibility; the general director of Jesenické Strojírny, known to have been a member of the *milice* and well-connected with the CP, was also felt to be in a weak position on employee relations issues. Beyond showing technical competence, the former *nomenklatura* were concerned in the early years of the transition to re-establish their managerial credentials using the socially acceptable criteria of professional, market-economic management. Their micro concerns with social legitimacy were exacerbated by the post-communist political climate that led to the passing of the 1991 Screening (Lustration) Act, which formally prohibited former senior communists from holding public office (see Chapter 6) – and management in a state-owned enterprise, even when legally joint stock, was deemed a public position.

The positions and security of senior managers depended in part on how employees or citizens responded to the lustration legislation, or whether they used it to settle old scores. The most obvious problems were created in the newly formed Montáže Jesenice, in which the new general director had formed a management team which included young managers who, in their pursuit of management ambition before 1989, had made the necessary statements of commitment by joining the enterprise militia. In the style established under state socialism, the general director received anonymous letters pointing out that two of his new directors had been *milice* members, and the general director, against his wishes, had to take action. In fact, he formally demoted the two individuals in question into middle ranking posts, whose hitherto occupants (both women) took on the formal posts of directors. This 'job swap' arrangement was a formal device, since the four people involved continued with their previous tasks.

Following 1 January 1992 when the Lustration Act took effect, it was in the interests of all former *nomenklatura* managers to move as quickly as possible into managerial posts in private enterprises. Some of those who were dismissed or driven into early retirement set themselves up in small firms, but for the majority, the only feasible strategy was to pursue the privatization of their enterprises as quickly as possible. The case of Montáže Jesenice again illustrates the point. It was relatively small and new, and very low in priority (or visibility) for government officials charged with the mass privatization scheme. When the list of the enterprises to be included in the first and second waves of voucher privatization was published, it became evident that Montáže Jesenice was being held back to the second one. Montáže Jesenice's general director worked hard – and successfully – to persuade the ministry to add the enterprise to the first wave list. In May 1992, it became a single-owner (the state) joint stock company, and it successfully progressed to privatized status.

These tables reflect snapshots of management composition, of course, taken at the points of fieldwork between 1992 and 1994. But, unlike expectations in Western Europe or the United States, there has in fact been relatively little change in membership of the management groups over the transition period under scrutiny. The changes that have occurred – such as in areas of personnel – are significant in themselves, but it has not been, and will not be in the near future, a custom for managers to exhibit mobility between regions and enterprises. Such immobility or loyalty (to put it another way) is evident within the sample.

Table 7.3 shows the average length of service of managers, and it can be seen that the loyalty to the enterprise is very strong. Of course, there are external factors that make years of service a highly imperfect measure of *voluntary* loyalty, e.g. the centrally controlled labour market before 1989 and the shortage of housing both before and after 1989. The vast majority of managers had joined the enterprises directly from a technical university, and, apart from a period spent in military service, had spent the rest of their careers in the same enterprise. In their late forties and fifties by 1995, they had spent an average (across the whole sample) of 21.8 years in the same enterprise. It is not surprising that, in spite of any disagreements that they may have had before 1989 (e.g. the men of '68), in interviews they still expressed a strong commitment to their enterprises. These managers found it difficult to conceive of working anywhere else.

After such long service, the post-1989 managers retained in varying degrees aspects of their pre-1989 values. They held their own enterprises, and their historical development, in high esteem, and expressed real pride in their

Table 7.3 Age and years of service by enterprise and level

	Vols		*Montáže Jesenice**		*Jesenické Strojírny*		*Agstroj*	
	Dir	*Dept*	*Dir*	*Dept*	*Dir*	*Dept*	*Dir*	*Dept*
Average age group	early 50s	early 50s	early 40s	mid 40s	early 50s	late 40s	mid 50s	mid 40s
% male	100	100	100	67	100	91	100	100
Average years of service	26.5	31	13.2	17.8	25.3	22.5	16.4	11

* The years of service include employment before 1989 as part of Jesenické Strojírny.

product and quality values. Our interviewees also spoke with feeling about the importance of the 'Czech identity', about the 'Czech way' of doing things, by which they meant a sense of self-sufficiency in which they were used to getting on with things by themselves. 'People in the Czech Republic were much closer as a community than elsewhere, because we help ourselves by ourselves – this is the Czech approach.' Or again, '[Czechs] want to have invented things themselves. This is the Czech way – a stronger sense of independence, and doing things their own way . . . Czech values emphasize nationalism and a sense of resistance.' These were seen as historical traits that had contributed to the survival of the Czech nation since the seventeenth century. It is also notable that this brand of nationalism became verbalized in an anti-foreign (especially anti-German) rhetoric, and strong judgements about the relative industrial (in)competence of former comrade nations in CMEA. Among these national-cultural and local-enterprise values and attitudes were also degrees of reproduction of the old socialist management values, concerning, for example, the responsibilities of managers towards their employees and their communities. Some managers in the old communist town of Volna and in Jesenice were often described 'pink' managers, because of their attitudes and policies towards social and employment policies.

In summary, the management groups of the four enterprises share certain important characteristics which form part of the social context of enterprise transformation in the transition period. In composition, the post-1989 senior managements were not significantly different from their pre-1989 counterparts. There have been changes in individual personnel, but even they tended to come from the same backgrounds located in the Communist Party's cadre policy. If anything, the revolution accelerated the career development of aspiring junior managers, and gave them a greater vested interest in the survival of the enterprise, in terms of which they had always defined their future. Their struggle with social legitimacy gave the new managements a direct stake in the 'appropriate' restructuring of the enterprises, and particularly in their rapid privatization. This would first enable them to persuade the new shareholders of their credentials for market-economic management, and thus put them in the driving seats of the privatized enterprises from which they would then be the key decision-makers in their own destinies. But, second, it would improve their chances of becoming fully accepted as esteemed and respected members of their local communities.

The continuity in office of formerly *nomenklatura* personnel had further ramifications for the values and priorities of post-communist management. We should not be surprised that, after years of working within the national-cultural and political-ideological environment of Czechoslovak state socialism, the managers of the enterprises continued to operate within a framework of values which incorporated a sense of nationalism, enterprise loyalty and social responsibility beyond those we would expect to find among Western capitalist managers. These structural and cultural aspects of the new post-communist managements provide very important starting points for our examination of the post-communist transformation of enterprise and management. They have crucial implications for the behaviour – actions and decisions – that managers displayed within the fluid institutional setting of the Czech transitional economy, and are constitutive of the new practices that with repetition will become the new institutionalized managerial patterns in the emergent market economy. Most of what follows explores the implications of these values, objectives, priorities and expectations as expressed by our enterprise managers.

The changing enterprises

Before examining in greater detail the processes of enterprise transformation, we shall provide a brief overview of the developments from 1990 to 1995. We do this in order to prepare the general picture, and to facilitate the understanding of the complex managerial processes within these changes. The first years following the collapse of the communist regime were felt by the enterprises as a period of shock, demanding immediate adjustments to radical changes in the environment. Although the state plan and the command economy in principle continued to exist for the first year, in practice virtually all predictable aspects of enterprise life changed. The three state enterprises – Vols, Agstroj and Jesenické Strojírny – had begun to experience greater independence arising from the 1988 legislative changes, and during 1990, following its separation from Jesenické Strojírny, Montáže Jesenice was given similar legal status. As state enterprises, and later as '100 per cent state-owned joint stock companies', the enterprises enjoyed a freedom of decision-making that almost disconnected them from their nominal legal owners, the ministries. This new autonomy left the new senior management teams suddenly 'free' to face a whole raft of problems that had accumulated over forty years: overstaffing, bureaucratic structures, ancient technologies, poor working habits and attitudes and the breakdown of the (discredited) internal control systems and managerial culture which had been based on the Communist Party. It was the new management teams – seen by the workforce as being remarkably similar in composition to the old one – which had to devise a new 'market-oriented' strategy, a privatization plan and internal structures and strategies to overcome the inherited problems.

While the managers had to face the old problems increasingly on their own, the environment of business in which they had operated with some stability for many years began to break down. The former CMEA was in a process of terminal decline, and the system of subsidies and financial credits which enabled state socialism to function became impossible to sustain. For Jesenické Strojírny, Vols and the new Montáže Jesenice, the economic changes wrought by the combined demise of central planning and the CMEA trading bloc were almost unbearable. The complete breakdown of their former soviet and CMEA markets led to Vols and Jesenické Strojírny management seeking to reorient their production to foreign markets in which they had little experience and few reliable contacts. The case of Jesenické Strojírny (and by implication Montáže Jesenice) is illustrative of the severe problems caused by the changes.

The detachment of Czechoslovakia from international Soviet policies led to the collapse of trade credit arrangements for developed countries that had been a source of so much external work – from then on, the survival of the enterprise demanded the making of hard currency deals. By 1991, Jesenické Strojírny's exports to countries with non-convertible currencies had declined rapidly to just 14 per cent of the 1989 level, and accounted for less that 10 per cent of its total deliveries. At the same time, it had reoriented its exports to hard currency trade, which had increased by over 450 per cent, accounting for 28 per cent of all deliveries in 1991. This trend continued during 1994, when, excluding domestic sales and those to Slovakia, Jesenické Strojírny exported fewer than 9 per cent of its products to the former Soviet bloc: that is, about 22 per cent of its exports. About half of these exports were for the SOVREP project. Within a few months of the revolution, the SOVREP project had transformed itself from a secure, prestigious socialist dream to an albatross-like financial nightmare. By 1992, Jesenické Strojírny had lost kčs10 million on a project which, in 1991, had accounted for nearly 40 per cent of all its deliveries. State credits had by then become a question of negotiation rather than certainty, and Jesenické Strojírny was owed nearly kčs200 million by the USSR. SOVREP was accepted as a loss-maker, but at least it kept Jesenické Strojírny workers employed.

Agstroj's problems were similar in outcome, but different in origin. The very economic success of Agstroj under state socialism was the source of its economic weakness after 1989. Its production capacity, which had expanded generously during the 1980s, bore no resemblance to its state of international competitiveness, to the industry-wide overcapacity and to the structure of market demand in world agriculture. With the imposition of import taxes in several former socialist societies, the total loss of the Yugoslavian market, the increased difficulties of developing world markets, particularly in the Middle East, and the virtual collapse of domestic demand following the depression of the early transition period, demand for Agstroj's products plummeted to only one-third of its capacity in 1993 – and it needed to hit two-thirds of production capacity in order to break even.

The three large enterprises (i.e. with the exception of Montáže Jesenice) have operated with or close to operating losses since 1990, and have adopted extraordinary accounting and restructuring devices in order to keep them afloat. One of the main problems was not so much that the work suddenly disappeared – after all, existing contracts often ran for five years or more – but getting payment for the work completed. Early commercial tasks in 1990 to 1992 therefore involved the renegotiation of contracts and the acceptance of unconventional (in Western terms) methods of payment, such as bartering. The maintenance of day-to-day financial continuity required unusual practices like withholding of payment to suppliers, which built up across the economy the huge stocks of inter-enterprise debt discussed in Chapter 6. Enterprise managements experienced this spiral of inter-enterprise debt as 'payment inability', whereby the system irrationality of inadequate circulation of money was felt as the increasing and simultaneous accumulation of both client debt and supplier credit to enormous levels.

Any early confidence in being able to find long-term Western clients and partners soon evaporated. The period from 1991 to 1993 was dominated by the process of preparation for privatization, all four enterprises being nominated for participation in mass privatization. Each enterprise established a small strategic team to put forward the basic privatization project, and this group additionally considered and advocated restructuring plans to be effected before the privatizing process began – contrary to the principles underlying Klaus's conception of mass privatization by which such restructuring was seen as the natural task of the new owners. In slightly different ways, each enterprise underwent fundamental processes of reorganization, in which decentralization of responsibility was the basic principle. Early on, each enterprise established new divisionalized structures, with further ambitions to turn them into profit centres. Jesenické Strojírny, at a very early stage, devised plans to turn the new divisions into 100 per cent owned subsidiaries, or 'daughter companies', of a new Jesenické Strojírny holding company – a concept the management sold to its new board of directors, and actually realized from the start of 1995. However, in all four cases, the paths towards new organization structures have been winding and stony, with a variety of deviations and obstacles *en route* (see Chapters 8 and 9).

Vols, Jesenické Strojírny and, after some bargaining, Montáže Jesenice were placed within the first wave of privatization, and were expected to develop plans involving the substantial participation of vouchers. Vols was quite successful in the auction rounds, and the new owners were known in January 1993. Altogether, forty-nine IPFs had acquired shares, of which the eight biggest owned more than 50 per cent. There were also more than 18,000 individual shareholders, including 3000 employees. The NPF continued to own nearly 20 per cent of the shares, which were placed in the second wave of voucher privatization. Although the balance of ownership has fluctuated since 1993, it has not changed significantly. As a result, the IPFs now control the private board of directors, with six members to the three internal managers, a composition that remained the same up to 1995. The NPF held back 35 per cent of Jesenické Strojírny's shares from the first wave of privatization, in the expectation that it could attract interest from foreign companies, which could raise a significant sum of capital. However, privatization was completed in 1992 without any foreign involvement, and the new Jesenické Strojírny a.s. had two significant IPF owners, each owning about 12 per cent of its shares. The NPF entered the remaining 35 per cent in the second wave of voucher privatization, successfully disposing of 25 per cent, but remaining a substantial minority shareholder in 1995 with a 10 per cent stake. Montáže Jesenice was the most successful of the enterprises in the privatization process, virtually all of its shares (with the exception of the 3 per cent retained by law for restitution purposes) being sold in the first two auction rounds. By the beginning of 1993, it was clear that four IPFs had between them acquired nearly 70 per cent of the shares, and they were each allocated a seat on the board of directors, with three internal directors.

The story of Agstroj following the events of the Velvet Revolution is somewhat different and far more complex than those of the other three enterprises, as a result of its own particular role in state socialism. Agstroj was considered by the new post-communist government as one of Czechoslovakia's 'crown jewels' (like Škoda Mladá Boleslav), and the NPF, which owned its assets on behalf of the state, was very hopeful that the enterprise could be sold lock, stock and barrel at a premium price to one of Europe's or America's large manufacturers. Despite some internal preferences for breaking the enterprise into smaller units, perhaps by entering some parts independently in the voucher privatization process, the state preference for keeping the enterprise intact prevailed, and Agstroj was withheld from voucher privatization in the first wave. Despite initial optimism, the NPF could not find a foreign buyer, and in 1993 it instigated complex negotiations between the government representatives of the NPF, Agstroj's management and its bankers. Arrangements were then made to 'privatize' the enterprise through what appears to be a legal device. Agstroj as a state enterprise merged with its engine supplier (Stroměsto Engines), which had been separated from its parent, Vojenská Stroměstská and privatized rather like Montáže Jesenice in the first wave. Upon merger with Stroměsto Engines, Agstroj adopted the latter's privatized status, despite its assets amounting to less than 30 per cent of the new Agstroj's total value. Just as the 'new' Agstroj a.s. was privatized by the absorption of its engine supplier, its traditional ball-bearing facilities were separated off into a new state enterprise called Agstroj s.p., which was to be entered into the second wave of voucher privatization. Key managerial changes have followed these complex processes. The new top management team was largely constructed from the former Stroměsto Engines, and the new private board of directors became dominated by the interests of the NPF. In 1994, the NPF 'sold' its 70 per cent stake in the still debt-laden Agstroj to the state-owned Consolidation Bank, which then effectively wiped out nearly kč2 billion of debt. In return, Consolidation Bank has placed two representatives on the board of directors, and influenced the replacement of senior managers in the areas of production and finance. During 1995, rumours abounded in management and the press that Consolidation Bank hoped to pull off a merger or some capital investment deal with a foreign company, in order to sell some or all of its stake in Agstroj a.s. The only foreign interest has come from a US competitor, Amfarm, which in 1993 entered into medium-term arrangements with Agstroj to supply machinery under the Amfarm brand name to its less sophisticated Third World markets. However, Amfarm has proven to be a reluctant suitor, and rather than giving Agstroj new capital, has provided commercial arrangements for selling products with little value-added and minimum financial surplus. The Amfarm deal has helped to push Agstroj's production up to near the break-even point, and has served to protect employment levels in the enterprise. Employment numbers have continued to slide as the management has attempted to come to terms with the diminished demand and the overstaffing that the enterprise had inherited from state socialism. By the end of 1990, employment had fallen to 9650, with gradual further declines until the 1995 figure, following the restructuring associated with privatization, reached 5900.

The development of Vols and Jesenické Strojírny has shown a similar pattern, having some initial success in increasing business in Western Europe in 1992 to fill the gap left by the problems of Eastern markets. But they were mostly able to bring off only small one-off contracts, and, in the case of Jesenické Strojírny, to sell single units rather than contribute to the large turn-key projects that are the really profitable contracts. This trend towards Western markets has been reversed since 1994 in Vols and 1995 in Jesenické Strojírny. Both enterprises have offices and representatives in the former USSR, and have been able to exploit their former reputations in the CMEA bloc, as well as price advantages, in competing with Western firms. Employment in Vols has declined slowly but surely from the 5600 present in 1990, to 4991 in 1992 and 4700 in 1993, settling around 4500 in 1995. In Jesenické Strojírny, employment levels declined quite dramatically from the initial 7000 in 1990. The hiving off of Montáže Jesenice reduced employment by over 1000 at a stroke, and by the end of 1990 there were 5862 employees. In the period 1991 to 1995, employment decreased by more than 30 per cent, reaching about 4100.

By far the most successful adaptation has been made by Montáže Jesenice, which has continuously shown a profit, albeit at a declining rate, over the period 1990 to 1995. In great part, this reflects the adeptness of Montáže Jesenice at reorienting its services towards the economies of the advanced capitalist nations, becoming increasingly involved in cooperative ventures with French, German and, more recently, Japanese companies, especially in the new field of power station assembly. Montáže Jesenice has achieved International Standards Organization (ISO) quality recognition for the whole enterprise, which has been a significant factor in the growing business – unlike Jesenické Strojírny and Vols, which have achieved ISO certification in only a few areas, and Agstroj, which is still groping towards it. Employment in Montáže Jesenice has fallen slowly from about 1150 in 1990 to fewer than 800 in 1995, but much of this decline has been in spite of Montáže Jesenice's plans, as workers have retired and some groups of workers have even set up in competition. The loss of skilled workers has been balanced by the employment of local casual workers, but this may have a potentially damaging long-term effect on the enterprise.

By the end of 1995, the enterprises had managed to survive the most traumatic period in their post-war experience, each having made its own unique response according to its business circumstances. It is possible to say that Montáže Jesenice has adapted most successfully and most quickly, with Vols and Jesenické Strojírny beginning to come out of the economic doldrums and Agstroj looking the most vulnerable to post-communist failure despite – or perhaps because of – being the brightest of stars before 1989.

In what remains of Chapter 7 and the next two chapters, we shall try to get inside these general trends and observations to see how the new enterprise managers effected them. We adopt the approach described earlier in the chapter, looking first at the processes of deinstitutionalization, associated especially but not exclusively with the immediate aftermath of the revolution.

Deinstitutionalizing state socialist enterprise and management

The failure of the central planning institutions was effectively felt in the enterprises from the start of 1990, before their formal demise. It was the policy of the interim government and of the first elected government in June 1990 to pull the state out of enterprise affairs, and managers who survived the revolution found themselves in practice in a position without external scrutiny. It was self-evident to most commentators and practitioners that the managerial and technical practices of state socialism, based as they were on the needs and demands of the command economy, would be neither relevant to nor proper for the post-communist regime that had, by popular but unquestioned consent, been conceived on the premises of a competitive market economy and private property. Yet, as has been central to our argument throughout, the formal institutional and socially constructed notions of management and organization are grounded in issues beyond those of pure technical efficiency. The notions of management and organization are reproduced at any one time from the formal and social processes of legitimation, which are themselves the product of the interplay between legal, structural definitions and the grounded realization of enterprise management at the point of the local enterprise. The repercussions of the Velvet Revolution, as opposed to pre-1989 periods in Czechoslovak economic history, rendered existing management and organizational practices both formally and normatively 'improper'. Consequently, existing managers were challenged both to adapt their economic (problem-solving, decision-making, resource allocation etc.) practices to the new, emergent conditions and to seek new normative grounds for the practices, authority, status and identity to which they explicitly and implicitly laid claim as managers.

The pressure on managers to change came from many sources, both outside the management group, and within it. The new voice of the people began to be expressed through Civic Forum, and became loud and inescapable during November and December 1989. Civic Forum set up groups in each enterprise, which involved men of '68, *nomenklatura* managers with the gift of foresight and even those who had been hitherto unpoliticized. With the power of national events behind them, they met directors in order to influence immediate changes at the enterprise level. Whether channelled through Civic Forum groups or not, there was no doubting the emotional groundswell of opinion from ordinary employees wishing to see major changes in managerial personnel. Some of those who applied pressure to the existing managers had had their own managerial careers denied or truncated because of their beliefs and external political activities, or their refusal to join the Communist Party. Having been limited in their ambition to technical functions, or, in the later 1980s, to reaching the lower slopes of enterprise management, the events of November 1989 offered them new opportunities to reassert their claims.

But the drive to change management and managers also came from within the managerial cadre itself. Some managers had joined the CP purely for the pragmatic reason that this would be the only way of pursuing a managerial career, so they were equally opportunistic in joining the haemorrhage of members that followed the revolution – and predated it in the later months of 1989 as people became more confident in the inability of the communist regime to resist the tide of opposition at home and abroad. Many other *nomenklatura* managers had seen the writing on the wall and despite being fully involved in the party and in the local political and social scene had anyway become frustrated by the processes necessary to sustain the system. Driven by perceptions of themselves as 'managers' *per se*, rather than 'state socialist managers', few of even the most senior directors put up much of a struggle against what became the inevitable – though some of the most autocratic senior managers were piqued, to say the least, that bodies such as Civic Forum could exercise power over their future and that of 'their' enterprise.

Before or at the same time as searching for new ways and ideas, managers adopted various methods of distancing, detaching and dissociating themselves and their organizations from the structures, traditions and practices that had typified the state socialist enterprise and its management. These strategies and processes of deinstitutionalization took various forms, but they struck deeply at the historical experiences that had hitherto been taken for granted by managers and employees alike. In our discussion, we shall focus on some of the more critical examples, by examining the expulsion, displacement or relegation of people and structures that were particularly associated with the previous regime; and the renunciation of former managerial ways and the formation of a post-communist managerial rhetoric that served to make sense of the surviving managers' past and continuing careers. In placing emphasis on these processes of historical rejection, denial and reinterpretation, we do not wish to downplay the importance of creative reconstruction, which will be given due consideration in Chapter 9.

The most obvious internal sign of deinstitutionalization was the dismantling of the dual structures that had been the backbone of local communist power in the enterprise. The CP basic organizations, the committees and the party apparatus were abolished, and the senior political functionaries in the enterprise were dismissed. The trade union offices were purged of their leaders. Then, in the first few months of 1990, attention was turned to the directors, senior managers and other managers with a reputation for their strong communist affiliations and loyalties. In this respect, local Civic Forum representatives played an important role. Depending on whom you speak to, these Civic Forum groups wielded enormous, often arbitrary influence, forcing managers to resign and leave the enterprise without any real justification; or they represented the new democratic voice, balloting departments on the acceptability of their heads before persuading former autocratic communists to relinquish their authority. In the words of one observer at Jesenické Strojírny, 'The period after the revolution was very unpleasant [for existing managers], with all the changes and with the insecurity.' In response to the popular call for visible changes in personnel, it was inevitable that senior managers had to be sacrificed – arguably to save others. Emotionally, people wanted to see the back of those managers and officials who had benefited from the old regime, and had acted as tyrants.

The enterprise director at Jesenické Strojírny was a case in point. As we have seen in Chapter 4, Engineer J was known as an arrogant autocrat, but at the same time his ability to exploit his contacts in the planning institutions made him a 'bit of a hero'. Since he was approaching retirement age, it was possible to dress up his dismissal and, according to one interviewee, 'he went easily'. Other accounts suggest that Engineer J was livid at his treatment and left in a state of acrimony. But those who served under him saw him as a nominal scapegoat: 'He was respected and liked, and would be successful today . . . Getting rid of him in 1990 was an example of change for change's sake . . . his head rolled symbolically' (Deputy Director, Jesenické Strojírny).

Montáže Jesenice's director, who was universally disliked for his domineering managerial style, was also dismissed peremptorily, but this was not the normal way of removing former senior managers from power. Within the sample as a whole, only seven of the twenty-seven directors (26 per cent) had been in a directorate position before the revolution, but most of the ex-directors had resumed their careers in middle management positions. Our findings do not allow us to follow precisely the fate of the other twenty former directors, because the research process was constructed to examine current rather than past managers. However, through serendipity, we do have a complete record of the 1989 directorate of Jesenické Strojírny, which makes interesting reading for those concerned with the dynamics of the post-communist economic elite (see Clark and Soulsby, 1996) – see Table 7.4.

It can be seen that only three directors were forcibly retired or dismissed, and each of these went on to start small businesses which have in fact flourished in Jesenice. Engineer J, the former enterprise director, is particularly interesting, as he started an advertising agency and other entrepreneurial activities which included the running of an investment privatization fund which has since become a major shareholder in Jesenické Strojírny, with a representative on the board. Apart from the former technical director, who

Table 7.4 Post-communist careers of Jesenické Strojírny's pre-1989 directorate

Pre-1989 position	Post-1989 status
General director	Enforced retirement; became part-owner of a number of small firms in a variety of businesses, including an IPF which acquired a significant share in the new privatized Jesenické Strojírny.
Economy director	Interim general director; demoted to department manager; recently elected to supervisory board.
Production director	Demoted to sales manager; recently transferred to strategy department.
Personnel director	Demoted to 'normal worker'; recently left enterprise for new job.
Technical director	Appointed General Director at Montáže Jesenice.
Investment director	Dismissed; set up own business.
Commercial director	Demoted to commercial manager; repromoted to adviser.
Engineering director	Dismissed; set up own competitive firm.

was competitively appointed by a panel which included Civic Forum representatives to the general director's job at Montáže Jesenice, the other former directors were demoted. Most were repositioned in middle management jobs, and have begun to make their way upwards again. The pattern is clear: with one exception, these senior managers have successfully redefined their managerial and business careers, either within Jesenické Strojírny or within the wider business community of the region.

In addition to dismissal and demotion, the former senior managers have been subject to other forms of dissolution and disgrace which have served to cleanse their earlier connections. We have already mentioned above the effects of the lustration legislation in which communist devotees were forced by public opinion to surrender their seniority, with potentially devastating effects on the management team. But, further, it was widely noticed that some former *nomenklatura* who had continued in senior positions, such as the general directors of Vols and Jesenické Strojírny, were in certain respects disabled in their transitional managerial roles. The general director in Vols is the most obvious and illustrative example, having been appointed under the communist regime and being thereby a significant reminder of the past in the present.

> It should be the general director's role to ensure strategic cooperation, but there are political reasons why this does not happen. Some people should not be in decision-making positions. The law about CP membership and the holding of office [i.e. lustration] is not clear . . . but these people have personal problems and are vulnerable . . . and it affects

their ability to do progressive work, to make unpopular decisions and to exercise effective influence with credibility. (Vols department manager)

Or similarly in Jesenické Strojírny, the general director's 'communist past can deprive him of power and influence, as it did for others too, in certain situations such as talking to the trade unions . . . [He] fears the trade unions' (Senior manager, Jesenické Strojírny).

In the close and small communities of Volna and Jesenice, it was not possible for such figures to conceal or disguise their former communist roles, and interviewees at all levels made reference to their pasts and to their likely problems in making the post-communist adjustment. In the early transition years, many surviving managers found it very difficult to overcome the inherited problems of legitimacy and credibility, despite the personnel changes that had taken place. Our interview materials provide repeated evidence of how they had begun to make sense psychologically and socially of the contradictions of their careers – concerning especially their struggle to be seen as bona fide market-economic managers despite their involvement as *nomenklatura* managers in state socialism. We can discern the evolution of two rhetorical devices that had the effect of distancing surviving managers' current status and credentials from their past negative managerial connections. Both devices took the form of 'retelling the past', of recasting state socialist management in words that could serve to support their claims to post-communist legitimacy, and make a sharp break from the enterprise management in which they were key players or being groomed for such roles.

Former *nomenklatura* respondents developed sophisticated interpretive schemes for understanding management in the past and its connections with the emerging market economy. One mechanism within such schemes was directed at explaining their own success in surviving the changes intact, while others had fallen by the wayside. Managers frequently drew upon a well-rehearsed distinction between 'political managers' and 'professional managers'. The distinction was so widespread and was pulled out so frequently in the same form that it is impossible to see as random – it was a shared, organized system of rationalization. One Jesenické Strojírny manager gave the most comprehensive exposition on the two concepts:

Before [the revolution] most decisions were made by the ruling party. Half the managers were not professionals but could make [important] decisions; the other half were professional, but could also decide. The first half were either retired, demoted or left for private work [after 1989] . . . Most good managers, the professionals, had to be members of the party . . . [in order] to have a chance.

When speaking of the 'politicals', the reference was always to those enterprise managers who had obtained their position solely or mostly because of political connections, and generally made little or no contribution to the enterprise beyond their ability to get things to happen in Communist Party circles – in practice no mean contribution, of course. Our respondents frequently questioned the managerial competence of such managers, who were seen in retrospect to have given all managers (i.e. including themselves) a bad name. On the other hand, the 'professionals' had been members of the Communist Party, because they had had no choice if they were to pursue a managerial career beyond a certain level; but, above all, they (that is, 'we') were also technically able or 'skilled'.

This distinction served as an important mechanism for salvaging the respondents' own and their surviving colleagues' reputations from their past connections, and for distancing themselves from the social inequities of the *nomenklatura* system that was the basis of the management legitimacy crisis. The distinction, and the interpretations which it spawned, offered a neat and satisfying justificatory tautology: only those who were competent could have survived the revolution; they had survived it, and therefore they could claim to be first and foremost professional, skilled managers.

In retelling the past, surviving managers developed another form of legitimating rhetoric. They felt the need to make sense of the behaviour and fate of the former directors, who had been deposed and displaced after the revolution. For older survivors, these directors had been close colleagues, and for younger survivors they may have acted as patrons and sponsors during their junior careers, guiding them skilfully through the difficult waters of party rules and procedures. Yet these same directors had been renowned for their autocratic, bullying, self-righteous and arrogant approaches, archetypes of the communist enterprise manager. The former *nomenklatura* among our managers had begun to develop a socially acceptable thesis about the communist managers they admired, which accounted for them as 'men of their time', and justified their sometimes rather 'strange' or arbitrary behaviour as 'suiting the previous system'. This rhetoric allowed the managers to understand, if not partially rehabilitate, their predecessors, and as a consequence some former directors received a lot of sympathy for their 'bad luck' in having been so successful under communism. Meanwhile, the inheritors of their managerial mantles and prospects, as worthy bearers of the label 'professional manager', could account for some of the post-1989 changes in personnel as some kind of political revenge or symbolic sacrifice. The references to Engineer J of Jesenické Strojírny often carry these kinds of themes. A surviving former *nomenklatura* in a senior position spoke glowingly of his former boss:

> [The former general director] visited countries, and had many close friends abroad. It was a pity for him to be born too soon . . . He used modern methods and tried to implement changes he had learned from the West and Western countries.

Needless to say, few of the lower level managers, nor those who had been deprived of their managerial careers under communism, saw it in quite this way!

The surviving managers and those promoted from outside the *nomenklatura* system rapidly established interim strategic teams in each enterprise, in part to respond to the problems of external institutional change. The creation of strategic units and teams was an articulate and symbolic declaration by the senior managers that they were no longer dependent on hierarchical structures of decision-making. While these strategy teams were charged with planning new forms of management and organization, aspects of which we shall consider in Chapter 9, the initial thrust of their decisions was to signal a break from the past.

The new senior managers realized that it was essential that the enterprises and their management *be seen to be different* from the communist period. The atmosphere of the early transition period was supportive of such a radical break. Speaking of this popular mood, one middle manager recalled: 'People needed changes even if they were bad.' This view was not unanimous, and many of those who had been committed to the previous system decried the tendency to seek change for its own sake. A leading trade unionist in Montáže Jesenice commented bitterly: 'Now, everyone thinks that all the past was wrong.' Even senior managers did not agree completely with the popular mood, which recommended the radical clearing away of systems, people and even memories. But the post-revolution euphoria and its associated logic could not be denied, especially by managers anxious to maintain their posts and to re-establish their credentials: 'The form of organizational change is important; revolution causes damage and chaos . . . evolution is a better way to create change. But in 1990, everything from previous times was thrown out' (Strategy manager, Jesenické Strojírny).

The hierarchical form of enterprise structure, representative as it was of state socialism, became anathema – a theme we expand on in the next two chapters. But parallel to this, managers attempted to present themselves as more suited to the new decentralized world. The rhetoric of the new senior managements and the 'leadership' styles they attempted to adopt shunned the autocratic orthodoxies of the state socialist world in favour of consultation, openness, listening, 'teamwork' and so on. Respondents in Montáže Jesenice, in particular, seemed impressed by a perceived change in management style:

> The directors meet once a week [with the general director]. These meetings are friendly and emphasize a move towards agreement – [this is] a fundamental change from the old management approach. (Former *nomenklatura* manager)

> Engineer G [Montáže Jesenice's general director] was a technical specialist, like Engineer H [his highly dictatorial predecessor], but his

behaviour has been a lovely surprise. He is ready to hear ideas from his subordinates, and, if they are good, realize them. (New young manager)

Management changes, yes there's a big difference – people now listen to my opinions. (New senior manager)

In Jesenické Strojírny, a demoted former *nomenklatura* director spoke enthusiastically of the new general director's adopted style: 'relationships are good [between managers]. The general director listens to subordinates, and is always willing to learn.'

Statements like these might seem mundane to a reader unaccustomed to hearing Czechs speak about communist management and managers. But these utterances were expressed in a tone of wonder or surprise, which emphasized the fact that it had been rare to experience directors or senior managers whose ear you could reach, and whose decisions you could influence. Some senior managers, speaking of their management style, claimed that they had always preferred to operate in a more open and receptive mode; others said that they would have liked to, but this had simply not been possible under the old regime. Most subordinates seemed to accept an argument which linked hierarchical form with autocratic style, so the emergence of a more consultative and considerate style would seem to presage a break from the past.

Managers had consciously decided to present their new, preferred style of management as a distinctive move away from the authoritarianism of the past, and they wanted to make this hiatus visible for all to see. It is another matter as to whether the changes were in their consequences cosmetic or real, and it is more questionable whether subordinates completely accepted the idea of a 'changed management'. Even the respondents cited above were not wholly convinced about the changes; their comments indicate a simultaneous scepticism about the extent or the depth of the changes. For example:

The management changes in Montáže Jesenice cannot be called a turnaround – more changes would be better. (New young manager)

Why is Montáže Jesenice just drifting? Because the top management are the same people – they are just behaving differently. (New senior manager)

This ambivalent attitude was held by many respondents below senior management. Senior managers have in various ways thrown off the appearance of being old socialist managers, but change has been less than it should be because deep down they are the same managers as before. We will explore this view in greater depth in Chapter 8.

The structural shifts away from hierarchy, the personnel changes and the evolution of new management rhetorics and styles have been major themes in the efforts of managers to distance the enterprises from their pre-1989 origins. The quest to detach management and organization from the past can be most poignantly illustrated by the ways in which post-communist managers acted to escape the legacy of the cadre and personnel department. No other function in the enterprise was subjected on the same scale to questions of managerial illegitimacy and disablement following the revolution than the personnel department (Soulsby and Clark, 1998). It used to be part of the state-owned enterprise functional blueprint, performing, as we described in Part Two, a central role in sustaining the political integrity of the enterprise in the state socialist context through operating and overseeing the cadre policy of the Communist Party. It kept records on the political activities of important staff, and reported to the local party. As a result, the personnel area of management was a detested and feared function.[1]

Being an institutional symbol of state socialism and of the *nomenklatura* system, the new senior management teams moved quickly to disband the department, to destroy or return political records and to reduce the staff (e.g. in Vols from 120 to 20) to reflect its more conventional (by Western standards) role. It was typical of the early transition period for the personnel department to be completely cleansed of its past associations, as former members of the Communist Party who staffed and administered the department were removed. It might be recalled from Table 7.4 that Jesenické Strojírny's former personnel director was alone in being demoted to the position of a manual worker, a reversal of career prospects that must have been particularly humiliating for someone who, only a few months before, had been among the most trusted of the *nomenklatura* managers.

Normal personnel activities were also affected by their links with cadre work, and by the time the department had been symbolically purged of its communist staff there were often few people left with the experience or qualification to run it. In Montáže Jesenice, for example, the new personnel manager described the situation as follows:

> [In] the management's intended changes to the personnel section . . . they wanted to devolve personnel to the [new] divisions, but only two people were 'qualified' and they needed four. So the secretaries were suggested as taking on these duties.

In Jesenické Strojírny, a manager used to work for the education (training) department:

> until 1989, the education section was part of personnel and had seven employees. After 1989, there were efforts to close the education section because of its association with the Communist Party. We won our fight to survive, but the CP members had to leave to allow it. Only me and two secretaries survived the change.

Changes to the staff in a highly sensitive area like personnel offered an immediate and popular way of distancing the post-1989 management from its state socialist counterpart, and made a clear statement to employees and other would-be stakeholders that 'we are different now'. But the process of deinstitutionalization was further reflected in strategic decisions about the structural status and location of the new personnel section. In Vols and Agstroj, the new smaller personnel departments were consciously reposi-tioned as subordinate sections in the reorganized economy (finance) and administration divisions, respectively, which, although still run by former *nomenklatura* managers, had an image less affected by the political blemishes of state socialism. Similarly, in Montáže Jesenice, personnel became a smaller less significant section, hidden away in the management services department.

The management of Jesenické Strojírny made the unusual move of maintaining the successor to the despised personnel and cadre department in Jesenické Strojírny as a central function. However, they tried to distance it from its predecessor by renaming it, demoting the former director to a very low position and installing in his place a former man of '68 who had been a sig-nificant political force in the Civic Forum opposition. The other enterprises also used the device of promoting to the post of personnel manager people who were known by employees to have a reputation uncorrupted by com-munist associations. The case of Agstroj offers an exception, in that the head of the new personnel department had worked in personnel as a manager in another state enterprise and had been appointed just after the revolution. It would appear that his origins outside Agstroj and the competitive nature of his selection were sufficient defences against the charges of political contami-nation.

Aware of the sensitive nature of the personnel function, most management teams took interim steps in 1990 to reduce the status of the activity, by tucking it away as a minor section under the auspices of some unrelated activity. Hiding personnel in the structure could only be a holding operation, given the importance of the management of human resources in an equivalent Western company, but it served to create a breathing space for memories to fade before it could re-emerge in a new form with new staff and a clean image. We shall pick up the further story of its re-emergence in Chapter 9.

Conclusions

We have begun in this chapter to examine the post-1989 transformation in management and organization that has taken place at enterprise level in each of the four cases which constitute the empirical base of our research. This has entailed in the first place a description of the general changes that affected enterprise management as a body. We have observed constancy and change in the membership of the post-communist management group, and shown that, at senior levels, processes of continuity prevail. From these circumstances, we have also inferred certain consequences for the priorities of the post-communist managers in respect of sustaining their own careers – in short, the need to control the processes of managerial and enterprise redefinition in such ways as to optimize their own technical and normative credibility. In a second section, we described the main changes which the four enterprises had experienced over the first half of the 1990s, highlighting similarities and indicating any differences. We shall return to these changes in a more analytical frame of mind in the following chapters.

In the last section of the chapter we identified ways in which the enterprise managements have responded to external institutional changes, especially those in the early phase of the transition, by detaching and distancing themselves and their enterprises from pre-1989 institutional forms and institutionalized practices. We have shown how the membership of the management team has evolved by eliminating, demoting and replacing *nomenklatura* figures who were too redolent of the past regime; how they have altered enterprise structures to reduce comparison with the prior hierarchical form and its sensitive functional areas of activity; how, relatedly, they have tried to cultivate styles of management that enhance perceived differences from management before 1989; and how the surviving managers had evolved legitimating rhetorics to explain and justify their continuity in office, while emphasizing their separation from the tainted image of state socialist management.

The distinction between deinstitutionalization and reinstitutionalization has its limitations, because either process of institutional change presumes, includes, foreshadows or re-emphasizes the other. We have tried to restrict our examination in this chapter to those aspects of management and enterprise change with a deinstitutionalizing slant. In the following chapter, we shall be dealing with those changes which highlight issues of coping with transience and creating new structures and practices.

Notes

1 On our first day at the enterprise, we were returning to the personnel department after an interview accompanied by an employee, and as we were going up the stairway outside the building he recalled the fear he always used to feel before 1989. In the garages below the personnel department, the enterprise *milice* used to store its weapons, and a march up these steps usually signalled that the employee had done something terribly wrong.

8 Continuity and inertia in enterprise transition

Despite the attempts to distance management and the enterprise from the past – the processes of deinstitutionalization described in Chapter 7 – the strength of the historical forces and legacies made complete detachment impossible, at least in the short to medium term. They remained a significant part of the *contemporary* social and economic environment in transition. The formal tasks of demolishing the legal institutions of the command economy took more time to effect than many predicted, because of the dangers of leaving an institutional vacuum which would allow an economic free-for-all. Moreover, the institutionalized practices of economic life which had developed over many years and had become part of taken-for-granted enterprise behaviour showed themselves to be very reluctant to disappear.

For many reasons, economic actors after 1989 continued to draw on their former managerial and work practices, reinforcing tendencies to institutional inertia, and so succeeded in reproducing an economic reality with strong pre-1989 resonances. It was thus actually undesirable for managers to dissociate themselves from their old ways completely – to do so, paradoxically, would have been a sign of management incompetence. The professional motives of competent managers in the post-communist economy were therefore sufficient to reproduce former institutionalized practices, and in doing so to create a transitional environment with *regressive* elements. But this tendency was further reinforced by their personal motives, which, as we have seen in the previous chapter, were tied up with their need to secure their managerial futures by overcoming doubts about their credibility in coping with enterprise survival.

At the same time that the former institutions were declining in practical and normative influence, future expectations about market economies were being developed and legitimated. In this latter respect, it was necessary for managers hoping to survive the short-term transition to adopt, and be seen to adopt, the characteristics of modern, preferably Western, management and organization, a process which would construct more *progressive* elements in the business environment. As in the case of reproduction of former practices, the reasons for the development of new practices were both technical-economic and normative. First, it was critical for the post-communist management to demonstrate that they could deal competently with the emerging market-related aspects of the transitional environment. Second, in the search to prolong their managerial careers, the new senior management teams, weighted with former communists, needed to establish their respectability as managers who could look after the interests of various stakeholders. The most important of these were: the liberal-economic government, which remained effectively their employers; the employees who had been enthused by new expectations; and future shareholders, including foreign investors, who would need to be convinced that the old communist values and ways had been eliminated from the managerial repertoire. In short, there was a need both technically and normatively to be seen as bona fide managers, despite the socialist backgrounds of most of them.

In this chapter, we shall examine the ways in which the post-communist managers set about dealing with this cluster of contradictory pressures – managing both the historical, regressive and the contemporary, progressive features of the transitional business environment, and proving themselves to be both technically competent and socially legitimate in their post-communist roles. We shall be looking in particular at how managers responded to the continuing importance of historical legacies in the context of simultaneous new economic pressures. We shall argue in particular that, while the reproduction of old practices might have been 'unfortunate' in an economy seeking radical change, it was also, for the most part, economically rational. This chapter focuses on the micro-processes leading to some degree of institutional inertia during the early transition period, and we reserve more lengthy discussion of the processes of reinstitutionalization – of managerial and organization redefinition – to the next chapter.

The basic thesis here is that the persistence of former managerial practices in the post-communist enterprise can be understood as efforts by managers to make both economically rational responses to transitional business problems of enterprise survival and socially rational responses to transitional personal problems of managerial survival. We begin by explaining the managers' everyday conception of the enterprise-in-transition as an organization in search of simple survival in conditions which the managers themselves understood in quite sophisticated ways. We next consider their response to issues of privatization, followed by how the senior managers successfully adapted former networking practices to support their own equivocal managerial status, and to deal with the regressive aspects of the transition economy. Having looked at the first attempts to reorganize the enterprises for privatization, we finally explore the ways in which managers reproduced pre-1989 conduct to resist the progressive implications of the decentralising structural changes.

Socio-economic transience and the strategy of survival

A central feature of the early period of socio-economic transformation was the uneasy coexistence of socio-economic pressures emanating from the continuing influence of historical legacies and the emergent influences of new forms of expectation and conduct. This period may be mainly but not exclusively associated with the time leading up to privatization, which was the middle of 1993 for the four enterprises under study, but extended until 1995 for many others. In line with the social-institutional arguments that thread through the book, we use the notion of *socio-economic transience* to refer to the transitional characteristics of the post-communist environment, which retains strong technical and institutional elements of the former state socialist system, while simultaneously developing powerful technical and institutional characteristics of the evolving market economy. In these circumstances, the concrete direction and outcomes of the process of transformation – that is, how the new social institutions actually develop – have to be understood in the context of how social actors respond to these contradictory pressures, and resolve the resultant everyday problems and dilemmas to which they give rise. In this spirit, we explore these issues of socio-economic transience as they were experienced and tackled by managers in the four post-communist enterprises.

This concept of transience is derived within the conceptual institutional framework developed in Chapter 2, but the underlying notion was expressed in a variety of more or less inchoate forms in the everyday theorizing of the managers involved. Speaking in 1993, for example, one respondent noted with more than a touch of ironic humour: 'We are going to the market economy, but everyone is waiting for instructions about how to get there' (Director, Jesenické Strojírny). In a more technical vein, a middle manager at Montáže Jesenice identified the same tension between the push of the new, and the pull of the old:

> Now Montáže Jesenice is going through a difficult time with reorganization into divisions, and being in the middle of a process . . . The organization structure is totally new, but [Montáže Jesenice] is still using some of the old systems.

In Jesenické Strojírny, a middle manager commented: 'top management is good according to the current environment . . . Top managers are working in a period of uncertainty – it is a transition period, not like the Western situation where you can move from A to B.' In early 1992, a senior manager at Vols had formulated the dilemma of coexisting forces of continuity and discontinuity more succinctly, in what he called 'bridge-time'.

> [Vols] has a good formal structure, which suited the command economy, but the market economy needs less formality. Currently Vols is in an [unstructured] situation. Now is the time to change the system, and it is very important to have an informal bridge from one [system] to the other.

Each of these formulations recognizes the need for or the expectation of some future state which is different from the past; as well as the inescapability of historical forces. In the words of a director at Agstroj, 'the past is an iron shirt'.

As a consequence of the uncertainties of the socio-economic transition, the managers were dominated not by the need to operate in a market-economic or profit-oriented manner, but by the need to manage the diverse pulls and pushes in the task and institutional environments to optimize the enterprises' chances of short- to medium-term survival. Managers in all the enterprises recognized that the circumstances of the transition were not conducive to the definition and accomplishment of the business and economic goals that lie at the heart of theories of the capitalist firm.

> The current situation in the Czech Republic means that only a strategy of survival is possible. There is poor utilization of capacity . . . This year we are holding on tightly, and working on [next year]. (General director, Montáže Jesenice)

The marketing manager of Vols defined one of his main tasks as: 'to ensure enough work for the factory to survive the transition period . . . [which he saw as] about three years . . . The main 'profit' is not monetary, but the sustaining of production continuity.' Observations that their enterprises lacked 'strategic direction' or 'real mission' were not so much criticisms, except in the eyes of Western observers, as a description of the essential nature of managing enterprises in the transitional period. The strategy of survival describes not only how managers responded on behalf of their enterprises to the external economic conditions of transience, but also how they understood their careers during this period – one of the enduring themes of this book.

Enterprise and managerial survival were defined in terms of both continuity of inherited managerial values and priorities, and the adoption of new post-communist ideas and knowledge. In Chapter 7, we spoke of the continuing values of the managers in the study, some of which reflected what was called their Czech identity, but others, of more direct relevance, defined basic assumptions regarding their work, their employees and their enterprises. Researchers on organizational cultures have argued that such basic assumptions are the most difficult to reveal, but this is surely a consequence of the stable contexts in which such research has taken place (e.g. Schein, 1985). As we argued in Chapter 2, in times of major institutional change, the most taken-for-granted values and beliefs are drawn to the surface of consciousness, creating a great sense of unease and discomfort among people. It is true of our managers that they struggled deeply and personally with the demands of the changed socio-economic circumstances; especially with the concrete economic dilemmas thrown up by the transition, and their own beliefs and priorities that had hitherto gone unquestioned. In their everyday decision-making within their particular enterprises, how could they apply the knowledge and values they held, derived mostly from experiences in the state socialist past, to the inherited and contemporary socio-economic problems of the transition?

The psychological struggle, which internalized the external ideological clashes of the new versus the old, was experienced by virtually all the managers, although some may have felt it more intensely than others. Despite inter-enterprise differences, the managers tended to define the process and ingredients of enterprise (and managerial) survival in a similar way. The overwhelmingly important priority was that of securing employment for their employees, and managers demonstrated an enormous sense of social responsibility in this context. Unlike in other former communist states, the impact of the economic policies of the Czech government was tempered by a tacit support for the large overstaffed enterprises, providing a tight labour market in many regions. The demand for labour in local economies undoubtedly eased decision-making in many privatizing enterprises. In Agstroj, for example, employment decreased by about 4000, or 41 per cent, from 1989 to June 1995 (see Table 8.1), and managers felt comfortable because most of those who had not been retired were able to find new jobs in a large town with an unemployment rate of about 3 per cent, and an intense shortage of skilled workers. Agstroj management still took decisions about redundancies with the destiny of the individual in mind. In the words of an Agstroj director: 'Agstroj is soft on the individual, which is typical . . . We are just not used to saying "we don't want you from the 1st January" – there is still a lot of social thinking. [Hardness] . . . is not in the Czech culture.'

It is a moot point as to whether the 'social thinking' is a Czech cultural phenomenon, rooted deeply in traditions of social democracy. Other managers saw such concerns for employee well-being and a reticence to make fundamental changes as a remnant from the former communist ideology. A different Agstroj director spoke of these continuing values among senior managers: 'they [the managers] are not red, but pink'. Many felt any social impact of economic decisions as a challenge to their role as managers, which they had historically defined in terms of maintaining and creating secure employment, rather than reducing it. The social consequences for employment levels of market-adjustment and restructuring were for many managers

Table 8.1 The reduction of employment in the enterprises

	Vols	*Montáže Jesenice*	*Jesenické Strojírny*	*Agstroj*
January 1990	5600	1150	7000	10,000
December 1993	4700	950	4200	5800
September 1995	4500	783	3800	5941
Percentage reduction, 1990 to 1995	19.6	31.9	35*	40.5

* After accounting for the formation of Montáže Jesenice.

crucial factors in strategic decision-making, and they identified strongly with the fate of employees, whom they saw as members of their community. Vols's metallurgy director put the point most poignantly in explaining that he lived in the same apartment block and on the same housing estate as many of his division's employees – they were neighbours and friends, he met them in shops, so how could he let them down? Although at the time of the first field visit his division was in real economic trouble, for him the *social* impact on Volna of laying off workers was inconceivable: 'The position of metallurgy in Vols is safe, because of the [social] effects on Volna of closing it down.'

In the small former communist town of Volna, in which there were few employment opportunities outside Vols, it is not surprising to find the directors resisting the 'immutable logic' of capitalism and 'downsizing'. In 1992, the strategy director suggested that the 'right' size of Vols was about 4000 employees, but the senior managers were not comfortable with the social and moral problems that reaching this target would have involved. Table 8.1 shows that Vols reduced employment by less than 20 per cent, compared with Agstroj's 41 per cent. The cases of the enterprises in Jesenice came between these two: a sign of the better labour market prospects in Jesenice than Volna, the former being a larger town with multiple employers, which made decisions easier to take.[1]

A strategic manager in Jesenické Strojírny decried the wholesale, unquestioned, taking on of new ideas from the West, proclaiming the neglected value of many aspects of the past. In particular, he identified 'a certain pride, a loyalty and a sense of social responsibility; [these were reflected in] . . . the enterprise's social policy, [which] was in substance good'. There was also a practical reason for maintaining employment in the conditions of the Czech transition, which had strong echoes with management in the state socialist economy. For reasons of macroeconomic policy and tacit support for the large state enterprises, the post-communist labour market, especially for the most skilled engineering workers, had remained very tight. New private firms were able to offer higher salaries, and often more interesting work, and all four enterprises were continuously in danger of losing their best employees. In the ironic words of a senior manager at Montáže Jesenice, 'the worst, they always stay'.

Continuing social values and economic practices informed the consequent strategic priorities which guided much of the early enterprise decision-making in the transitional environment. The strategy of survival, for practical as well as social-ideological-moral reasons, was based upon a policy of finding enough work to keep people employed. This strategy involved all sorts of unusual management practices, and the seeking of new contracts which were evaluated according not so much to classic capitalist criteria of maximizing revenue or profit as to satisficing criteria of sustaining existing employment levels. The financial director at Montáže Jesenice in 1992 explained how divisional performance targets were derived from knowledge of existing projects and the number of employees in the division, not from market-imposed financial criteria. Anything achieved beyond the targets was seen as a bonus.

The strategy of employment stability thus entailed the sustaining of a sufficient level of production, which itself required maintaining domestic contracts with existing clients, and, to counteract the loss of foreign trade in Eastern markets, increasing deliveries abroad. The reorientation of production towards the West was particularly important because of the need to solve the financial crises perpetuated by the spiralling of inter-enterprise debt, or, as it was known within the enterprises, 'payment inability'.

Each enterprise had so much 'money' tied up in the debt–credit balance that by most Western standards they might have been considered to be financially unviable. In Montáže Jesenice, for example, the notional stock of workable money was some kčs35 million, representing the excess of what it was owed by clients over what it owed suppliers. However, suppliers had not paid up, so Montáže Jesenice had a strong incentive not to pay its bills. Because of the shortage of real cash, Montáže Jesenice had to borrow money from the banks to pay its wage bill, and subsequently paid high interest rates on its loans. The financial situation of the other enterprises was identical in principle, but on a larger scale. Additionally, both Jesenické Strojírny and Vols were owed giant sums as a result of the collapse of the Soviet Union, and Agstroj had huge outstanding foreign debts from Middle Eastern customers which had been subjected to international trade bans. Not surprisingly, the problem of payment inability was the routine obsession in the finance offices, and it was the litmus test of financial management to be on good enough terms with banks to be able to keep the business afloat.

Enterprise strategy during the first years of the transition was dominated by short- and medium-termism. Survival was foremost in management thinking. Based on a mixture of inherited pre-1989 values and priorities and the enterprise realities arising from socio-economic transience, the satisficing survival strategy placed employment criteria first and foremost, in the service of which commercial and financial activities were pressed. Thus was created the internal environment of enterprise decision-making.

Waiting for new owners: The power vacuum

The transitional strategy of survival was a form of muddling through in difficult, ambiguous circumstances, but all four enterprises and their managements shared an ambition of greater clarity – to become privatized. Ownership and control were perhaps the most obvious expressions of the equivocal status which state enterprises held in the early transitional environment. In 1990, the new government attempted to pull the state out of detailed economic management by withdrawing from planning matters and deinstitutionalizing the command economic environment. However, at the same time, the enterprises retained their state-owned legal status and awaited clarification of how they could become private. This created a fundamental strategic dilemma for the enterprise managements. They needed to meet increasing market-economic expectations and proceed smoothly towards modern management patterns and organizational structures in order to underline their legitimate claims as post-communist managers of potentially competitive enterprises. But simultaneously they had to confront the demands of external environments still influenced by the declining command-economic institutions and associated patterns of business and trade. A parallel internal feature at this time of environmental transience was not so much the rapid development of new Western management ideas, rhetorics and principles – which took further root following privatization – but the continuing importance of former practices and values.

During 1990 to 1992, Vols, Agstroj, Jesenické Strojírny and Montáže Jesenice found themselves without any clearly articulated long-term direction, but overwhelmed, as we have seen, by the need to survive. With the impotence or elimination of the central planning institutions, and anticipating the process to privatization, the senior managers of the four enterprises had neither central state organs nor private shareholders to act as an effective external focus of accountability for organizational policy and performance. In this power vacuum, senior managers in principle had virtually complete discretion about how to steer their enterprises towards the new era. However, the external realities of the business and the internal values and ambitions of the managers themselves acted as joint constraints on their choices. At all levels of the enterprise, privatization was held as necessary for longer-term enterprise salvation and was an actively promoted cause. In general, managers hoped that the appearance of 'concrete owners' would overcome the problems of strategic drift, and offer almost a guarantee of economic improvements. Some saw privatization as an opportunity to make the complete transfer from 'state enterprise manager' to 'business owner' by participating in the design of competing privatization projects (e.g. in Agstroj and Montáže Jesenice); others were more practical, believing that privatization was a necessary step towards ensuring the success of their own careers.

As part of their strategic thinking, the managers considered the possibility of attracting interest from foreign capital as a means of privatizing their enterprises. Both Jesenické Strojírny and Agstroj, for example, were appraised by the NPF as holding out real opportunities for foreign direct investment. As it turned out, none of the enterprises was successful in interesting foreign buyers. An examination of our findings suggests one or two possible explanations of the *Czech* side of this question, since it was obvious from our interviews that most managers – especially the senior managers – were not exactly heartbroken by this 'failure'.

The strategy director of Vols exemplifies the typical response. He spoke of the enterprise almost having its fingers burned in initial negotiations about a proposed joint venture with a large German company. In his view, the German company had tried to exploit its financial power to the detriment of Vols, so managers decided to pull out of the proposal, and declared themselves to be 'happy to be alone'. Some of the fears expressed by Vols's managers were for its workforce and local community, whose futures might have been less certain were a foreign company to take effective control and, by implication, use its Western management methods (e.g. rationalization) to sort out the enterprise. This attitude towards foreign capital, and towards German firms in particular, was quite commonplace: a German firm 'had been interested in Montáže Jesenice, but [we] did not want to work with them, as we felt we would be used for cheap labour – the Germans were only thinking of money' (General director, Montáže Jesenice).

While the benefits of foreign capital involvement were obvious to all the enterprises, struggling as they were with updating and improving their technologies and technical systems, there was clearly strong resistance at the higher levels. An enterprise representative on the supervisory board at Jesenické Strojírny, who had been a very senior manager before the changes, made the point clear:

> Foreign investment would allow investment in production, but the rest of the Supervisory Board would not like foreigners buying [into] Jesenické Strojírny . . . In the first wave [of privatization] 25 per cent [*sic*] was especially prepared for foreign buyers to get foreign capital, but there was no buyer . . . [They] only wanted to buy the design team, not the production facilities. (Middle manager, Jesenické Strojírny)

Jesenické Strojírny's financial director expressed a similar view: 'In 1990 there were possibilities of capital investment from abroad, but they only wanted to invest in the profitable bits, and still exercise power.' The view that foreign capital only wanted to cherry-pick, rather than take on full responsibilities for the enterprise, was anathema to the strong sense of enterprise loyalty and the social thinking that still permeated senior management.

In the managers' responses to FDI there are strong elements of nationalism: the Czechs may have had forty years of state socialism, but they still know their own business. A corollary is a particular kind of anti-foreign (specifically anti-German) sentiment, which is also identifiable. These Czech values and associated 'social thinking', and the perceptions of actual foreign corporate conduct which reinforce them, suggest an underlying cultural resistance to FDI which may penetrate deeply into the mind-sets of both management and the workforce. We have many stories and quotations which illustrate a degree of distrust of foreign capital, with the feeling that its social and cultural costs would outweigh the benefits of a direct financial injection.

However, there is another aspect to this question that can be seen in the last quotation above – that is, a political dimension. It was in the interests of the senior managements, particularly former *nomenklatura* managers, to maintain tight control of the privatization process and thereby to exert continuing influence over the processes of redefining post-communist management. The implications of the Czech values of independence and self-learning for the emergence of management as an institution cannot be underestimated. They coincide with and reinforce the political preferences and sectionalist interests of senior managers, who have shown themselves to be keen to keep control of their enterprises and of their careers in the unique historical circumstances of the Czech Republic.

Internal and external networking

In Chapter 4, we saw how socio-economic networking developed as institutionalized senior management practices for ensuring the survival and health of the enterprises under the hierarchical structures that administered the central plan. Given the *nomenklatura* system based on the organs of the Communist Party, it was not surprising to find that external networking activities had informally utilized the channels and contacts within these structures. In Chapter 7, we saw how the membership of the new directorates, as social bodies, showed a strong resemblance to the former *nomenklatura* cadres. One of the initial conundrums that confronts any Western researcher examining post-communist management is how a communist manager in 1989 can become a capitalist manager in 1990 – a puzzle not lost on the managers themselves, who have since struggled to convince everyone that this was not just possible but rational. To understand the continuity of the former *nomenklatura* elite it is important to develop sociological accounts that explain how the internal cohesiveness and integrity of this social group was maintained, as well as economic arguments about how they could better manage the problems of the transition than those from outside the ex-communist cadres. Their claims to technical superiority were based mostly on their monopoly of managerial experience before 1989,[2] and the fact that they were well-connected to other managers who themselves were still in a position to help in enterprise survival. In effect, these connections could be shown to be powerful enough to overrule the incipient, but uncertain, market-economic tendencies in the emergent environment, in much the same way that they had previously undermined the formal rule of the command-economic hierarchy.

The *nomenklatura* and educational origins of many of the post-1989 managers suggest that they shared many common values and interests, having belonged to both internal and external networks of mutual contacts. As we have argued through the book, the senior managements have in some respects been in a precarious state because of the inherited non-legitimacy of many of their members. This was clearly demonstrated in the 'job swap' incidents at Montáže Jesenice reported in Chapter 7, where public outcry at the directorate status of young, formerly 'militant', communists could have destabilized the balance of managerial expertise assembled by the general director, himself a figure of some political importance under state socialism, both inside Jesenické Strojírny and within the structures of the district Communist Party. The managerial response, perhaps a hallmark of the behaviour of close social networks, was to devise the protective mechanism of job swaps, in the knowledge that the formality of the membership of the top group could be re-established after privatization.

The post-communist senior management groups shared interlocking, mutual interests derived from their common pasts, and this has tended to bind them into a social dynamic of self-protection. In Vols, for example, ex-*nomenklatura* members of the directorate were thought to be vulnerable in the same way as the general director, both because of their backgrounds and because they were part of a team led by someone generally understood as being managerially disabled. Although the general director was valued for his good industrial connections (see below), his perceived professional weakness served to keep the senior management team even more tightly integrated; if the general director had fallen, it would reveal the vulnerability of his fellow directors by taking away the cover of their mutual protection. One middle manager approaching retirement put it thus:

> the [senior] managers are not yet at a good level of competence; they have improved a little, though not as much as they should, because of the general director, [who] . . . is not good . . . Vols is now waiting for privatization and the top management will change in personnel . . . [but] for some people, this general director is better for them, because another one could want different managers [around him . . . without him] other managers could lose their jobs.

The implication here is plain: that the former *nomenklatura* managers formed a sort of mutual protection zone. There was a similar story told in Jesenické Strojírny, this time by a senior manager who had experienced the inner social dynamics of the directorate:

> [The general director] chooses whom he wants, and I am not sure whether they are the best. [He] is locked into a relationship with all the other directors, and they have to support each other, even though there may be friction, because they are closely connected. Only [Engineer X] was not connected with the previous regime.

In Jesenické Strojírny, the director's team was further bound together by the fact that the general director was supported in his application for the post by a team of colleagues who had, on his accession to the general directorate, been raised into senior management positions.

In Chapter 4, we cited a young Agstroj manager's description of the state enterprise as a 'big jug of wine' nourishing the *nomenklatura* management. Although speaking historically and unwilling to go into contemporary details, he alluded to the enduring effects of such systems of mutual interest for the post-communist enterprise. It was common among the more critical, especially non-former *nomenklatura* managers, to speak of the internal networks as mafia-like. One man of '68 in Vols, for example, still saw life in Vols and Volna as being influenced by 'relationships between communist groups and the mafia'.

The evidence suggests that senior management in each enterprise tended to operate as tightly structured networks, based around common backgrounds and experiences, but also cemented by mutual interests in perpetuating their careers under post-communist conditions. Their perceived vulnerability served to create tighter bonds, and may also have protected the less competent of the survivors.

The processes of continued networking need to be understood within a wider context than being merely social mechanisms for managerial survival, although there is little doubt that this was both a major intention and a major consequence of the behaviour. It is equally self-evident that the enterprises benefited economically from both the perpetuation of the former *nomenklatura* managers and the socio-economic networks they brought to and enacted in their managerial work. In particular, external networks of contacts constituted for the post-communist enterprises a crucial resource in their struggle for survival in the uncertainties of the transitional economy. As we have seen in Chapter 4, 'competent' state enterprise directors and deputies, as well as those trusted managers who had worked in the commercial function, would have developed strong connections throughout the relevant task environment of their business. Contacts within the industry among former partner enterprises, within the industrial ministries, in the old VHJs and FTOs had mostly survived the revolution in various ways, just as our managers had. Business friends often went on to hold new positions in the state sector, the emergent privatized sector or the new private sector. Being able to access and activate these contacts was understood to be critical to enterprise survival.

Respondents recognized the role of former contacts in the current environment when they assessed the strengths of the post-communist directors.

> [The general director of Jesenické Strojírny] is an impressive and very clever man. He knows lots of people, and knows the ways to [get access] to foreign and Czech trade. (Middle manager, Jesenické Strojírny)

> The driving force for change [in Montáže Jesenice] is the general director. He has a strong personality, and has many important contacts from the past, especially in Jesenické Strojírny and other factories. (Senior manager, Montáže Jesenice)

Montáže Jesenice's general director also spoke about the importance of personal networks:

> [It is] very, very important to use contacts with both Jesenické Strojírny and other enterprises. For example, most of our assembly work is on

cement works, and most cement works have cooperation with firms from abroad, which invest money in them . . . good contacts from the past allow Montáže Jesenice to get assembly work . . . Lots of work comes as part of bigger engineering projects, coordinated by private and state enterprises. It is important to have contacts with such firms.

Another respondent in Jesenické Strojírny assessed the general director as a 'good networker', who still used his old networks. These two general directors were understood as having managerial qualities which made them relevant to the post-communist environment, but their counterpart in Vols was seen as being managerially very weak and inadequate. However, his essential contribution to Vols was the networks to which he had belonged in the past, and whose members he could mobilize in order to secure orders, maintain production levels, protect employment levels and hence promote enterprise survival. As such, he acted more like a figurehead, and left the important strategic decisions to a small managerial coalition.

Other managers were also assessed, and assessed themselves, in terms of the value that their contacts have for solving problems of the transitional environment. 'Of course I keep in touch with my old contacts. For example, when I am doing a job in Jesenické Strojírny I turn to my old friends' (Middle manager, Montáže Jesenice). One female manager involved in the job swap arrangements in Montáže Jesenice spoke of the former *nomenklatura* manager concerned: 'The organization did not want to lose him, because he is very expert and experienced . . . He has lots of contacts in the business.' The Montáže Jesenice manager in question also saw the importance of his contacts:

> I still have many personal contacts [from the past] and I still use them. I exchange a lot of information with old Jesenické Strojírny contacts, and also with economists in other assembly enterprises who are [now] competitors . . . [We] often get together under the auspices of the general directors, who are well-connected into the industry.

The financial director of Vols, one of the three surviving *nomenklatura* directors who had held on to their pre-1989 posts, was well-connected with the banks and emergent financial institutions. He was so successful at gaining access to money to deal with payment inability and to keep the business going that he had a reputation as a 'financial magician'.

In contrast, the new managers who had not been *nomenklatura* could not compete in this way. For example: 'The enterprise had good contacts with foreigners, but my personal contacts are limited, because of politics [in the former regime]. Only the highest level [of managers] were allowed contacts' (Middle manager, Jesenické Strojírny). The quantity and quality of post-communist managers' external contacts was directly related to their position in the pre-1989 regime. Since, for a variety of reasons, the ability to utilize socio-economic networks was understood to be decisive in helping enterprises to survive the problematic period after 1989, the ex-*nomenklatura* managers were considered as bringing not only significant managerial experience to the new world, but also a valuable resource. The importance of networks can also be judged in the external appointments that were made to senior and middle management positions.

After the revolution, the new general directors acted swiftly to attract certain senior personnel who had been released by the changing and collapsing role of the central planning institutions. In fact, as we know from Chapter 3, the VHJs had begun to diminish in importance as the 1988 state enterprise legislation took effect, so by 1990 there were already some very well-connected former VHJ managers looking for new jobs. There is some evidence that the new enterprise managements looked to secure the careers of former colleagues who had been close and useful colleagues before the changes, and were themselves bearers of very well-established socio-economic networks. Just as those internal demotees in the enterprises have tended to be recycled into more responsible jobs since the revolution (see Table 7.4, p. 151), so the enterprises picked up several VHJ and FTO directors and managers whose careers had been prematurely curtailed.

Agstroj, for example, had been very close to the industry's VHJ and FTO, which in the early months of 1990 had made redundant many experienced former *nomenklatura* managers. One former sales director of the VHJ, Agrov, had been appointed to the post of marketing manager, and his previous job had involved him in formal and informal contacts with the ten most important enterprises in the Agstroj's industrial sector, plus the FTOs. He described how his earlier job had brought him into close relationships with sales and trade managers in the enterprises, and said that this network of friends was still the basis of much of his work in the post-1989 Agstroj. Agstroj also appointed Agrov's industry-wide metallurgical expert to a senior management post, and his former contacts had been one possible factor in his decision to put forward a competing privatization project for his division – which was unsuccessful.

The senior managers of Jesenické Strojírny also decided that their future would be enhanced by offering senior positions to former managers from the central planning institutions. They had re-engaged the services of a former Jesenické Strojírny deputy director who had been promoted in the 1980s to the VHJ in Prague, and also in 1994 had given a part-time directorate post to a senior administrator from the Ministry of Industry who had lost his job. But most significantly, in 1990 they had attracted back to Jesenice, to take up a new post of strategy director, a manager who had left Jesenické Strojírny for a senior post in Prague after 1968. The importance of this appointment is manifold, and we will make reference to it again when we consider issues of organizational structuring below. But, in the view of one middle manager, '[He] is the most powerful manager. He has contacts in the ministry and could force through some central changes' (Middle manager, Jesenické

Strojírny). The economic significance of these networks cannot be underestimated in the conditions of transience that pertained in the early 1990s. As we have seen in Chapter 6, the problems for mechanical engineering enterprises had become intense during the early transition years, with the collapse of previously secure foreign markets, as well as reduced demand at home.

Regarding foreign trade, both Vols and Jesenické Strojírny continued to have very good contacts in the countries of the former Soviet Union. These markets were felt to be vital in the longer term, because both enterprises had strong regional reputations resulting from the past, and could deliver quality goods at prices that were cheaper than those of Western competitors. In the short term, business in these areas was decimated by the changes, but the quality of the contacts permitted the managers at Vols to devise transitional methods with very strong echoes from the past. As Vols's marketing manager commented in 1992: 'We expect a long-term future [in the former Soviet Union] after short-term problems. We have used bartering as the main method to overcome the problems for three to five years.'

One arrangement had involved the delivery of traditional engineering products to Russia in return for a huge quantity of railway track, which could be reprocessed in the foundry as raw materials. Springing from the quality of personal contacts in Russia, and the kind of trust and practice that was more typical of international trade in the CMEA, this arrangement suited both parties under transitional conditions, where Russia already owed substantial debt. The products were 'sold', production levels were sustained, workers were productively employed and the physical exchange proved a more reliable compensation, given the weakness of the ruble at the time. The sales director of Vols continued, with a certain touch of humour: 'We have other imminent deals with Russia – to be paid in dollars. I am an optimist, I hope the Russians will pay up. Bartering and such deals are a reflection of our historical contacts.' Bartering was also practised in the other enterprises as an indispensable instrument for the strategy of survival, and had to be effected through strong socio-economic networks, which in turn could only have been activated by former *nomenklatura*.

All the enterprises continued to have and use former contacts in the enterprises that succeeded the FTOs. Many of these contacts served as representatives of the enterprises in far-flung countries. 'Without contacts you have no business success in your market' (Senior commercial manager, Jesenické Strojírny). Contacts in the former FTOs were particularly important, because such trade enterprises had inherited offices and client networks from the past. 'We [still] have dealers in foreign countries from former days' (Director, Jesenické Strojírny). Following the revolution, Agstroj had exported to some Western markets using an export agency, which had in its earlier incarnation been an FTO centred on another large engineering enterprise in Bohemia. However, Agstroj had been let down, so managers reactivated contacts in its former FTO with some success.

But contacts were also essential in dealing with the downturn in the domestic market. In this context, the ability to operationalize old VHJ and ministry contacts was central to the management strategy of enterprise survival. The contacts of surviving and promoted *nomenklatura* directors and of new appointees were often used to circumvent the forces of the embryonic market place. As a middle manager in Jesenické Strojírny commented, 'In the past, VVV was Jesenické Strojírny's VHJ. This formal link was broken in 1988, but the close historical relationship ensures continuing cooperation'. We have similarly seen, throughout this exposition, that the relationship between Jesenické Strojírny and Montáže Jesenice has been maintained on the same basis. In Agstroj, the VHJ background of the marketing manager also gave the enterprise good opportunities for cooperating on projects, or on the mutual provision of supplies, thus by-passing the market process. In Vols, the marketing manager claimed that selling the enterprise's products in the Czech Republic is a set of 'clear simple tasks, because there are good contacts with [for example] the other metallurgical plants'.

Senior managers brought socio-economic networks into play to great effect to cope with the interim problems of the economic transition – particularly maintaining output and employment during the immediate post-revolution industrial decline – but it was equally clear that former contacts would not offer a complete, longer-term solution to enterprise survival. The old networks began to falter over time.

> I am still using the contacts which were the pre-revolution customers . . .
> But as the personal contacts have left their enterprises, these networks
> are breaking down. (Director, Montáže Jesenice)

> Old partners are still very important in . . . [our industrial] sector because
> there is still no competition; we are still the only firm with a [specialized
> piece of equipment]. Personal relationships and contacts are very impor-
> tant in my work, I know lots of peers to whom I can turn . . . [But] many
> communist contacts who were experts have been swept away because of
> politics after the revolution. (Middle manager, Montáže Jesenice)

A director at Jesenické Strojírny makes the same kind of point:

> In the former Czechoslovakia, there are over 400 places where we have
> completed work. We try to keep up contacts. We make trips to reconnect
> clients in the former state enterprises, for example. Some of the enter-
> prises have now been split up, which makes it necessary to find new
> contacts as well as relying on old ones.

Most directors knew the limits of their old contacts. The well-connected marketing manager may have used his former VHJ network 'lots', but he knew he had to seek out new contacts.

The socio-economic networks of the former communist managers were obviously very important in getting the enterprises through the early painful years of transition, reproducing former practices as a significant aspect of emergent post-communist management and reinforcing in some degree the social structures of business that had developed under state socialism. Of course, the importance of networking served to underline the indispensability of the experience and knowledge locked up in the former managerial cadre; just as the continuity of former *nomenklatura* managers in senior enterprise positions virtually guaranteed that networking would become an important crutch to fall back on in the solution to the problems of socio-economic transience. In this interaction, enterprises were helped to survive, and the surviving managers were given a solid rationale to explain their economic utility and their managerial legitimacy.

Organizational restructuring: The first moves

The strategic teams that were established from 1990 (see Chapter 7) undertook a number of complex tasks in order to secure the survival of the enterprises until privatization could give the anticipated greater assurance of longer-term success, but rated the process of privatization itself as the main goal. Despite espoused government policy, most senior managers saw it as crucial to them and their enterprises to reorganize and restructure so as respond to the progressive elements and expectations in their business environments. Thus, organizational redesign became the central feature of enterprises' *formal* responses to external changes, especially in their ambitions to privatize. This early restructuring process was uniform across all four enterprises, in that it took the form of radical decentralization – or, as it turns out, given the regressive elements of socio-economic transience, *over*-radical decentralization.

Having rejected the former hierarchical, functional structures as inappropriate to management in the new era, the strategic management teams turned to known Western organizational designs, importing the charts, integrative mechanisms and motivating systems of the divisionalized structure. The divisionalized form was accepted by senior managers, almost without criticism, as the structural answer to transitional problems, in that it was visibly different from the centralized functional bureaucracy known to be 'normal' in large-scale Western enterprises operating in similar industries, a first step towards 'marketizing' relationships between the major business activities – a phrase with strong, positive post-communist resonances – and a clear and visible statement of intent to get a grip of managerial and labour productivity.

The first structural responses to the environment of transience were common to each enterprise.

> In 1989 [*sic*] there were moves towards a divisionalized structure in Agstroj, with the aim of giving more autonomy to the individual production units, getting them to take more care of themselves . . . they had to learn to work on their own [after everything had been managed from the centre]. (Director, Agstroj)

Decentralization in Agstroj actually created ten divisions, reporting to a strategic centre, but the 'structure had to be changed again, because there were too many divisions and the span of control was too great' (Plant director, Agstroj). Even with a lesser degree of decentralization, managers found it more difficult than expected to operate the structure. A middle manager explained: 'The structure is different [from before 1989], but in some cases it is only a formal change, not real. The divisions should be more autonomous but the present state means that it is not really working.'

The experiences of Jesenické Strojírny were much the same. The strategy team was headed by a well-connected director who had been reappointed in 1990 from Prague. This director had worked in the old organization and management department before 1968, and had, with his colleagues, been responsible for the design of a very progressive, decentralized structure, which, following the onset of normalization, had reverted to the traditional functional form. Respondents noted his insistence on implementing a variation of the old, discarded model, and in 1991 the enterprise adopted a multi-divisional form, which soon ran into troubles like those encountered at Agstroj:

> the first major change was creating a structure in 1991 with sixteen independent plants, selling products to each other. This was not successful because each factory [used its new autonomy and] effectively employed too many people. They protected their people and services [and] overall it was inefficient . . . [Moreover] the general director had too many managers to control.

We can understand more about the failure of these structures by considering the motives of the divisional and middle managers who operated them – a point we shall return to in the section below. In the meantime, it should be noted that the other two enterprises underwent a similar experience. Montáže Jesenice designed a new structure from its inception in 1990, and introduced it in 1992. The structure was a hybrid, defining the operations units as divisional profit centres and the support units as departmental cost centres. This form threw the enterprise into disarray and conflict and very soon needed more attention.

> Now Montáže Jesenice is going through a difficult time with reorganization into divisions . . . All divisions are going their own way, free to earn

divisional profits. The organizational structure is totally new . . . and some areas are chaotic. (Divisional manager, Montáže Jesenice)

Vols too almost immediately introduced a divisional structure, but, unlike the other enterprises, was less ambitious from the start, despite the ultimate ambition to move to profit centres. The new divisions did create some inter-unit conflict, but in the first phase the divisions still basically operated and contributed as cost centres.

The massive shift to decentralization and its embodiment in a multi-divisional form seemed to be a consensual move, indicative of the new managerial rhetoric that had evolved in the first few years. It is plain that these new structures appealed strongly to the post-communist managers, especially for legitimatory reasons. These new structural forms possessed features that were very important symbols of the new democratic, market-economic society. To reiterate an argument from Chapter 7, they were a manifest declaration of separation from the past, because they offered organizational characteristics at variance from the hierarchical, autocratic, conformist patterns of the national and state enterprise. In principle, the structures symbolized freedom, autonomy, independence, initiative and responsibility, all values lacking in communism and popular in the post-communist backlash. They not only signalled desirable changes to employees and the wider community, they also held out real prospects for the status of the many state socialist managers who had survived the changes. The multi-divisional form was blatantly Western in its origins, and it suggested management mechanisms and ideas that were visibly modern, with a flavour of the new market-economic era. The new structures were not just seen to be necessary, efficient responses to the emergent capitalist economy, but demonstrated that managements whose credentials were deeply implicated in an unjust and anti-meritocratic past could take on, apply and implement more appropriate management ideas and practices.

In other words, the managers could be seen to be actively interested and involved in the success of the post-communist enterprise, thereby storing up greater credibility for the future. Moreover, as our managers revealed during early interviews, the simple divisional structures were not the end of their ambitions. Extending the rhetoric of decentralization, independence and responsibility even further, the divisions as cost centres would evolve into marketized profit centres, which would then be spun out as autonomous market players under a holding structure. Senior managers could see not only an ideological advantage in openly espousing such radical decentralization; it is likely that many could also see ways of creating a financially beneficial organizational environment for their own managerial careers.

In their anxiety to demonstrate their new managerial wisdom and conversion, and given their small direct knowledge and experience of capitalism, it is likely that the enterprise managements moved too quickly towards market-economic forms when their socio-economic environments were still too influenced by behaviour and patterns from the past. Since much business was still being conducted according to former economic practices, the new structures were more likely to distract managers from the tasks of survival. In short, there is a suspicion that managers had opted with enthusiasm for divisionalized structures as a response to progressive, normative pressures in the reinstitutionalizing environment (see below), rather than to the immediate business needs of their task environment.[3] However, as we shall argue below, the most intensive impediments to the new structures originated from within the enterprises, as divisional and middle managers struggled to come to terms with the internal organizational environment created by divisionalization.

Management responses to organizational changes

While the senior managers were coping with the tribulations of the transitional environment by drawing on the trusted practices and networks that had seen them through the economic problems of state socialism, middle managers were trying to face up to the problems posed in their own changed environment. Having been used to working passively and obediently in the hierarchical structures, many of them found it difficult to adjust to, sometimes even more difficult to trust, the decentralized systems of management and organization which swept through all the enterprises from the start of the 1990s. Senior managers soon began to realize that real obstacles to their structural designs lay not so much in technical systems and structures – although there were undeniable weaknesses in the technical support that could be given for the new informational needs of the multi-divisional form – but with the attitudes and behaviour of the employees. This included manual workers, such as the unskilled employees who had developed poor working practices in the past; and especially middle-ranking managers, whose positive support and attitudes were necessary for making a success of the new divisionalized structures. A director at Jesenické Strojírny complained: 'The most difficult thing is to change the thinking of lower and middle managers in the factories.'

At greater length, Montáže Jesenice's general director located the source of middle management attitudes in the work they did in the past. In describing their mentality,

> I would use two words: passivity and laziness. For example, in the past in the commercial department they were used to just sitting down and turning work away. Now, instead of showing initiative to find business they still sit by the phone waiting for clients to ring.

As a middle manager in Jesenické Strojírny explained,

> The current mentality, and it is the same everywhere in the Czech Republic, results from the previous period. People did not have the

opportunity to show that they are best, or to exert themselves, and there is rather a big group of employees who are still waiting to see what will happen. The most active, assertive people have already left . . . for better opportunities.

The new organization structures which were developed to take the enterprises into the new post-communist era created a completely new environment which formally demanded that middle managers be active rather than passive, and seek responsibility rather than shun it. These requirements disqualified many former managers from immediately taking on the new duties. As a middle manager said in Vols, 'the older generation of managers should leave . . . because thirty years of managing in the old regime has an effect on a manager's competence'. One of the issues here was to unlearn bad habits, but another was how to overcome the new fears and suspicions created by the changed management environment. Some of the fears were simply personal and psychological, as one particularly honest middle manager in Vols revealed about his redefined job:

> The problem with the central plan was that everything was written and there was no place for 'activity' . . . Sometimes [now], when I need to take a decision, I just feel confused. Work is based in [management] teams, but many members are unable to take decisions without getting confirmation from above. I worry so much about my responsibility for the decisions that sometimes I cannot sleep.

The general director of Montáže Jesenice experienced such reactions from middle managers. Having served under the previous plant director, who had been notorious for his autocratic rule, they could not take responsibility for the smallest decision without checking at the very top. These personal worries about ability to cope were supplemented by mistrust and suspicion about the way the new support systems worked. For example, the introduction of divisionalized structures in all four enterprises required both responsible decision-making in the divisions and the communication of accurate economic information for control purposes. In each enterprise, middle managers showed themselves to be unable or unwilling to play this new management game. In Vols, the strategy director described what had happened:

> [Vols has increased the] . . . degree of decentralization to the divisions, [and changed] the relationship between centre and divisions . . . Divisional strategic plans [were] accepted as the method of bottom-up corporate planning . . . Investment will be developed through these decentralized strategic plans [rather than through] centrally determined investment . . . Some divisions have been more forthcoming than others . . . Some have become more market-oriented than others because of the people involved.

Middle managers found the pursuit of decentralization threatening not only to their managerial competence, but also to their feelings of security, their experiences and their established practices of controlling their managerial environments. In the past, they had grown accustomed to operating in an environment of mistrust and fear, and, when asked for information – economic or otherwise – that reported on their own or their colleagues' performances, they would routinely 'clean it up' to minimize questions. The fear of punishment which was characteristic of state socialist management continued to create problems for the new central units in getting a clear picture of the problems and performance of the new divisions. 'Divisions are keeping [undeclared] reserves of money, which is an old custom. They do not understand the economics of the whole company, but we cannot get the whole picture' (Finance manager, Montáže Jesenice).

The general director of Montáže Jesenice was aware of the problems of the withholding and biasing of information.

> The thinking of people is changing very slowly . . . For example, the new structures are not trusted because people are worried about losing their jobs . . . [The quality of information] is rather worse than better, because in giving me information [managers] . . . worry about my judgements. For example, they underestimate performance forecasting figures because they worry that I will cut their budgets if they do not reach the target figure. This is a throwback to the old system when if you did not fulfil the plan you would lose money.

With his financial director, he used informed guesswork to counter-bias forecasts.

Placing greater independence of divisions in the hands of managers inexperienced in exercising responsibility and fearful of making mistakes is a recipe for failure. In paradoxical fashion, the initial radical decentralization in some respects created the conditions for its own downfall. The examples above demonstrate how information can be manipulated within systems, but when managers are conscious of the need to reduce costs in order to meet financial targets, they can go about eroding the very technical systems upon which decentralization is founded.

> [Before] nobody was bothered about costs. Now client departments have to think about costs . . . because each department is controlled by costing methods . . . [e.g.] their use of computing services is tracked by flows of accounting data . . . When departments realized that they had to pay for their . . . [computer] terminals, they gave them back. This means that the use of the terminals decreased by 50 per cent and [the technical system] . . . was being under-used. But the cost still had to be borne by the enterprise. (Computer manager, Jesenické Strojírny)

But resistance was not reserved for middle managers: even the divisional managers, usually members of the senior management team, found the implications of divisionalization difficult to handle. In Vols, for example, the creation of divisions and the anticipated move towards profit centre status made explicit the vulnerabilities of certain areas of Vols's business, with the metallurgy division being particularly exposed for its overstaffing, out-of-date technology, weak market position and other inefficiencies. The implications for employment in the division, and as a result for the community of Volna, were immense, and managers, even at the most senior levels, found the proposed marketization of Vols's internal structures difficult to accept. It was impossible for these managers to ignore the legacy of the enterprise's close integration in the social community, because, from a very personal viewpoint, they found it inconceivable to be associated with a policy that made their neighbours unemployed in a local economy with, in 1990 to 1992, few real alternative job opportunities. By early 1993, Vols's top management had shelved the idea of profit centres, because the resistance had made unreliable the quality of information and decision-making at divisional level. For many directors whose attitudes were still affected by social thinking, this outcome came as a personal relief.

In Jesenické Strojírny, the new divisional structures served to exacerbate inter-functional and inter-plant rivalries and conflicts that had been a normal, but submerged, part of organizational relationships for many years. Under the former hierarchical system, there had always been some structural tension between the commercial, production and technical departments, which naturally arose in large-scale project work that took years to complete and entailed the resolution of product specification, production synchronization and product delivery problems. The new highly decentralized structure, however, created free-standing, profit-seeking divisions which served to reduce the degree of integration between these functions, in a business which, for the most part, demanded close cooperation and collaboration. Suddenly, there were a number of individual production divisions (e.g. heavy and light machinery products), which could earn revenue and profit by selling single machines to customers; the commercial division which was in charge of the most profitable business of turnkey contracts, and commissioned services and machines from the individual support and plant divisions, but received the contracted payments directly from clients; and the technical division, which had to sell its services to each division. The plant directors felt that they had limited opportunities for profits because of their marginal involvement in turnkey projects, and that they were more or less servants at the beck and call of the new, powerful commercial division, which, to underline the point, moved into delightful new office premises during the changes. It did not go unnoticed that the general director hailed from a commerce background. Early resistance and disagreements in top management reinstituted a degree of recentralization in the short run, but, unlike in Vols, the dominant coalition of general director and strategy director was so powerful that more radical decentralization towards independent 'daughter companies' soon returned to the agenda.

Montáže Jesenice experienced the same initial problem with the new divisions, which, in seeking to maximize their own objectives, were acting to subvert the integration essential to its business. Both financial and commercial managers identified this tendency:

> The organization needs to be internally well-connected, and the process of decentralization challenges this principle. (Finance manager, Montáže Jesenice)

> Lateral communications need improvement to meet contracts, especially in the preparation of foreign contracts. Divisions are keeping information to themselves about potential foreign clients [in order to claim them for their own division]. This is happening at all levels. (Commercial manager, Montáže Jesenice)

It is evident that, after 1989, many managers at all levels were quite unhabituated to the assumptions that underpin the Western model of divisionalization, and unfamiliar with the attitudes and behaviours necessary to make it work. Decentralization brought out old managerial reactions that had been born and bred to respond to state enterprise environments, and the new managerial ideas and systems were weakened if not undermined by such behavioural responses. Whether through the enactment of old 'pink values' in protection of employment and functional empires, the reproduction of old practices like information distortion and hoarding, or the inflammation of latent inter-functional tensions, the new structures were effectively resisted from the inside, while being over-progressive for the prevailing environmental conditions of socio-economic transience. Decentralization had gone too far too quickly.

Conclusions

In this chapter we have continued the examination of the processes of institutional change in the four former state enterprises that have participated in this project. Building on the work in Chapter 7, we have addressed at the level of organization and management those issues that arise from what we have called socio-economic transience: the ambiguous coexistence of economic and institutional relics from the command-economic past, and the emergent economic and institutional expectations of a future market economy. Managers have devised basic, uncomplicated strategies to deal with economic problems emanating from such an environment, formulated around a concern for short- to medium-term survival, rather than longer-term growth with a clear direction. For various reasons, we have identified the primary rule of this strategy as the maintenance of optimal employment levels. Since the major part of the post-communist management body – especially at senior directorate levels – had been implicated in the former regime, they had very strong incentives to make a good job of enterprise survival. Managerial survival itself, especially before the arrival of new owners in the privatization process, hung on their early transitional success.

A necessary, rational and effective part of the strategy has been the reproduction of managerial practices that had their origins in solving the enterprise problems of the command economy. One example is the socio-economic networks that ex-*nomenklatura* managers had nurtured before 1989, and maintained as critical post-communist resources which could be enacted in order to ameliorate the dilemmas of socio-economic transience. In addition to being a relatively effective recipe for enterprise survival in these circumstances, the reproduction of former practices had the paradoxical effects of reintegrating the surviving managers as a social group, while reinforcing and sustaining the regressive components that demanded such responses in the first place. In other words, while such practices were undeniably important, if not essential, ways of responding to the remaining non-market elements in the business environments of the enterprises, at the same time they were potentially mechanisms for resisting the development of a new management body and weakening the embryonic and delicate market processes. The logical consequence is that to the extent that these old management customs remain a critical part of the post-communist management repertoire in the longer period of transition, they are likely to become *reinstitutionalized* as a significant and enduring characteristic of the Czech way of managing a market economy – underlain with a new set of post-communist rationales. We will take up this point in Chapter 10.

Our discussion suggests a further consequence of the perpetuation of former state socialist managerial attitudes and practices. We have seen in this chapter that some reassertions of former managerial patterns have retarded the processes of reinstitutionalization by virtue of a reluctance to ratify new ideas. Managerial responses to the new divisionalized organizational structures have been sociologically understandable because of their lack of experience of, and the symbolic significance of, the new behaviours demanded by the changes. Managers continued to reproduce what had been perfectly rational responses under the social and organizational conditions of the command economy, such as withholding or vetting information. Sometimes such responses were almost innocent; at other times they reflected values and attitudes that had been part of respondents' self and professional definition as bona fide enterprise managers. Either way, managers at even senior levels were able to undermine the new structures that represented the new market-economic world.

We now turn to the last substantive part in the jigsaw. Having discussed the processes of deinstitutionalization and institutional inertia, associated with the distancing of management from the past while simultaneously using old practices to deal with the transitional present, we move on to consider the nature of reinstitutionalization, as managers attempted to take on and promulgate the values and knowledge directly linked to private enterprise and the market economy.

Notes

1 In fact, Montáže Jesenice recruited its site employees from all over the Czech Republic, and many of its skilled workers had voluntarily left for better paid jobs in private firms – the management was very concerned about the low level of employment.
2 We have already noted in Chapter 7 the additional development of a legitimating rhetoric that these surviving managers had been the professionals: that is, the technically competent part of the *nomenklatura* cadre.
3 One senior manager at Montáže Jesenice was so keen to learn about Western structural ideas that, as organizational researchers, we were quizzed about other alternative forms. His eyes lit up at the very mention of 'matrix structures'. Then came the instant request for us to send him more information.

9 The redefining of Czech management and enterprise

In the previous three chapters we have analysed the transforming task and institutional contexts of the post-1989 Czech(oslovak) socio-economic transition, and have examined how the external processes of deinstitutionalization and institutional inertia have been reflected and reproduced in the behaviour of enterprise managers, as they have confronted the ambiguities and contradictions of post-communism. We now take up the question of how, during the transition period, the post-communist managers have gone about redefining the technical and normative components of management and organization in order to validate their claims to be bona fide managers of bona fide private enterprises. We consider the strategies of reinstitutionalization, which have in general involved making visible connections between managers' own values and practices in the transition period and those already accepted in established capitalist economies as being both efficient and legitimate.

The chapter is structured around two sets of issues: first, the reconstruction of the enterprises as market-economic institutions, with features of the capitalist corporation, including productivized, profit-oriented, market-oriented activities which take place within an appropriate structural milieu; second, the emergence of post-communist management grounded in market-economic rationality, and presentable to the national and international business community as being knowledgeable and competent in dealing with the contingencies and vicissitudes of a global economic environment. Since a central aspect of this second issue involves questions about the development of market-economic knowledge, rhetoric and practices within the management body, we consider the processes of and constraints on management learning. The two processes of reinstitutionalization are, of course, heavily interconnected, because the adoption of the 'right' organizational characteristics is not only a technical question of managerial competence, but also a deeply symbolic act, being direct proof of the credentials and credibility of the surviving managers.

The enterprise as private company

We have already considered ways in which the state-owned enterprises began to change in response to the transitional environment that they confronted during the early 1990s. These changes were partly a result of the decisions taken by the senior managers to deinstitutionalize former state socialist systems and structures, and partly a response to the conditions of transience that tended to reinforce the appropriateness of past practices. In Chapter 8, we examined the early, contested attempts to create new decentralized organizational structures, and in Chapter 7, we remarked on the processes of reorganization that effectively reduced the status and visibility of the previously tainted personnel function. In this section, the processes of organizational restructuring again come under scrutiny as we examine them from the perspective of reinstitutionalization and redefinition. The most notable change has been the taking on of privatized status, and we start by looking at the relationship between the new ownership structures and management decision-making.

Boards of directors, management discretion and corporate governance

From 1993 onwards, the former state-owned enterprises, which had become in the interim period of privatization state-owned joint stock companies, took on the status of private joint stock companies. For Jesenické Strojírny, Montáže Jesenice and Vols, this was accomplished wholly or mainly through participation in the voucher privatization process; at almost the same time, Agstroj merged with its engine supplier and became 'privatized' in the process. The new boards of directors met from mid-1993 onwards, though the managements had in practice collaborated with the larger shareholders for several months. The structures of ownership were quite diverse, as was the influence exercised by new external board members over executive management; but there were also identifiable patterns.

In the three large enterprises, the state continued as a significant shareholder, particularly in Agstroj and Jesenické Strojírny, where, respectively, 70 per cent and 35 per cent[1] of property was still held by the NPF. Ownership of the remaining 30 per cent of shares in Agstroj was so dispersed that IPFs were virtually locked out of any external influence. In Vols, Jesenické Strojírny and Montáže Jesenice, several IPFs had managed to accumulate enough shares to be able to nominate their own representatives. Concentration of ownership was at its highest in Montáže Jesenice, where 70 per cent of shares had been bought by four funds, whose representatives formed the four to three majority on the board of directors. Eight IPFs owned over 50 per cent of Vols, but there has emerged one dominant IPF, whose representative, the owner of a successful management consultancy business in Prague, was elected chair of the board, and the external members took a majority of six to three. In Jesenické Strojírny, only two IPFs managed to accumulate 10 to 12 per cent of shares each, and they took a seat on the board of directors alongside the NPF, with one member who represented the many thousands of dispersed individual shareholders, who personally owned 4 per cent. After the second wave of privatization, the NPF's shareholding reduced to less than 10 per cent, and the position of the two IPFs, one a local fund partly owned by Jesenické Strojírny's former enterprise director, Engineer J, was consolidated.

It is evident from our interviews that, in the early period following privatization, the senior managers continued to exert a great deal of uncontested influence over most strategic issues in their enterprises, probably resulting from the IPFs' lack of relevant experience and the internal managers' monopoly of knowledge of the business. In 1993, for example, the general director of Montáže Jesenice observed:

> The board of directors accepted my plans. [With] . . . the management being in a minority [on the Board], some problems are inevitable, but up to now there has been agreement after long discussion [with management decisions] . . . The representatives only want to know what I do, to approve or disapprove. They let me get on with managing.

The financial director of Jesenické Strojírny offered a similarly positive view of the early board of directors: 'The board is well balanced. The investment funds give good advice . . . [but] management proposals are usually successful because they are well prepared.' This initial passivity of the IPFs was also identified in Vols:

> The first AGM was held in October 1993 . . . Beyond looking after shareholder interests, the investment fund representatives leave management to the managers. [This approach was exemplified] in the confirmation of all senior personnel in their managerial and directorate posts. (Strategy director, Vols)

The stronger the continued interest of the NPF in enterprise ownership, the larger was the external involvement in internal decision-making. At Jesenické Strojírny, for example, the NPF representative was understood as 'both an active and a powerful member of the board'. Unsurprisingly, the NPF was particularly concerned with the state of management in Agstroj, where there were changes in the internal senior team resulting from its 'backdoor' privatization via its merger with Stroměsto Engines in July 1993. One Agstroj director noted:

> [Its shareholding] gives the NPF . . . strong control over Agstroj, but this is better than being under ministry control. We [Agstroj] can act effectively as a joint stock company. The NPF mainly exercises power over financial matters.

It is noticeable over the first two to three years of privatized status that the external members of the boards of directors became more bold in their decision-making, and began to find ways of exercising greater influence over internal management. Following the failure of the NPF to find buyers and the continuing weak performance of Agstroj, this process was specially clear. In 1994, the NPF had sold its share of Agstroj to the Consolidation Bank (see Chapter 6), which therefore took over the two NPF seats on the board. Interviewed in September 1995, one director described the changing state of affairs:

> Major financial and property decisions must be approved by the statutory organ in Prague, and Agstroj management only makes decisions about the everyday running of the business, and on contracts up to a certain value . . . The board meets every fourteen days, and the Consolidation Bank now exercises greater central control than last year.

The greater control included replacing two senior managers with external appointees whose direct remit was the reassertion of hierarchical discipline over the enterprise. We shall return to this matter below, when we consider the continuing processes of reorganization.

The trend towards greater external influence was less obvious and restrictive in the other enterprises, but was present. In Vols, for example, a senior director in late 1995 explained:

> Influence processes in the board are getting more obvious. At the beginning, influence was wielded 100 per cent by the management, and while the results were good, there is no reason to change . . . If performance is poor [as has happened over the past year], the externals may well use their power more, and apply their own expertise.

At the same time, our Jesenické Strojírny respondent suggested a similar process: 'power has shifted towards the board of directors, with its external representatives, thus excluding many top managers . . . The board [now] prefers to make everyday rather than [strategic] decisions because they are easier.'

It would appear that the external representatives of the IPFs were developing greater confidence, and taking a much greater interest in internal decision-making of the enterprises (Brom and Orenstein, 1994). Indeed, the same Jesenické Strojírny respondent suggested that the representatives had begun to use their directorships as a means of pursuing their own interests, or those of their investment companies. We noted in Chapter 6 that some critical economists had identified the tendency for enterprise executive decision-making to become intertwined with sustaining the financial interests of the banks that owned the ICs who owned the IPFs. The IPF representatives in the four enterprises had real power to resist senior management preferences or to insist on their own. There appeared to be an enormous scope for bargaining at the board level, with external representatives nominating their preferred suppliers (Jesenické Strojírny), offering their own marketing, advertising (Jesenické Strojírny) and consultancy (Vols) services, recommending appointments to senior management positions (Jesenické Strojírny and Agstroj) etc. The importance of these activities for the general maintenance of the socio-economic networks discussed in Chapter 8 should not be overlooked.

The story of Montáže Jesenice provides an interesting conclusion to this section on changing ownership patterns and control. Made independent of Jesenické Strojírny in 1990, Montáže Jesenice management had always retained close business and personal relationships with its former 'parent'. In fact, while the contracted assembly work it did for Jesenické Strojírny diminished initially, since 1993 the proportion began to increase again. In their separation they had continued to own some common property, including a factory site in Jesenice, which Montáže Jesenice wanted to convert to manufacture assembly equipment. Late in 1994, the Jesenické Strojírny and Montáže Jesenice boards of directors agreed an equity for property swap, in which Jesenické Strojírny took a 20 per cent stake in Montáže Jesenice in exchange for its half share of the factory site. As a result, Jesenické Strojírny also received a seat on Montáže Jesenice's board, diluting the control of the previously influential IPFs. Through a variety of arrangements that have not been transparent to the outsider, by the beginning of 1996 Jesenické Strojírny had increased its stake in Montáže Jesenice to 51 per cent, effectively welcoming its former plant back into the fold. Montáže Jesenice's loss of independence was made plain in Jesenické Strojírny's annual report, presented at its 1996 AGM, where Montáže Jesenice was included as a significant property, and its results were hailed as part of Jesenické Strojírny's consolidated performance.[2] This is an ultimately ironic commentary on the process of privatization, where, for Montáže Jesenice at least, the market economy has effectively turned back the clocks to incorporate market-independent relationships within the hierarchical system of corporate governance.

Organizational restructuring continued

We have argued that enterprise restructuring has been a major tool in the hands of senior managers: a means of expressing their claims to both market-economic management technical competence and renewed managerial legitimacy in the face of their communist pasts. In Chapter 8 we used the example of divisionalization to illustrate both the attempted break from the past attachment to hierarchical and centralized forms, and the reluctance of senior and middle managers in the face of significant changes in their managerial environments. In this section, we wish to emphasize restructuring as an instrument of reinstitutionalization and redefinition.

The decisions of the new privatized boards of directors immediately confirmed virtually all the surviving enterprise managers in their positions,[3] and thus served to reduce the felt vulnerability of the former *nomenklatura* who dominated the senior management ranks. Since the new boards of directors also opted to play a fairly passive role in enterprise management (see above), it was possible, even encouraged, for the strategic management teams to proceed, perhaps at an even faster rate, with their radical decentralization plans. In each enterprise, managers accepted such restructuring as the one true path to the private corporation, and some managers revealed a strong emotional commitment to this policy; though it was underpinned by, and articulated in the form of, market-economic rationality. This is not to say that all managers accepted these ideas as the whole truth, since many expressed personal doubts about their relevance to the Czech situation, and were critical *on a personal basis* of the remedies prescribed by Western knowledge. In this sense, the new rules of Western management remained contested, but the institutional demands of post-communist reality were too powerful to allow effective expression of individual scepticism. We would argue that emotional commitment and the withholding of criticism are characteristics strongly suggestive of a dominant process of institutional patterning, whereby the new decentralized forms – whether based around product or geographical divisions, profit-centred business units or autonomous subsidiaries – have been accepted as appropriate market-economic structural redefinitions and copied into the post-communist enterprise (Fligstein, 1985). While it might be possible to argue for more technical, task-environment type rationality in the case of Vols, for instance, even in this instance the normative-emotional appeal to Western management knowledge and patterns was plainly a fundamental and overwhelming motivation behind the decision-making process.

We saw in Chapter 8 that the decentralizing reforms, which in the early years took the form of divisionalization to cost centres and profit centres, were in general over-radical – again a hallmark of institutional isomorphic or patterning processes – and had been turned back by managerial resistance. The success of privatization gave the managements a fillip to re-engage with these structural changes. Jesenické Strojírny provides the extreme example. The embarrassing and expensive reversion from extreme divisionalization in 1993 had led to the retirement of the strategy director (see Chapter 8), to be replaced by a man who, however, shared a similar ambition to drive Jesenické Strojírny towards a holding company structure. These strategy directors were of the same age and had worked together in 1968 to design divisional structures in the spirit of the Prague Spring; their design being rejected by the course of normalization, their commitment after 1989 was seen by many as a rather personal crusade. The new market-economic circumstances breathed new life into this old solution and further vindicated the completion of a holding ('mother') company structure, with multiple 'daughters' operating more or less autonomously as profit-seeking companies. The holding company concept offered a structural form which fully reflected the new logic of internal marketization and the imported managerial rhetoric of decentralization. Thus justified and rationalized by reference to Western ideas, the holding company scheme, the personal ambition of the new strategy director and the general director (whose influence had itself been ratified and strengthened by the new board of directors), could be put forward as a logical means of modernizing the post-communist enterprise.

There was continuing resistance to the increased marketization of relations between the divisions on the grounds that the most profitable and fundamental business of Jesenické Strojírny was turnkey contracts, for which high degrees of integration and cooperation between structural units were required. But the general director, the strategy director and the commercial director (whose new daughter company would have most to gain by being in charge of turnkey operations) formed the most powerful of cabals, each with a seat on the new board of directors. The post-privatization confidence and influence of the general director were crucial in promulgating the holding company. The one outspoken voice opposing the changes at senior directorate level and within the board of directors – the human resources director who had been appointed as a man of '68 in 1990 (see Chapter 7) – was replaced in 1994 by a former external member of the board who had lost his job in a ministry in Prague. Opposition from the other divisions also collapsed, possibly in the face of the obvious material gains that were to be had by the divisional heads, who by January 1995 had become general directors of new private companies and held a variety of paid directorships on the many boards of directors that sprouted up across the new holding company structure.

Commenting in 1995, one middle manager in a daughter company spoke of the initial experiences of the holding companies:

> The holding structure is in place and operational, and power has become more concentrated – top management has lost part of its power which has shifted to the board of directors . . . There are problems with the structure. It is very complicated with problems between the daughters – there is now a contract for everything [which delays work]. For example, it takes time and is delaying for us to wait for the necessary paperwork from [the former Commercial division] . . . The holding company sustains itself because the [more] powerful people gain from the arrangement – more have a share of the small profits because there are eight boards of directors [instead of just one].

When asked about the similarities with the old hierarchical planning system, when everything went upwards for approval, he replied 'Why not? The people are the same.'

Montáže Jesenice held steadfastly to the hybrid functional-divisional form it had introduced in 1992, changing only certain managerial responsibilities within the structure. The main change in its case came from the Velvet divorce, having to register its Slovakian assembly division as a separate private daughter company (a wholly owned s.r.o.) in Bratislava. Since the vast majority of the working employees of the division had anyway lived and worked in Slovakia, the spinning out of the daughter, which was still actually controlled from Jesenice, was inevitable and logical. As we have seen above, the post-privatization period has witnessed the gradual reabsorption of Montáže Jesenice by Jesenické Strojírny, where it is now understood almost like the plant it had been before 1990.

The structure of Vols remained much the same over the whole period of study, with slow progress towards realizing the benefits of divisionalization. In contrast to the realization of the holding concept in Jesenické Strojírny, Vols's senior management continued to hold it as a long-term aim, its appeal being its modernness and difference. Their gradualist approach to restructuring continued to be a major feature of the post-privatization period, and this was probably at least in partial recognition of the expense of perpetual reorganization at a time when survival remained a key issue. In 1995, the strategy director put the case for fully marketized arrangements in a relativistic framework:

> It is not official policy to move Vols to a holding company, though it is a strategic idea that is part of senior management discussion . . . [X division] might in the near future become a daughter company . . . [As] a new daughter [it] would have more freedom to make decisions, but [would have the advantage over competitors of being] within the bigger organizational context of Vols (for example, paying cheaper rent for facilities) . . . there would be more and tougher discipline from the managers, and workers would readjust . . . The same logic could be applied to some [other] divisions, but not all.

The rhetorical appeal of marketization and holding structures was similar to that in Jesenické Strojírny, but the forces of power in its favour were more balanced. Vols's senior managers had continued to subscribe to the ideas, and had absorbed their logic. However, following privatization, the agents of new strategic ideas and structural reformulation had changed. As the strategy department at the centre was being reduced in influence,[4] so the board of directors employed on annual contracts the services of the strategic consultancy firm owned by the new chair of the board of directors, an IPF representative. It is too early to identify the strategic or structural preferences of the consultants, or whether they will serve as agents of institutional patterning in the introduction of particular Western ideas and methods.

Whereas the stories of both Jesenické Strojírny and Vols imply that they have been makers of their own destinies within the economic constraints of the transition, Agstroj has been the object of a multitude of forces that have left the managers with little room for manoeuvre. Their initial attempts to enact a policy of divisionalization were only successful to a limited degree, and they were forced to pull back to a more centralized form (see Chapter 8). In 1995 Agstroj continued to have a moderate form of divisionalization, with each division having the same functional departments.

> [The divisions] . . . had been decentralized following the pursuit of a holding company structure, [and it] . . . was not working well. The organization was felt to have become too decentralized – with duplication of resources and activities [and poor communication]. Agstroj had to be reorganized from scratch . . . They also needed tighter financial controls, so there had to be a recentralization, a kind of tougher centralization, and there was friction when divisional managers found that their decentralized responsibilities had been withdrawn. (Director, Agstroj)

This recentralization had been the response of the Consolidation Bank to the pressing economic problems of the enterprise. It used its power on the board of directors (see above) to replace two directors, and made an external appointment of a new production director who reinstigated a centralized structure in which all operational plants reported through him.

In the context of our study, it is the very extremeness of the Agstroj case and its circumstances that serves to demonstrate the significance for our managers of Western managerial ideas *per se*. The strong rhetorical importance of and attachment to structural change as decentralization that we have found in each enterprise is illustrated in the quotation above. Divisionalization in Agstroj was espoused only as the first move in reorganization, a move towards the goal of the holding company concept. As a structural form, in the eyes of the enterprise managements the holding company embodied the ruling assumptions underlying post-communist political and economic rationality: decentralized power, independence and the relentless pursuit of marketization as the governing principle of economic coordination. Managers' allegiance to the structural idea was more symbolic than realistic, particularly in the case of Agstroj, where, by 1995, the harsh realities had created the conditions for a financial stringency that could not be delivered through structures which enhanced decentralized responsibility and managerial discretion. But managers still clung to the underlying tenets.

Establishing structural units

Within the accepted framework and rhetoric of decentralization, senior managers made decisions to establish new structural units that reflected accepted themes of market-economic rationality of the reinstitutionalizing environment. In the first place, structures were introduced to reflect those functional activities that had no rational place in the institutionalized business environment of state socialism, notably strategic management, human resource management and marketing. Second, interpreting the demands of the post-1989 transitional environment in terms of the Western injunction to focus business sharply on core production activities, managers used various structural devices to detach from the enterprise the inherited weight of unprofitable work and social welfare provision.

During the transition period, each enterprise introduced new functions to mimic within their structures the business expectations and norms associated with a market-economic company. We commented in Chapter 7 on how the former personnel departments, which had been heavily implicated in the enterprises' communist structures, had been deinstitutionalized and, in three of the enterprises, publicly relegated in status to a 'section', even concealed in places that put the old cadre and personnel department out of harm's way. Following privatization, however, these three units began once more to resurface, enjoying an enhanced structural position as a 'department', and their heads were given enterprise-level responsibilities. In 1995, Agstroj was partially reorganized, and the director of what had been called the 'administration' division was retitled director of 'personnel'. There was a general reshuffling of responsibilities with the other enterprise divisions, leaving in the renamed division a variety of activities with a more broadly personnel flavour, including public relations and ecological matters. Personnel in Montáže Jesenice also began to resurface in the 1994–5 period, following a structural reshuffle. The management services department, in which personnel had been hidden, was divided into two new departments and its activities were reassembled as technical-commercial services and a new personnel section. Although the new department retained section status and its head was formally regarded as having middle management status, she contributed to senior management decision-making and reported directly to the general director. The evolution of personnel in Vols followed the same pattern, when, at the beginning of 1995, the new personnel department regained its independence from the finance (formerly economy) division, with which it then stood as a structural equal. Following privatization, senior managers evidently felt it 'safe', even efficacious given the problems of recruitment in the shortage labour markets, to enhance the structural profile of the function.

The rehabilitation of the personnel function took a very different form in Jesenické Strojírny. It had retained its structural location in 1991, and it was the only enterprise in the sample whose head of personnel had the progressive title of director of 'human resources', operating at a directorate level. The position of the function represented a continuation of its historical structural importance, but the adoption of the new title signified a symbolic move towards a redefinition in modern Western terms. However, in 1994, the strategic influence of the function began to weaken. Following a number of disagreements, especially over the introduction of the holding company structure, the director of human resources (a man of '68) was demoted and replaced by a part-time director more sympathetic to the general director's objectives. At the beginning of 1995, the new holding structure decentralized everyday personnel issues to the daughter companies, and the structural influence of human resources waned. The decline of human resources continued when, in the summer of 1996, the external members of the board of directors voted its director off the board in order, effectively, to increase the balance of power in their favour. By 1996, the position of personnel had reached about the same position, though via a different route: formal and informal representation at the level of senior management, but with control over human resource issues being largely at an operational level; the reputation of the personnel departments had been mainly restored, and, as we shall see below, they were being mobilized by the senior managements to help to secure their post-communist careers (for more details, see Soulsby and Clark, 1998).

The cases of strategic management and the marketing function were somewhat different from personnel, in that they had had little representation in the pre-1989 state enterprise. We have seen in Chapter 7 how the surviving managers set up strategic management teams in order to address the issues raised by their new independence in uncertain conditions. This structural innovation has turned out to have only a transitional life, but the role of strategic teams cannot be underestimated in terms of redefinition and reinstitutionalization of management and organization. We noted above that Vols had by the beginning of 1996 reduced the status of the activity by reallocating its powerful exponents, but a similar process can be seen in the other enterprises. In Montáže Jesenice, the influential deputy director in charge of strategy was reassigned to other duties, and in Jesenické Strojírny, the strategy director retired after seeing through his pet holding company idea, and his successor within a matter of months lost both his position on the board of directors and his top-level position, as the strategy team was relocated under the central finance department.[5] It would appear that a separate strategy function was killed off by privatization, and the strategic tasks of long-term planning and reorganization have been taken on by the top management teams and the boards of directors.

Like strategic management, marketing had had no functional equivalent at enterprise level under state socialism, but within the accepted framework of decentralization, the enterprises created structural units entitled 'marketing', 'marketing services' and the like. In each case, the function was not conceived as strategic, and was located as a section, or even a sub-section, within the more traditional department or division of commerce. As introduced, the marketing sections were in all instances small and poorly staffed, and were evidently still seen as performing a role of lesser importance than sales. In a sense, this low-key role was understandable, since it proved very difficult to staff the departments with experienced staff. A director in Montáže Jesenice probably spoke for many managers in the four enterprises when he acknowledged the absence of special marketing expertise.

There were experienced staff, especially in Jesenické Strojírny, where the progressive policies of the previous director had included ensuring that his commercial acolytes spoke directly to foreign clients; and in Agstroj, where, as we noted in Chapter 8, senior management appointed as marketing manager a man who had been a sales director in its former VHJ (that is, the only organization, apart from the FTOs, in which something akin to marketing would have taken place). Even so, the limited spread of marketing skill and understanding guaranteed that the function was very narrow in its influence within the organization. The marketing manager in Jesenické Strojírny commented: '[It is said that the enterprise] is more market-oriented since 1989, but I am not convinced. Other managers and employees think that the marketing function is me.' It is possible that the marginalization of marketing was a consequence of its near irrelevance to the transitional environment, dominated in the early days in particular by the economic and business relics of state socialism. We described in Chapter 8 how the main weapons in the senior management armoury of survival techniques in these circumstances were the former socio-economic networks which former *nomenklatura* managers could enact. The prolonged and successful employment of such methods could easily have retarded the full structural and managerial development of a marketing function. But we shall return to this topic below.

The rationality of state socialism had led enterprises to accumulate a vast array of activities and assets which either had no economic-productive purpose (e.g. the local provision of social and welfare services) or were highly subsidized and, in themselves, unprofitable plants constructed to secure relative production autarky (such as metallurgical manufacturing). The fall of state socialism and the emerging institutionalized environment undermined the logic of these organizational features. The new senior managements quickly assimilated central themes of the latest Western market-economic logic, which proclaimed that efficient companies 'stuck to the knitting' and 'concentrated on core activities'. Over the early 1990s they made decisions to refocus their enterprises by detaching or redefining the costly legacies of the past. The most obvious method adopted has been to create structural units, first to 'productivize' former social assets and second to accumulate poorly performing economic assets.

The productivization of social assets has been a key process in the redefinition of the post-communist enterprise (see Soulsby and Clark, 1995). The enterprises tried to dispose of the social facilities like apartments, hotels, flats, recreation and holiday centres, kindergartens and sports stadia which had become financial burdens. Some were given away (e.g. kindergartens and schools to the municipalities), others leased to external agents who would pick up the running costs (e.g. cultural clubs, sports facilities), yet others sold privately (e.g. hotels in resort areas). Some of these properties were so undesirable that the enterprises found it very difficult to get them off their books; further, some managers with 'pink tinges' had a greater attachment to the enterprises' social functions within the community, and to the welfare of employees and their families. It became a normal practice in these circumstances to keep the assets 'within' the enterprise, by redefining their legal relationship and status (e.g. as a daughter company) and their objectives (to become profitable). Thus hotels and holiday centres were given some independence from central management, sometimes by giving the unit manager a financial stake in the new company.[6]

Where such assets could not be sold off, the enterprises set up special units to manage their disposal over the longer term, rather like a micro version of the NPF. Such was the case of Jesenické Strojírny, which created a daughter company called 'services' precisely to manage the remnant social properties while seeking mechanisms of disposal. Jesenické Strojírny services is one example of a 'sink structure' – a means of collecting together the costly, non-profitable bits of the former state enterprise into one unit, in order to allow the whole enterprise, and other daughters, to appear more profitable. In the case of this daughter, the property was almost entirely the former social assets of the old state-owned enterprise, of which the worst problem was the housing – because of the horrendous maintenance costs for flats that had been neglected for many years, combined with the government-capped rents that limited income from them. Problematic or unprofitable production projects were also bundled up into special units for the accounting purposes of isolating their worst excesses from the mainstream of enterprise activity. Jesenické Strojírny's problematic SOVREP project, inherited from before 1989, was a case in point. Jesenické Strojírny devised two small daughter companies, one of which was located in Slovakia, to manage the SOVREP project, contracting productive work to other Jesenické Strojírny companies while keeping the financial uncertainties from affecting them.

A similar interpretation is possible of Agstroj's contrivance to hive off its historical but failing ball-bearing production facilities into a new, separate state enterprise, Agstroj s.p., following the privatization merger. Agstroj s.p. was based on this old plant, but also acquired for good measure the former Agstroj's neglected apartments and various non-productive assets. The stated aim was to privatize this sink unit in the second wave, but this was not realized. It was still hoped that privatization would go ahead during 1997.

Where it had proved impossible to sell off or otherwise dispose of those activities that had become in the post-1989 world a cost burden to the enterprise, senior managers sought a policy of damage limitation. At best, they tried to productivize formerly non-profitable or social activities within corporate structures. Invariably this involved the creation of special units, the consequence of which was to make the enterprise more acceptable in market-economic terms, by presenting a more production-focused, slimmed down definition of the privatized enterprise. Given the scale of their social and unproductive properties and the problems of off-loading them in the transition period, demonstrating a mastery of and commitment to the rhetoric of 'core production activities' was probably at least as important as its actual realization.

Redefining management

Processes of management learning

Alongside the structural changes that were influencing the nature of the post-communist enterprise went changes in management values, knowledge and practices. Indeed, as we have seen, senior managers rightly saw their role in restructuring the enterprises as a means of both demonstrating their developing managerial awareness and asserting their claim to have market-economic knowledge that could be seen to be appropriate to managing in the new era. Although the focus here is on reinstitutionalization, it is not possible to explain the transformation processes without some reiteration of historical themes. We have seen in Chapter 8 that out of necessity managers approached post-communism with retrospection, drawing on relevant and rational (to them) methods from the past to cope with their everyday problems. State socialism in various ways furnished the managers with examples, experiences and knowledge that have proven to be significant resources in the development of their self-definition as post-communist management. The redefinition of management and organization has included the acquisition and integration of applicable management knowledge for the post-communist economy, and therefore has evolved from the blending of pre-1989 and post-1989 influences (see Soulsby and Clark, 1996a).

It should also be remembered that, like the majority of other Czech and CEE enterprises, our enterprises have not attracted FDI during the transition years (in contrast, see Child and Markóczy, 1993; Markóczy, 1993; Villinger, 1996; see also Whitley, 1994; Radice, 1995a, b). Foreign owners or capital partners might have directly imported their own Western management ideas and practices, or imposed them on local Czech managers, a transitional solution which our managers would have been reluctant to accept (see Chapter 8). In their absence, the management and enterprise redefinition have been accomplished through more or less indirect absorption of Western influences.

Management learning, as a process of knowledge acquisition, can be seen as a prerequisite for cultivating managerial competence in the new and changing institutional conditions. At any one time during the transition, the state of management knowledge and rhetoric has been shaped directly and indirectly by both new and old values and ideas intermingling with both foreign and domestic values and ideas (e.g. Soulsby and Clark, 1996a). The current stock of management knowledge then informs the development of the post-communist management practices which are brought to bear on the everyday problems of the privatizing and privatized enterprise. The acquisition of management knowledge in any particular enterprise depends on a number of specific factors which filter the ideas into or out of the concrete learning process. For example, we have already alluded to national-cultural factors that may make Czechs more open to domestic ideas than foreign

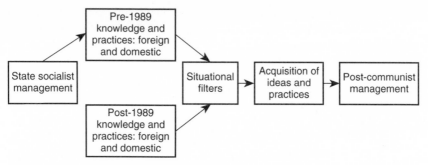

Figure 9.1 The process of post-communist management learning

ideas, and their attitude to FDI is a fine example. Further, the predominance of former *nomenklatura* over non-*nomenklatura* managers in the senior management teams may predispose the enterprises towards recycling pre-1989 ideas (e.g. Jesenické Strojírny's 1968 organization structure; see below) and practices (e.g. networking; see Chapter 8) in preference to acquiring and applying new ones. These situational factors are crucial to understanding the actual processes of redefinition that take place. Figure 9.1 presents a summary of this argument.

In understanding the nature of management learning and its resultant impact upon post-communist management and enterprise, it is necessary to distinguish between the acquisition of knowledge as ideas, values, concepts, theories etc., and the operationalizing of those ideas into a set of observable practices, techniques, methods and systems. It is arguable that management has not been truly redefined until the conduct and behaviour of managers have changed, leading to new patterns and forms of control and coordination. On the other hand, the notion of management has changed at least in some degree to the extent that managers accept, espouse, advocate and even propagate new ideas, values and so on. Consonant with common usage, we will speak of the acquisition of ideas as the development of managerial *rhetoric*, and this is sharply differentiated from the development of management *practices* – in most instances, the latter presuppose the former, but not vice versa (Reed, 1984; Willmott, 1987; Watson, 1995; Soulsby and Clark, 1996a).

In the context of surviving former *nomenklatura* managers, the significance of the acquisition and mastery of Western management rhetoric cannot be understated, because of its legitimatory value. These managers participated in an enthusiastic quest for any visible means of personal and professional legitimation, and the support given to them by knowledge with a close and indisputable connection with market-economic rationality was inestimable. On the other hand, a glaring gap between rhetoric and practice would once again make senior managers vulnerable, and beg comparisons with communist management.[7] Needless to say, the enterprise managers were continually on the look-out for new ideas to add to their stock of knowledge, and used a variety of sundry sources, from the informal scanning of management and business magazines to formal attendance at business seminars run by Western experts and the reading of Western textbooks which often adorned the old state socialist cabinets and shelves in managerial offices.

However, the most important source of new managerial knowledge was via contact with management consultancy firms, sometimes Czech, sometimes Western – but mostly Czech national firms which could point to strong Western connections and credentials, such as their representatives having being trained in France, or using techniques tried and tested in the United States. All four enterprises used consultants to a greater or lesser degree, but had a healthy scepticism based on having had their fingers burned. Two of the enterprises had been successful in getting European Union PHARE funding (Jesenické Strojírny) and European Bank of Reconstruction and Development money (Agstroj) to finance expensive projects with the direct participation of West European consultants, whose fees would otherwise have been beyond their budgets. Consultants had been employed to work at all levels of the enterprises. However, they were felt to offer special expertise in those areas of organization and management that had been identified as the post-communist weak spots – notably corporate strategy, structural redesign, marketing research and management, accounting systems and quality management. This seemed to be a short-cut to the acquisition of the more fashionable management and organizational ideas and practices, although they were acquired at a price.

One of Agstroj's directors was quite open about the quality of the external advice: 'Many consultancy firms have set foot in this place without the slightest idea of the conditions . . . [Their advice] cannot be applied here . . . It is "kind uncle's advice", simple and unrealistic.' Similarly in Jesenické Strojírny:

> [We have had] . . . bad experience of two firms, one Swiss and the other American with Czech representatives . . . [They] were ineffective, because of their need for quick returns, a lack of long-term commitment and an inability to get deep.

The managers had a declared preference for working with Czech consultants, because they were thought to be better able to understand the complexities of the transition environment. Foreigners were seen to be more likely to be peddling over-simple solutions at over-high prices. All the enterprises had since the early years reduced their use of consultants as a result of a sense of poor return on investment.

There had been good experiences of external advice. A group of international MBA students based in Switzerland had spent time in the metallurgy division of Vols, and by adapting Western strategic analysis techniques to the enterprise's conditions had offered advice that helped to turn the division around. Both Jesenické Strojírny and Montáže Jesenice worked with another consulting firm for a number of years, with the conscious aim of developing senior management expertise and conduct. This firm was ideally compatible with the values of the managers; the seminars were run by a Czech former academic who had spent a period in North America where he had acquired an MBA. His six-monthly seminars focused on developing the positive attributes of the former *nomenklatura*, with whom he probably shared a common background, and offered some very important mechanisms for making sense of their management careers.[8] It is probable that his ideas had a substantial effect on their growing post-privatization confidence as worthy post-communist managers.

By using consultants as a resource, managers have improved their personal stock of management knowledge and imported into their enterprises techniques and practices (with supporting rationales) that reflected recent developments across a whole range of international management. In this sense, consultants have acted as the concrete agents and media for the copying of institutionalized patterns and practices across national boundaries (see Scott, 1991). In proportion to their involvement with business consultants, Czech management and enterprise have been exposed to important Western management fads and fashions (Huczynski, 1993) and have adopted ideas and techniques in accordance with the institutionally preferred values and methods of the particular consultants, rather than in rational response to the technical demands of their transitional task environment.

We now move on to examine more closely the evidence for management redefinition, by identifying features of the new rhetorics and practices that became expressed in the four enterprises. We limit our discussion to certain fields of management where the state socialist experience had left wide gaps in experience and knowledge. In particular, we examine the emergence of personnel, marketing and quality practices.[9]

Personnel management and managing the personnel function

We have followed the progress of the personnel function during the previous two chapters, noting in particular the ways in which its historical role had rendered it vulnerable after 1989, and making it critical for new management to exercise control through the symbolic processes of restructuring and restaffing (see Soulsby and Clark, 1998). Within the newly structured and restaffed function, there is evidence that significant elements of the rhetoric and practices of Western human resource management were being embraced. Some Western personnel ideas began to permeate the enterprises, but it is not clear at this stage of research to what extent the ideas have infiltrated beyond rhetoric into real management practices. Neither is it entirely obvious to what the degree senior managers have tried to adopt Western ideas as a whole package, or apply them in a more piecemeal fashion.

In the light of the role played by the *nomenklatura* system under state social-ism, senior and personnel managers recognized that the establishment of unambiguous, depersonalized and transparent practices for management recruitment and promotion was one of the most pressing problems of post-communist organization. Most senior managers in the enterprises claimed that they had achieved their positions on merit, having successfully gone through a *konkurs*, a competitive appointment process. However, as we have already seen above, contrary to the meritocratic rationality of Western recruitment practices, it was possible for very senior managers to gain their posts through patronage and sponsorship. Respondents in Vols, for example, commented on the sometimes personal nature of appointment practices and on the lack of transparency in promotion criteria. In the early 1990s, managers continued to be selected and elevated by the general director or his senior colleagues. Managers could be arbitrarily transferred to new positions even when they had no technical expertise in those areas. Independent of the technical merit of the device, the 'job swaps' case at Montáže Jesenice demonstrates further the facility with which senior managers could overrule the espoused rhetoric of transparency by offering managerial protection to colleagues. Some managers described a 'usual pattern': they would be telephoned by a senior manager, called to a meeting and asked directly if they wanted the position. Respondents expressed the fear that, if they refused to accept, showed reluctance or asked for more time to consider the position, then the 'telephone might never ring again'. In the interviews, however, former *nomenklatura* frequently made reference to the *konkurs* as a means to explain and justify their continuing senior managerial responsibilities. Thus, although Western conceptions were a normal part of the rhetoric of post-communist personnel management, respondents suggested that the reality was far more uneven in practice, and possibly actually unusual in the case of higher levels of management recruitment and promotion.

While the personnel departments were often cut out of the decision-making process when it came to important management appointments, they were involved in designing their special contracts and reward packages once in position, organizing internal and external training sessions in support of the related expectations and obligations. Senior managers realized that the nature of the employment relationship had to change in order to overcome the problems of weak, passive management behaviour, and to create the sort of distance from employees that would enable them to assert greater and more effective control over the labour process – and thus break away from the way things were before 1989. The actual nature of the redefinition has been strongly influenced by what senior managers have understood to be normal or typical of management reward systems and expectations in the West. As such, the transformation of their enterprises towards market-style companies has involved the creation and implementation of remuneration structures for managers and technical staff which are like those of Germany or the United States. Such recipes have been propagated by both foreign and domestic business consultancy firms, and have been commonly discussed in the burgeoning Czech business press. One of the most important consequences of the new contracts offered to senior managers has been the increasing 'privatization' and individualization of the employment relationship at this level.

Over the period of transition covered in this book, the senior managers of the enterprises have succeeded in establishing a more Western level and degree of compensation, with the new personnel function at the centre of the process. Instead of basing their material benefits on privileged access to goods, property and services, as had been the case of the old *nomenklatura* management (Soulsby and Clark, 1995), the post-communist managements of the four enterprises have used methods from Western management practice to assure the economic benefits of their positions. The consolidation of privilege into monetarized rewards has created a structure of remuneration which formally and materially differentiates senior managers from other employees, and also maintains secrecy and confidentiality about enhanced salaries and perquisites. Improved employment conditions for managers in the four enterprises included performance-related pay (PRP) and the provision of company cars as normal parts of the remuneration package. In Jesenické Strojírny, for example, even company cars were the basis of finer gradations of social differentiation at management level: German cars were given to the senior managers, while middle managers could only aspire to the more traditional Škoda. In the name of offering rewards for responsibility and task performance in order to support managerial status, such mechanisms have served to reinforce the tendency to increase socio-economic inequalities within the enterprises, and hence to distinguish clearly the position of manager from lesser statuses.

At Jesenické Strojírny, the director of human resources had implemented a programme to redefine contracts of employment for senior managers which were annually renewable and based on an appraisal scheme. According to one middle manager:

> A big difference is that normal employees sign a contract that is indefinite, but top managers have a rolling one-year contract. Performance is reviewed annually by the top executive committee, if [managers are] not good enough then they can be fired. Workers know that there is such a contract, but don't want to understand [that the] top management are more on the risk side [now].

Jesenické Strojírny has implemented a PRP scheme, and the details of the managers' pay and other rewards have become confidential. With management salaries made private, it has become impossible for other employees to appreciate the speed at which managerial remuneration has increased, compared with their own. For example, the basic salaries of Jesenické Strojírny's senior managers increased by 102.5 per cent in the two-year period 1993 and 1994, whereas those of middle managers rose by 31 per cent and of ordinary workers by 34.5 per cent. Furthermore, a confidential consultants' report that had been circulated around certain Czech enterprises indicated that Jesenické Strojírny's rate of increase in salary differentials was very low compared with what was going on in many other privatized enterprises. The importance of these changes to the reward system and the intensification of economic inequalities has to be understood in the context of the very narrow band of wage differentials that had been the experience of people working in Czechoslovak enterprises before 1989. One manager, a man of '68 in Jesenické Strojírny, commented that there was a feeling among some employees of unhappiness and resistance to the new style of business and management:

> Sometimes it is very difficult for employees to accept new changes . . . [compared to the] past . . . For example, how they [managers] behave . . . In trying to apply the new standard of management they [the managers] decided . . . who would have top power, and . . . who should receive a car. People at first couldn't accept this and opposed it. And managers tried not to notice this [opposition]. But they have [had] to return something to the employees . . . Employees work in new more comfortable environments . . . [However,] it is true that it looks [as though] managers have more benefits.

This trend for senior managers in particular to benefit substantially from new personnel practices, which have individualized their contracts, monetarized their rewards and consolidated them in higher salaries and other perks, may be contrasted with the consequences of the popular managerial-rhetorical theme of focusing on core production activities, which has influenced the restructuring of the enterprises (see above). In each enterprise, the personnel function has been formally involved in the reshaping of these social activities, whereby many of these now-peripheral activities have been disposed of, and the strategic aim following privatization has been to retain only those services which would be found in a typical large Western-style company (e.g. subsidized staff canteens). The effect has been to reduce the social wage which employees used to receive indirectly through access to the enterprise-subsidized social and welfare activities, and in return they receive a monetarized, but insufficient compensation. In making these changes, the managements have rejected the traditional involvement of the now weakened trade unions, who at best have been regarded as only worthy of consultation, and as lacking any real power or role in the management of employee-related matters. It is evident that those with responsibility for any remaining social and welfare activities run them in accordance with the wishes of the shareholders and managers of the privatized enterprises.

The adoption of Western personnel rhetoric and practices has made the Czech enterprises and their managements more like their Western counterparts, and the personnel department before and following privatization has been a crucial instrument in the reinstitutionalization of both the human *management* resource and human resource management *qua* function. Senior managers have been able to use the newly established, new shape personnel functions to control the design of new contracts of employment and reward systems for managers, which have not only served to support their claims to be bona fide market-economic managers, but also furthered their own economic interests as a group. Personnel managers also gained from this process, since the design of modern management contracts can be claimed as a triumph for the more 'rational' (i.e. normatively more acceptable) management of senior human resources, and hence a step towards the ultimate recognition of personnel management as a professional expertise. In short, both parties are validated because they can successfully refer to socially recognized and sanctioned Western management knowledge and practices – the touchstone of post-communist managerial legitimacy. More concretely, the outcome of this application of Western management knowledge has been the design of new management contracts and a tighter organizational focus. The resulting monetarization of managerial rewards and benefits, taken with the reformation of social and welfare activities, has tended to augment the level of financial reward which they, the senior managers, have been able to receive and to increase visibly the degree of socio-economic differentiation within the enterprises.

Developing a marketing orientation and function

For each enterprise, the most important of the contemporary transition-economic problems was to find new, preferably Western, clients. Such clients brought hard currency, rebalanced trade following the collapse of the Eastern markets and, in the longer term, introduced the Czech enterprises into Western markets where a more secure future was seen to lie. Yet, for the most part, the enterprises and their managements had had little experience of marketing – especially export-marketing – either as function or as a set of practices. Despite this, from the earliest field visits senior and commercial managers demonstrated an excellent grasp of the general principles of the market and of the rhetoric of marketing management. The senior managers realized that survival in the new era demanded that enterprise management as a whole develop what they called a marketing orientation, by which they meant a number of qualities in direct juxtaposition to former 'commercial' management. The marketing and senior managers identified three features, at the same time both values and principles, of the marketing orientation: first, a view of the customer as being the central consideration; second, a proactivity of vision in dealing with potential customers; third, a degree of innovativeness and creativity in the approach to selling and promotion.

For the Commercial director at Vols, 'The key idea of marketing is how to satisfy the customer . . . and [the new department of] marketing services is working as a team to develop marketing goals and a plan.' The marketing managers at each enterprise in their own ways identified the demands on their new departments as emanating directly from the evolving market features of the transition environment and from the post-1989 independence that was suddenly thrust upon the enterprises. They had to find new (especially Western) customers, and this required demonstrations of planning and initiative from marketing personnel. Jesenické Strojírny's marketing manager noted the new requirement of his function: selling 'is now a people problem, and we need to create a system to see to the needs of the customer'. It is significant that the managers defined the marketing orientation less in terms of any inner characteristics, and more by contrasting it with the perceived weaknesses of the past that were still present in 1995. Such was the novelty of the values and practices required by marketing management that the new orientation inevitably flew in the face of the practical experiences of most staff involved in the respective commercial departments and divisions.

The background of the marketing manager of Agstroj as sales director in Agrov gave him as good a marketing experience as is likely to be found in the Czech Republic, but he also commented on the new values necessary: 'The [marketing] philosophy has changed, and has to be part of all employees . . . You need new techniques for the new environment . . . With no central plan or central control, Agstroj has to sell directly in foreign markets.' One Jesenické Strojírny director, who had been directly involved in the recruitment of marketing staff, related the problems to wider issues regarding the consequences of a strict engineering training that typified employees: 'There is an emphasis on [technical] qualifications in the Czech Republic, rather than on the qualities or attitudes of people. There are 4300 people in Jesenické Strojírny, but only a few, mostly designers, are creative.' His colleague, the marketing manager, believed that passivity even affected the mentality of the younger managers. 'When we have meetings . . . the younger managers complain that the FTOs have been abolished. They are still waiting for the government to establish new contacts. Instead, they should go out and find the contacts for themselves.' This point reinforces the comments cited above from the general director of Montáže Jesenice, who complained about the failure of the commercial department to show the initiative necessary to find new business.

A Vols director also contrasted the past with the present, implying a continuing problem in this area: 'Commercial work was easy in the past . . . and marketing was unknown . . . Now marketing is, or ought to be, important, because we need to find new customers in the West . . . it could be a problem.' The lack of proactivity in the so-called marketing function was a major problem, and one that endured until our latest meetings with the managers in 1995 and 1996. A strategy manager in Vols said in a comment about the recent integration of the technical and commercial divisions:

> Marketing remains our weakest function. The integration [of technical and commercial] was rational because of the high technical knowledge needed to work with customers; on the other hand, we need people with

more marketing-creative skills. Czech universities are just not teaching this new subject enough.

Marketing managers had attended seminars, short courses and other Western consultancy sponsored activities, and also pointed proudly to American marketing textbooks and business magazines. There is no doubt that they had assimilated the value-premises and ideas of 'marketing', but they suffered from a number of glaring problems in establishing a flourishing department that could contribute to enterprise performance. At the obvious level, the staffing of the marketing function was a typical concern of the enterprises; in the words of the Montáže Jesenice marketing manager, which many of his peers in other enterprises would confirm, 'Marketing is a department but it has no experts.'

The weakness of marketing ability was blamed by many managers for the inadequately slow responses to the changed circumstances of the post-1989 era:

> By 1989, it was possible to market [its products] directly [instead of through FTOs] to get higher profits, but managers were not very skilled at marketing so no one started to be more active. There were lost opportunities and Agstroj lost two to three years to competitors. (Middle manager, Agstroj)

The lack of training and of experience was one factor in the failure to develop practices and techniques that could be perceived as providing the function with a recognizably 'marketing' identity. A further problem was that during the transition period commercial activities did not attract the kind of budget that could support deeper training and the development of the marketing research and promotional activities of the modern marketing function. In these conditions, the search for new customers took the form of extending and enhancing former practices that were well-known before 1989, and hence less risky and expensive, e.g. developing glossier, more modern, multilingual brochures and flyers; continuing product presence at traditional trade fairs plus some experimental, often low-key, appearances at Western ones; using historical social contacts. While socio-economic networking might be classified as a good industrial marketing technique for enterprises in the mechanical and heavy engineering sectors (Lodge and Walton, 1989; Hakansson and Johanson, 1990; Wilson and Mummalaneni, 1990; Johnston and Lawrence, 1991), it was less a thought-out marketing tactic, and more a resort to known practices that were still relevant in the transitional economy (see Chapter 8). Given the low budgets and the lack of expertise, resort to old practices was rational, yet at the same time it held back the application of new ideas and possibly hindered the emergence of a modern and influential marketing function. Agstroj's marketing manager, with his experience of 'marketing' under state socialism, took it almost as an insult that he could learn much from books, conferences etc. '[We don't need them]. Agstroj has a long tradition in exporting, so we are utilizing that long-term experience.'

This comment was made in the context of using old contacts, and he was not typical of the marketing managers. However, it does underscore the complacency engendered by a reliance on old practices to deal with the problem of finding new Western clients and markets, which senior managers realized was a key to the future success of their enterprises, despite their fear of becoming dependent on Western companies. During the transition, the marketing departments were less involved in devising ways of knowing about and caring for clients, and more concerned with finding Western *partners* to work with. In this respect, Agstroj's strategy was a typical, if extreme, example. Its commercial collaboration with Amfarm was forced by a very weak market position, and while it had brought in little capital, it did offer outlets for Agstroj's products in foreign markets. The other enterprises actively sought any way of gaining access to the West. A senior manager at Vols noted:

> Important decisions have to be made about relations with German firms. Partner firms are very important for getting new customers in Western economies, because a [joint] product can be promoted by the 'good name' of the German partner firm. We often have a better design [than the Germans] but we have to use the German design in order to sell [the machine]. When Vols has a recognizable brand name, we can make our own decisions.

Enterprises like Vols and Jesenické Strojírny had had a strong reputation for quality on CMEA markets, so conceding dependence to German brands was difficult to accept; given their Czech traditions, this made them culturally reluctant partners with foreign companies. It is equally understandable that in the later transition period both these enterprises began a re-expansion on their own into former Soviet markets where their names still carried kudos.

Given the lack of expertise and finance, and the continuing prominence of old trading practices, it is no wonder that the marketing function did little over the period to improve its structural marginalization, which in turn reinforced the other problems. The weak influence of marketing in practice contrasts sharply with the waxing of marketing rhetoric among all senior managers, and the acceptance of its role in the post-communist enterprise by virtually everyone else. Senior management of each enterprise recognized the importance of marketing in successful Western companies, and placed great store on presenting the modern facade of marketing in their management talk. However, under existing institutional conditions, the symbolic presence of a marketing function in the privatizing and privatized enterprises seemed at least as critical as, and certainly more realizable than, a fully operational and expert substructure. From the surviving managers' points of view, the central consideration was to be seen to be doing something to introduce changes in line with the new 'market imperative'.

The pursuit of quality

We have already seen that the four enterprises had complete faith in the quality of their products, their production processes and the skills of their employees. Such loyalty was typical not only of the senior managers, but even of those employees whose careers had been truncated by the communist domination of the enterprises before 1989. Further, there is little doubt that within the context of CMEA and developing economies, the four enterprises had very strong reputations for their machines and services. Yet, following the collapse of communism and the decline of the traditional markets, all this added up to nought. The drive for Western clients had a major impact upon the enterprises' strategies, which had to conform not just with the technical realities of product and production in which the managers had so much confidence, but with the *institutional* realities of Western markets of which managers had little understanding. In much the same way that quality has become a buzz word in Western management vocabulary over the past decade or so, it was necessary for the Czech managers to demonstrate that they could speak quality.

Quality management was not a new function in the enterprises. Before the changes, each enterprise had, within the production department, a section devoted to quality, though its job was, in the words of the Jesenické Strojírny quality manager, 'more like quantity than quality control . . . It was a set of agreements about what it was necessary to do to achieve quantitative targets by designing reliable systems'.

Training was more in the principles of physics than management. Western norms of quality management affected the enterprises through the demands of prospective Western partners and clients, which, in assessing tenders or contracts, looked less at the actual products and services and more at their current certification in respect of quality – in particular, ISO 9000. This was not merely a matter of applying for and receiving a judgement. It was a time-consuming process of preparing exhaustive paperwork according to special criteria, changing employees' conduct to conform to possibly unusual and unknown practices, and being subjected to a quality audit and inspection. Not only did this take time, when enterprises were desperate to find new business, but it was also, by Czech standards, outrageously expensive. The quality manager at Montáže Jesenice, who was to lead the process of quality certification, recognized the importance: 'We are facing the problem of becoming part of Europe and . . . all activities need ISO approval.' ISO 9000 was probably easiest for Montáže Jesenice to achieve, simply because the enterprise is relatively small, and it only needed to evaluate one set of activities. In each of the other enterprises, each division or daughter needed its own certification. But even so, it took three years for Montáže Jesenice to make the grade, at an enormous upfront cost. In the view of Montáže Jesenice's general director:

> ISO 9002 was very difficult and very expensive. [We created] . . . an internal team and cooperated . . . with twenty different advisers for different activities in the company . . . [After] one year trying to understand and explain to workers what was required . . . [there was the] creation of documents and manuals, . . . [then] implementation . . . We have to pass a test audit every year, which is good business for [the German consultancy firm, based in Prague].

Not counting internal person hours, the successful development of ISO standards had cost the enterprise over kč800,000, though its very possession had been essential in their successful tendering for foreign assembly business (e.g. a large Japanese contract).

Jesenické Strojírny and Vols had also been through these processes several times, and by 1995 had achieved the standard in several activities. All three enterprises had used the same quality consultants for final audits, but had given a lot of business to the expanding Czech consultancy industry. The process was evidently for most managers not one of choice. It was seen as distracting a lot of time, energy and funds from other issues of modernization and survival, and, in the opinion of the Vols strategy director, was used by Western firms to thwart the competitive edge of Czechs:

> It is in our own interests to produce a high standard of production, and we are now trying to reach [ISO] certification . . . In the Czech Republic, we know we have to introduce quality standards, but the setting of high [and expensive] standards may be regarded as a deliberate barrier to entry.

Agstroj had not, up to 1995, succeeded in satisfying ISO norms. The process began only in 1994, after production managers had attended a seminar to learn about the philosophy of Western quality managers. They accepted a proposal by a group of Czech management consultants, but Agstroj's quality manager believed that the enterprise was starting from a position of conforming 70 per cent to the ISO standards.

Both Jesenické Strojírny and Agstroj had also decided on a strategy to adopt some form of total quality management (TQM), and all four enterprises had stumbled over the problems of getting the behavioural aspects of new norms and systems accepted.

> It is hard work, so we are trying to use consultants on the shopfloor . . .
> The quality strategy is understood but is hard to implement . . . [because of] making the strategy spread across the whole organization . . . It is a

long process which mostly depends on the way people accept it . . . The main problem is operationalizing the norms. (Agstroj Quality manager)

In Jesenické Strojírny, the quality manager made much the same point:

> In terms of quality management the development of ISO 9000 is important. The problem is teaching people the new approach – it is not a technical problem . . . After [ISO] certification, we will go for the Deming brand of TQM. The problem with this is that the cooperative aspects seem too much like old socialist brigades, and it is difficult to teach workers the difference.

Similarly, the strategy director of Vols noted both the technical and the behavioural problems: '[It is] one problem that [technical] norms, paperwork and manuals are required . . . [It is quite another] how to persuade people to follow the rules and systems.' There is little doubt that the copying of ISO standards and TQM systems into the enterprises is an example of coercive isomorphism (see DiMaggio and Powell, 1991). The managers have reluctantly chosen these expensive routes to finding new foreign clients for primarily institutional rather than technical reasons. The process has not been seen as an easy option, because of employee resistance to the conduct presumed in Western quality norms and systems. Comments in 1995 and 1996 revisits indicate that despite the success in the initial quality audits, new working practices have not been consolidated, so the enterprises could face problems in future annual test audits.

Conclusions

The propositions in this chapter have related specifically to the ways in which the post-communist enterprise has been redefined and reinstitutionalized in such ways as to pursue the twin goals of enterprise and management survival. Throughout we have suggested that the senior managers have been in the driving seat, and that their values and priorities, based on their historical and contemporary experiences, have been reflected in the strategies and decisions that they have taken. It is our contention that central to understanding the structural and managerial changes since 1989 has been the fact that the senior managers have been predominantly from former *nomenklatura* positions, and have therefore had to deal with anxieties about personal and professional legitimacy and credibility.

The arguments and the materials presented offer interesting insights into the power and influence of senior managers, and especially their relationship with Western management knowledge, which has offered them a vehicle for modernizing their image and practices. The rhetorics of markets, marketization, decentralization, competition, differentiation and quality are examples of the systems of ideas and knowledge which have been borrowed, adopted and, to some degree, applied by the post-communist managers, affecting the structures of their enterprises, and the emergence of new functions and practices that had been hitherto more or less unknown to them. The new privatized organizations and their managements are thus in many respects very different from their state enterprise predecessors, and this result is no accident of evolution or unmediated adaptation to new environment demands, be they technical-economic or institutional. Rather, these are the outcomes of deliberate, motivated decision-making, affected, amended, resisted or supported by other interested human agents with a stake in the enterprises: other managers, other employees, the new shareholders and so on. These processes mean that the managers have not had it all their own way.

Given the theoretical perspective presented in this book, the processes and strategies of reinstitutionalization should be understood within two contexts. First, the socio-economic transitional environment provided the social, economic, political and institutional conditions of transience, in which the enterprises had to operate and survive (see Chapter 6). Second, the decisions of senior managers created the parallel internal processes of deinstitutionalization, institutional inertia and reinstitutionalization, in which context they have attempted to move the enterprises forward to stable and socially sanctionable forms (Chapters 7, 8 and 9). The developments in organization structure and human resource management are cases which demonstrate the relevance of conceiving the transformation process as an interleaving of the three forms of institutional change, artificially separated in order to tell the more complex story analytically. In the next, and concluding, chapter we recap these arguments in the light of the wider theoretical and empirical objectives of the book. We also look forward to the future development of Czech enterprise and management as the post-communist economy takes on a more permanent institutionalized form which will have been the direct consequence of, among other factors, the transition management decisions and practices which have enabled the enterprises to survive.

Notes

1 In fact, in respect of Jesenické Strojíny, the municipality had been given 9 per cent of the shares as part of the privatization project, but the NPF represented these shares, giving it control of nearly 35 per cent.
2 At the time of writing in late 1996, it is unclear what effects this take-over will have on Montáže Jesenice's direction and management.
3 The partial exception was Agstroj, where a number of significant Agstroj directors (including the post-1989 general director, a former *nomenklatura* director) were relocated in the new state-owned 'Agstroj' which was created from a former plant. But the new directors of the privatized Agstroj were drawn predominantly from the former Stroměsto Engines.
4 The strategy director, quoted above, moved to a new senior management post at the beginning of 1996 and his influential assistant was about to retire. With the finance director, they had been commonly recognized as being the driving forces behind strategic decision-making in the post-1989 period.

5 The position of Agstroj was unclear at the time of writing.
6 In an example notorious within Jesenické Strojírny, in 1993 one of its resort hotels
   was turned into a private business (s.r.o.), with the former manager putting up 50
   per cent of the capital and Jesenické Strojírny agreeing contractual arrangements
   for sharing its financing and profits. The new owner used irregular, not to mention
   illegal, methods to develop the hotel, and the human resources director, under
   whose wing it resided formally, had to face a lot of criticism for a poorly defined contract and inadequate management control. Following formal bankruptcy proceedings, the hotel was renamed and appeared as the property of the new structural
   unit discussed in the text.
7 The careers of senior managers in the Czech Republic are invariably tied to the
   same enterprise in the long term, and so they are more open to exposure than
   managers in, say, North American and British companies, where career paths can
   allow them to escape before being 'found out' for empty managerial rhetoric.
8 In the interviews with senior managers there were well-rehearsed arguments about
   the past, and it is quite likely that this particular consultant had worked with the
   managers on re-evaluating their biographies along the lines described in Chapter 7.
9 Accounting and finance offer interesting areas of study, but our materials are less
   strong in these instances (but see, for example, Seal *et al.*, 1996).

Part IV

Conclusions

10 Economic transformation as institutional change

In the final chapter we bring this exploration of management and organizational transformation to its conclusion. There are two major aims: first, to review the main theoretical and empirical contributions of the book; second, to pull together arguments in order to compose a synoptic picture of patterns of organization and management as they have emerged from our examination of Czech enterprises. The evidence and interpretations presented in the preceding chapters remain the central focus, although, in the second case, we have placed our findings within the context of broader themes of the Czech economic transformation.

Reviewing the arguments

The field research on four former state enterprises has yielded a wealth of materials which have been used to explore organization and management under conditions of socio-economic transformation. Since transformation refers to profound changes in socially accepted ways of conducting economic activities in general and organizational and managerial activities in particular, a social-institutional approach has been proposed as a vehicle for optimizing the opportunity to understand these processes. By conceptualizing transformation in terms of institutional change – itself constituted by the interaction between three sub-processes of deinstitutionalization, reinstitutionalization and transition management – the arguments have been able to focus on the social and system tensions that inevitably result from the movement from one relatively stable set of arrangements towards another putative socio-economic order based on new rules, methods and patterns.

The arguments in the book have been structured in order to apply concepts and propositions derived from the social-institutional approach to the transformation process in the Czech Republic. The theoretical principles were established and discussed in Chapter 2, before we turned in Part Two to the description and explanation of the institutional nature of Czechoslovak state socialism as both command-economic system and enterprise management. Within the economic conditions created by the command system, the strong political-administrative pressures to conform to the goals and rules of the planning institutions were shown to lead to a whole range of technical problems which made it difficult for the enterprise managements to fulfil their plans efficiently by adhering strictly to their formal role. These technical problems were exacerbated by massive problems of personal and professional legitimacy in the period of normalization, when many employees withdrew their goodwill from the process of production. As we saw in Chapter 4, the consequence was that enterprise managers developed their own decoupled practices, which took on a *socially* accepted character as appropriate for dealing with the very problems that *formally* approved management failed to solve. The extensive use of social networking and bargaining within the economic structures, of information fiddling and production fixing and so on, acted both as a temporary cover-up of systemic failures and as a form of slow, institutional erosion of the system itself. The imminent system crisis was supplemented by the continuing social crisis at the level of civic life, and when, in the face of external events, power was no longer deemed sufficient to impose the formal institutions on everyday economic and social life, the end was in sight. After forty-one years, state socialism had left an enormous impression on Czech society, and relative to most other state socialist countries in the region, the Czechoslovak command economy in 1989 approximated to a rigid, centralized, autarkic, bureaucratic, neo-Stalinist model. The starting point of the changes was therefore relatively close to a pure type of state socialism, and its structural and behavioural legacies have continued to play a formative role in the post-communist transformation.

Part Three reported on the chief empirical questions concerning the transformation of economic institutions. While Chapter 6 examined the process of transition at the level of the political economy, Chapters 7, 8 and 9 drew heavily upon the management experiences of enterprise change, as revealed by the respondents in the study. At each level, we utilized the language of institutional change as a vehicle for presentation and explorations, considering the deinstitutionalization of the command-economic structures and associated behavioural patterns, the reinstitutionalization of the economic system and patterns of management and organization consonant with market-economic values, and the management of the regressive and progressive elements simultaneously present in the transitional environment.

The dominant modes of organization and management implicit in the state-owned enterprise were deficient and unprepared both technically and normatively for the demands of the socio-economic transition. The struggle inherent in the transformation process has therefore been about not only developing the occupational competence of managers in the changing economic circumstances but also re-establishing their professional credibility and personal legitimacy. The technical and normative redefinition of management and organization were especially vital for the surviving former *nomenklatura* managers who, after 1989, faced an indeterminate future without the authoritative support of either the command-economic institutions or the communist apparatus. Unlike many other approaches to the economic transition, we have viewed its accomplishment as the accumulating outcome of the conduct of economic actors operating with both motive and power to get things done in accordance with their own values and interests. In this respect, we have had a privileged opportunity to examine the influential role of new enterprise managers whose decisions have helped to restructure and redefine the emerging form of Czech organization and management. Their motivation could be partly accounted for by the values, expectations and practices that they learned during their previous management incarnation under state socialism. Many of these senior managers held their present posts because in the past they had been able to satisfy the political demands of the cadre *nomenklatura* system; as a result, they not only gained access to authority, material rewards and privileges, but also, in employees' eyes, carried the stigma of communist association. The post-communist management group's aims to survive and develop their careers in the new era depended on them being able to distance themselves from the past and dress themselves in the new mantle of market-economic management. The analysis has also demonstrated in some detail how managers have continued to enact inherited institutional practices and methods in their everyday efforts to make sense of the ambiguous technical and normative context which is the transformation.

The research evidence provides significant support for a number of propositions which are at the heart of the social-institutional framework. First, rather than focusing exclusively on the ways in which the transformation process has been influenced by contemporary factors, we have recorded the enduring significance of *historical* factors in the unravelling of the economic transition. In the discussion of societal transience, institutional inertia and the role of state socialist legacies in management and organization, we have noted the impossibility of presuming a socio-economic present and future unaffected by the past. For these reasons, the transitional period could only really be understood from the foundations of reliable knowledge about state enterprise management practices in their command-economic context, however articulately economists, politicians and policy advisers have defined and delineated the rules of a market-economic institutional system. Historical factors have influenced the present at least partially through their embodiment in institutional rules and forms, which were reproduced in institutionalized practices and routinized in everyday life. Thus institutional traces and residues necessarily linger on in the conduct of social actors at their workplace, and to project a transformative trajectory without weighing their relevance, as transition economists often do, is to limit the chances of successful explanation.

Second, the arguments reinforce the institutionalist view about the role played by *normative* factors in shaping socio-economic order and transformation. The processes of legitimacy acquisition and attribution have been central to the analysis of the behaviour of economic actors under conditions where they, and the institutions they represented, were normatively deficient. It is inadequate to conceive of the transition in purely technical-economic terms, as is implied in the transition-economic conception of formal institution building and policy setting, or in the contingency-theoretic view of organizational change as system responses to external economic pressures. The normative-institutional dimension helps to make sense of managing the transformation as well as transforming management, both of which require that things are done legitimately, or at least are seen as being done legitimately.

Third, the evidence validates the usefulness of examining the processes of institutional order and institutional change as the *on-going social accomplishment of human agents*. Specifically in an economic context, it is indispensable to building a thorough account of the economic transformation that macro-economic processes are understood not just as a set of constraints on the conduct of economic actors, but as the social construction of economic actors through whose interactions structures and systems are produced, reproduced or challenged. We have repeatedly shown how the institutionalized practices of enterprise managers have reflected and reinforced wider institutional forms, but they have also served to challenge and undermine them. Management practices such as decision-making at the level of the enterprise have a cumulative effect on the shaping of the economic transition, influencing the actual pathway of institutional change. The processes of socio-economic stability and change are therefore underpinned and enacted by micro-institutional processes of reproduction and contestation.

Fourth, since the actions of social agents are given such an important role in the social-institutional approach, it is a critical objective to identify *underlying human motives and strategies* in considering the processes of institutional change. In reality, institutional stability and change are political processes, not processes of reproduction or repudiation which are socially passive, spontaneous or innocent of motive and power. In the face of social contestation, institutional order is sustained by processes of legitimacy acquisition and attribution, supported by the underlying threat of coercion by those whose interests are served by the status quo. Processes of institutional change are underwritten by the motivated and strategic actions of concrete social agents, who have emotional, intellectual and practical stakes, personally and sectionally, in the outcomes of the transition. Our examination of the processes of deinstitutionalization and reinstitutionalization at the level of the enterprise has found substantial evidence for the contestation of the redefinitions of post-communist management and organization, especially by middle managers. However, it also points to the substantial influence of enterprise managers on emergent concepts and practices. These managers had enough power and status, and a collective interest in the ways management was being defined, perceived, rewarded and legitimated, and enterprises were being restructured and privatized.

Czech organization and management: Historical limitations and future possibilities

In 1989, many transition economists had approached the transformation of the former state socialist countries with a certainty and a confidence in their prognoses and policy recipes for the delivery of a fully fledged, Western-style market economy. Within a few years, observers realized that socio-economic transformation was more than a technical design problem.[1] Our own analysis highlights the complex normative and behavioural foundations of economic order and change, and points to the impossibility of shaking off historical legacies and residues in understanding the nature of transformation. But questions remain about the emergent institutional forms of the Czech economy. To what degree have Czech enterprises and their managements adopted features associated with the Western business corporation, taken as the model of market-economic organization and management? In what ways have the emergent forms of organization and management taken on characteristics that are distinctively Czech, reflecting the socio-economic legacies of the country's experience?

The empirical scope of this book is of course limited in strict statistical terms to the experiences of just four enterprises and sixty or so managers, and it is necessary to be wary of generalizing too far. However, given the aims of the research project, we shall offer a summary portrait of the post-communist Czech organization and its management as they appear to have developed in the early 1990s. Before we do so, it is important to understand the parameters of these conclusions, recognizing the scope for diversity in Czech organization and management, and to contextualize them within the broader trends of the economic transition.

Inter-enterprise differences

The adoption of Western institutional forms and practices has varied from industry to industry and from enterprise to enterprise. Since we focused on organization and management in former state enterprises, any conclusions must recognize the essential differences between enterprises privatized through the mass privatization scheme and others, whether set up anew or privatized through foreign investment. The consumer goods and the food industries, for example, have seen major inflows of foreign capital and foreign competition, which have placed technical and normative pressures on domestic firms to change rapidly and to adopt Western-style features of management. Similarly, in industries where small firms have flourished, such as retail services, small labour-intensive production and trading, strong competition has focused the minds of managers on modern management techniques. We would contend that the case enterprises have experienced similar problems to, and share key features with, a large proportion of the former state enterprises in Czech industry. In certain respects, the four enterprises are typical of many such organizations during the transition period: they tend to have a relatively strong relationship with their communities; they manufacture and assemble large, specialized mechanical engineering products, in general for industrial clients; their former partners were often in the old CMEA trading bloc; they have been all privatized without the assistance of FDI.

The arguments in this volume have emphasized the common problems faced and solutions adopted by the enterprise managers in the sample, but it has become evident at various stages of the story that, even within our small sample, the emergence of organization and management has taken diverse routes. Each enterprise is of course unique in various respects, and this reflects the actual path of its historical development, its specific inheritances from state socialism, its products and technology, the nature of its community and the ways in which its new management has sought to deal with the problems of its particular transitional environment. It has not been the aim of this book to dwell on these differences,[2] but some passing comments are appropriate before we end, in order to put the conclusions into perspective.

Vols stands out as being the gradualist of the four, making minimal, incremental changes to its employment, its products, its management body, its social assets and so on. Our view of Vols is that it has been deeply affected by the nature of its state socialist past and of its local role. Vols is located in what was known as a communist town, and the role of the enterprise and its managers has always been oriented towards looking after its isolated, dependent community. The managers at all levels expressed strong social commitment to Volna, and some of the senior managers were referred to as pink managers – that is, their social(ist) concerns affected their ability and/or willingness to make decisions for purely economically rational purposes. In such circumstances, it is not surprising that the transformation has been enacted as a slower, more gradual process, with a tendency towards a change and retrenchment pathway. The enterprise's decisions to revert to former Soviet trade are consonant with such a portrait.

In contrast to Vols, Jesenické Strojírny may be classified as the radical transformer, having from an early stage adopted a policy of fundamental decentralization, and, despite opposition, driving forward the implementation of the holding company project. It also embraced for some time the progressive rhetoric of human resource management, and attempted methodically to develop a strong organizational culture. Jesenické Strojírny had always been the most forward-looking of the enterprises even in state socialist days, when its attempts to divisionalize during the late 1960s were brought to an end only with the repressive impact of economic normalization. The autocratic and well-connected (hence well-protected) enterprise director encouraged innovative and even deviant management practices, and this sustained a culture with progressive elements. In 1989, Jesenické Strojírny stood in a relatively advantageous position, with managers who had fairly up-to-date knowledge, even experience, of Western management ideas in the realm of, for example, structural design and marketing.

Among the four enterprises, Montáže Jesenice holds a singular position. It was created in 1990 from Jesenické Strojírny, and its relative smallness and new independence allowed it to be a flexible and dynamic transformer during the transitional period. It was the most successful of the enterprises during privatization, acquired quality standards most rapidly and found new clients in different markets. However, there is no doubt that the senior managers of Jesenické Strojírny did not like its assembly plant being separated, and it remains to be seen whether their success in bringing Montáže Jesenice back into the organizational fold will allow Montáže Jesenice to continue to benefit from its smallness.

Agstroj had been the most successful of the state-owned enterprises before 1989, but its path towards transformation has been difficult, if not regressive. It has been unable to find sufficient new markets for its gigantic production capacity, has had limited success in the privatization process or in its desperate search for new capital, has continued throughout the period to make operating losses, is unable to repay debts and has been stunted in its attempts to take on modern decentralized organizational forms. Agstroj is still, albeit indirectly, accountable to agents of the state and requires the financial support of the state to prevent its bankruptcy. Agstroj has more than the others been dramatically hampered in the transformation process by its past, and its strategic and operational management are dominated by the overwhelming financial burden of its economic position. Early attempts to be progressive in management and organizational changes have therefore been repulsed by the need for hierarchical and centralized stringency.

These few paragraphs illustrate that the four enterprises have approached the economic transition in different ways, and these can be described at the most local level of concrete economic behaviour. The uniqueness of each enterprise can result from a wide variety of historical and contemporary factors, and generate a range of different pathways towards their own transformation (Greenwood and Hinings, 1988; Laughlin, 1991). Despite these differences, the overwhelming sense of the findings is that the four enterprises have more in common than not.

Key organizational issues in the Czech transition

In order to contemplate these commonalities from a broader perspective, we need to consider several relevant issues of the economic transition. By raising questions about corporate governance, banking and finance, market relations, the new management class and the role of the state, this discussion examines the vulnerability of the incipient institutions of the capitalist market economy that is unfolding in the Czech Republic, and contextualizes conclusions about Czech organization and management in transformation.

Corporate governance and the new owners

The longer-term evaluation of the processes of economic transformation must reflect an understanding of the development of appropriate institutional mechanisms of corporate governance: that is, systems, rules and practices of external control and supervision that replace the previous centralized use of bureaucratic authority and permit market-derived signals to influence internal management decision-making and enterprise performance. There may be some debate over what sort of market economy will prevail, and hence over how corporate governance can ensure that managements respond in the interests of shareholders, but the processes of organizational and managerial transformation should give some clues about how new practices of external control are emerging, especially following privatization.

> The complicated institutional framework that ensures the proper governance of the corporation constitutes the very core of the capitalist infrastructure that is completely missing from East European societies. The task of privatization is to construct such a governance structure and institute it in an environment in which there is a pronounced lack of available personnel and a potentially unfavorable political structure.
>
> (Frydman and Rapaczynski, 1994, p. 56)

Where the enterprises adopted a private legal status as a consequence of their participation in the mass privatization process (see Perotti, 1994), the nature of corporate governance depends on the motives and objectives of the ICs, the IPFs and their representatives on boards of directors, which affect the way they conduct their control function (Brom and Orenstein, 1994). Our research, being focused mainly on internal management processes and changes, gives us only limited clues about the directions in which corporate governance has moved in the four privatized enterprises, but within the documented features of the Czech transitional context we can make a number of observations.

In Chapter 9 we commented on the developments at board level in the four privatized enterprises, and noted that, after an initial phase of passivity, the IPFs acted to strengthen their position on the boards and become more pro-active in matters that might normally be considered to be internal management concerns. From their position on the boards, the representatives have been able to encourage internal management to take decisions that serve their (the representatives') interests, e.g. to employ their consultancy services or to do business with their preferred contacts and suppliers. Other observers have noted that the ultimate owners of the largest IPFs and ICs – that is, the big commercial banks – have used their ownership connection to consolidate old business, or to open up new, financial business with the newly privatized enterprises, thus locking ownership patterns into commercial arrangements (e.g. Brom and Orenstein, 1994; Coffee, 1994; Takla, 1994; Laštovička *et al.*, 1995).

In particular, such conduct suggests that IPFs, their owners and representatives have used their new proprietorial status as a means of cultivating collaborative business contacts, and this strand of evidence and line of argument has some significance for the future of Czech market capitalism. The IPF representatives at one and the same time may represent the IPF or IC (or bank) which appointed them or their own firms, and may have used their positions on the boards of directors to bring off preferential transactions with the enterprise in question, thus tying them into socio-economic networks which we have already described as a continuation of normal business practices from the past. Under such circumstances, it would not be in their interests to move for bankruptcy or radical management change which may itself threaten their own business interests. For these reasons, it is difficult to see how their presence could constitute external control or monitoring of the strategic prioritizing of internal management decisions in the interests of all shareholders.

Transformation and the shortage of new capital

All the four enterprises were privatized directly or indirectly through the voucher system, and could thus be considered as typical of Czech industry. A specific feature of mass voucher privatization has been its inability to deliver the new capital and investment required, particularly in the heavy and mechanical engineering sectors. Domestic savings and funds were inadequate for the effective recapitalization and development of Czech industry (Šik, 1993, p. 194; Frydman and Rapaczynski, 1994, pp. 15–16), and neither the banks nor the other financial institutions have offered substantial sources of new capital for the privatized enterprises.

The largest banks, successors of the monobanking system, have had to service the bad debts inherited from before 1990, and, in their questionable business practices of continued lending to their old, former state enterprise clients, have reproduced accumulating bad debts as a feature of the transition economy. As ultimate owners of the largest IPFs and through their loans to their old clients (to whom they are now also linked by ownership), banks and other financial enterprises have effectively committed a lot of the available domestic capital to large privatized enterprises which may not be the business activities most likely to invest it in new products and technologies. Through the voucher privatization, the banks' IC subsidiaries also successfully acquired shares in competing banks, and there evolved a substantial cross-holding of shares in the financial institutions. There is a danger that such banking practices, of lending to old 'safe' enterprises and using new proprietorial authority in the privatized enterprises to consolidate or expand financial business, will spread across the financial system as institutionalized features. If one of the main objectives of the banks has been to develop their own business through enterprise ownership, there can be little incentive for them to encourage their subjects to seek new capital by share issues which would at the same time dilute their IPFs' ownership and influence.

In the absence of adequate amounts of or channels for domestic capital, the only other way of financing the modernization of the Czech economy has been through foreign investment. For a variety of reasons (see Chapter 8) the managers in our enterprises have not been very favourably inclined to FDI, being very wary of the motives of foreign investors in setting up commercial relationships or joint ventures. Like many other former state enterprises, our enterprises failed during and after the privatization process to attract FDI, a not insubstantial proportion of which has been largely placed in a few high-profile deals. The size of FDI inflows has not been sufficient to renew or update the capital base of a largely old-fashioned engineering industry.

Lack of capital provides a major challenge for a transitional economy. Most enterprises have been unable to attend to questions of their long-term strategic development, and investment and new product development suitable for Western markets have progressed at a very slow pace, sustaining the enterprises' vulnerability during the transition period. The current state of the banking and financial sector simply exacerbates the problems of the enterprises. Twelve banks have collapsed in the four years from 1993 to 1996, often as the result of bad or possibly illegal lending practices, creating a lot of uncertainty and bad debt problems that will not go away. Such symptoms may not add up to a crisis, but they do have major micro- and macroeconomic implications: inhibiting the modernization of the viable private and privatized enterprises; forcing enterprises to continue the survival strategies (see Chapter 8) longer than would otherwise have been necessary; encouraging the drift back to traditional markets, such as the former Soviet Union (see Chapter 8), where enterprises could count on their former reputations and where clients have traditionally been less concerned with modern product specification; and slowing down the elaboration of post-communist industrial structures.

Post-communist management and the nomenklatura legacy

One of the most conspicuous findings of the research has been the degree to which former *nomenklatura* managers have retained positions of power in the privatized enterprises, and this raises questions about the longer-term implications for the institution of management. Three years after the enterprises had succeeded to privatized status, the positions of these managers have become secure and the influence they exercise in enterprise decision-making is likely to remain for many years. While issues of post-communist legitimacy are still on the political agenda, as illustrated by the debate during 1996 about renewing and extending the lustration legislation, most managers in the four enterprises are far less vulnerable to challenges about their communist pasts because questions of managerial legitimacy are now rarely asked at enterprise level.

The more significant questions concern the degree to which you can teach old dogs new tricks – given the twenty, sometimes thirty, years of experience of state socialist management, how far can new management learning be more than superficial? At one level, there can be little doubt that the managers, particularly the top managers, have absorbed the concepts and vocabulary of Western management knowledge, but there is the suspicion that the advocacy of new ideas and practices has been located within political games to renovate the image of the managers themselves. The demise of the strategic role of HRM in Jesenické Strojírny, following its initially powerful sponsorship from the top, is a case in point. From the perspective of effective organizational transformation, the ability to express the concepts and values of TQM, marketing or HRM is not enough – both the ideas and the practices need to seep deeply into the enterprise. As one senior Jesenické Strojírny manager commented, 'All the top managers have changed their views, but the workers still don't even know the words.' Many middle management respondents in the case enterprises continued to ask questions about the competence of their seniors, implying that they had not been convinced by their superordinates about the depth of the organizational and management changes that were taking place.

We have noted that senior managers have found it rational, and probably socially comforting, to reproduce their former socio-economic networking practices as a means of overcoming difficult problems in the transitional environment, and that such conduct will continue, at least for the next few years, to maintain the economic significance of past connections in the present conditions. These networks will diminish slowly in relevance and importance, their communist origins will be forgotten and their foundations will be replaced by new social rationales: for example, the new business clubs and associations which are shooting up in the larger towns as meeting places for senior managers. Since many of the post-communist, former *nomenklatura* managers are relatively young – in Jesenické Strojírny, for example, the majority of the senior management team are in their mid-forties – they may have up to another twenty years at the top, and reproduce practices with subtle, increasingly distant, resonances of the pre-1989 enterprise.

The vibrancy of state enterprise legacies in the longer-term future of the Czech economy will depend on other factors, such as the quality and nature of Czech business and management education. Universities have been importing Western business ideas in great profusion, and British and American MBAs have been introduced in a number of institutions. Drawing on personal anecdotal evidence, student-managers seem to have a healthy scepticism about unadulterated Western management knowledge, but many graduates and academics involved in the delivery of business education see themselves as educational entrepreneurs who can make nice side-earnings out of Western ideas and knowledge packaged as a product to be sold on the management market. Subjects with a hard and direct impact on business, like financial management, marketing, information technology and strategic management, are therefore highly desirable and attractive for academic specialization, while studies of personnel, human resources and organizational behaviour remain underdeveloped, with less academic take-up and support. The consequences of this pattern of management education are not yet clear but, given the importance of human resource issues in the modern business world, the longer-term balance of management expertise and competence may be unfortunate.

New management through new private business

The transformation of Czech management and organization depends not only on what has happened in the large former state enterprises and the new privatized sector, but also on developments in *private* business since 1989. In Chapter 6, we noted the rapid expansion of new private businesses following the deregulation of ownership and the programmes of reprivatization and small privatization. As mentioned above, it might be expected that this business sector, comprising flexible and dynamic small and medium-sized firms, is where modern management techniques will most easily take hold, and where the longer-term institutions of management and organization will be formed. Yet there are doubts about the ways in which new businesses have been created and run.

This partly relates to the banking practices which have made it hard for small, more risky, ventures to acquire capital. There have been many questions about the origins of capital in some firms which have expanded rapidly in an environment of capital shortage. One controversy concerns the role of 'dirty money' in business start-ups and expansions, and many people, when asked, have stories to tell about new firms in the community. At the same time, it has also been suggested that senior politicians and liberal economists have turned a blind eye to the sources of business funding because of their enthusiasm for encouraging the rapid expansion of this sector. In opposition to this expedient attitude, some have argued that the moral foundations of new capital do matter, since they send out signals and expectations about the effective institutional norms of business and management (e.g. Reed, 1995).

A supplementary issue concerns the backgrounds of the most successful local entrepreneurs. The evidence reported in this book, and some as yet unreported findings emanating from on-going research, indicate that there are different types of small business person. First, there are skilled workers and technicians who started craft or service firms, often, to begin with, as a part-time occupation to supplement employee earnings – such firms tend to grow only very slowly. Such people may have been the beneficiaries of the restitution process, receiving small property back into the family. Several groups of skilled Montáže Jesenice employees broke away from the enterprise to set up as competitors in small-scale assembly work; other employees started building services, or reopened a family restaurant. Second, there are senior managers whose position allowed them access to inside information on the worth of small properties hived off from large enterprises, giving them business bargains as well as an opportunity to escape the uncertainties of life in a state enterprise. Third, there are the former *nomenklatura*, who left, 'retired' or were ejected from the large enterprises in 1989 to 1990; and a related group made up of sons and daughters of former *nomenklatura*. These last two groups were in a privileged position, not only because they had the chance to accumulate money and resources from their earlier advantages, which, in the early period after 1989, went a long way in buying property; but also because their socio-economic networks allowed them to build up business rapidly within an industry related to their original enterprises and their own expertise. Our research has revealed several examples of such entrepreneurs, of which the most eminent was Engineer J, former director of Jesenické Strojírny. Engineer J left Jesenické Strojírny in 1990 and started a marketing agency, which conducted business not only with Jesenické Strojírny, but also with Jesenické Strojírny's former state socialist partners at home and abroad. With others, he later started a travel business centred on enhanced sports facilities which, while under his control, Jesenické Strojírny had built and expanded over the 1980s. His third business venture was an IPF which has since 1993 become an influential player in Jesenické Strojírny.

The stories about the development of the local economies of Volna and Jesenice belong to another book, but these short excerpts suggest that, to a lesser or greater extent, an important section of the emergent private business sector has fallen under the control of the same type of person who has continued to dominate the new privatized sector. Some of the same questions and doubts must therefore apply, concerning, for example, the willingness and ability of management to abandon old ideas and practices and to assimilate and implement new management knowledge. In short, our evidence from both within the enterprises and within the local economies indicates that the influential business and management class of the transitional economy comprises largely converted *nomenklatura*. In that many social scientists believe that the motivational force behind a healthy market economy must derive from an active, entrepreneurial capitalist class like that found in the West, the values, objectives and interests of former *nomenklatura* acting as a class may result in rather confounding outcomes. At the least, this may slow down the rate at which local and national economic transformation can be accomplished in the way desired by transition economists.

The continuing role of the state?

The final issue to be raised concerns the degree to which the mode of the Czech transition has realized a greater independence of the economic institutions from the hand of the state. Of course, there can be no doubting that the collapse of the central planning institutions has diminished the authoritative significance of the state as an economic actor, and the political rhetoric and posture of Klaus and his ruling right-wing coalition have reinforced the view of a free-market, liberal economy. However, as we noted in Chapter 6, the reality of the mediating role of the state in economic affairs has meant that, possibly necessarily, the transformation has been rather less extreme.

The state has played a central role in the design of the privatization process, and, despite the assertion that the restructuring of state-owned enterprises should proceed *after* the establishment of new private ownership, the reality was very different. In the four enterprises, senior managers went about restructuring from an early stage, and one of the aims was to make the new organization look more modern and rational in the eyes of their major stakeholder – the state. The consequent ownership patterns were the often unintended results of the mass privatization process designed by the government and its advisers. After the first wave, the state, through the NPF, continued to play a significant role in the external control of those many enterprises which had not been completely sold – in our sample, Jesenické Strojírny, Vols and Agstroj. Even after the second wave, it is estimated that the NPF is the largest owner of productive property in the Czech Republic.[3] Only at the end of 1996 was the government planning a more radical sell-off of the large banks, which, as mentioned above, have remained 30 to 50 per cent owned by the NPF, as well as owning, through their ICs and IPFs, a substantial proportion of voucher-privatized assets.

The state continues, tacitly and indirectly, to influence the economic transition in a variety of ways. Through the behaviour of the large banks, and by using institutional devices like the Consolidation Bank, the state has controlled the burden of bad debts and restrained the free-market economic processes of bankruptcy – the case of Agstroj, as told throughout the book, is illustrative. This has strongly influenced the structure and dynamics of the labour market, sustaining unrealistically low rates of unemployment, far below any comparable transition economy let alone any other major European country. It is likely that there is still a shake-out of overstaffing to come, but at the same time the conditions encourage enterprise managers to hold on to their labour resources for fear of being unable to recruit in the future. Meanwhile, the state continues to regulate rents, holding them below market levels and discouraging the geographical mobility of labour.

The rhetoric of liberal economics does not accord with the reality of the state's practical policies. It has been argued that such a wily set of policies has been the foundation of the strength of the Czech economic transition, sustaining a public commitment to the democratic-market ideal by implicitly subsidizing social stability. This in itself may or may not be criticized, but from an institutional viewpoint it remains important to emphasize that the state has continued to play a substantial role in the emerging form of the Czech economy.

Patterns of Czech organization and management

We are now in a position to summarize the features of organization and management that have developed in the post-communist transition, especially in those privatized enterprises which have had little direct association with Western corporations. Specifically, we are concerned with assessing whether the forms have emerged as reflections of Western management models, or whether historical and contemporary influences have led to patterns of organization and management which are distinctively Czech.

We begin by indicating the ways in which Czech enterprises have developed as a response to a Western role model. First, senior managers have acquired and mastered many aspects of the ideology and rhetoric of Western management. They are relatively fluent in the languages of marketing, human resource management, quality management and so on, so that the outsider, and even the uncritical insider, would be impressed by the transformation of these born-again industrial capitalists. The degree to which this knowledge has been successfully applied – for example, in the areas of marketing and personnel management – is less remarkable. Second, with mixed success but continuing commitment, the enterprises have all undertaken processes of decentralization in management and organization. This feature is exemplified by the managers' obsession with organizational designs and changes that have moved sequentially through the forms of increasing internal marketization, culminating in the dream of the holding company and its daughters. Third, to different degrees, all the enterprises have been downsized, reducing the excesses of overstaffing and therefore becoming more like their Western counterparts. Fourth, the enterprises have all sharpened their production focus, lessening their former social role and dispensing with many of their 'unproductive' activities and assets. Such actions have displaced the costs of social provision to the community and the state, and have potentially had significant implications for the previous institutionalized relationships between economic enterprise and social community. Finally, the managers have undertaken policies explicitly oriented to making their own role and status more closely attuned to their Western counterparts. Post-communist employment management has introduced changes in contracts and reward systems that have increasingly institutionalized social and economic inequalities between managers and employees that are similar to the West. In this way, the political separation of organizational groups that had typified state socialism has given way to standard capitalist forms of social and economic differentiation.

Despite these trends towards more market-economic forms, there are reasons to reject the simple view that the privatized enterprises have been successfully converted into Western-style corporations. Not only has there been a gap between the acquisition of the ideas and their application in practice, but alongside the adoption of new Western ideas has coexisted an array of old values, customs and practices which continue to find their expression in everyday organizational behaviour. First, many of the same types of people – former *nomenklatura* – are still in influential positions, and, as we have argued throughout the book, they have tended to manage the enterprises in ways that have safeguarded their own interests and preferences. Their values still contain observable traces of 'redness' or 'pinkness' and place great emphasis on securing the social support of the employees and the surrounding community, especially in enterprises (like Vols) whose communist roots and social role were deeply engrained in the conscience of managers. Managers exhibit a proud sense of Czechness and a parallel scepticism towards Western ideas, Western capital and Western motives. The managerial value system is at once nationalistic and community-focused (rather than parochial, in a pejorative sense), and acts as a natural barrier or filter to the extreme market-economic practices that the dominant politicians and transition economists would like to see adopted. Second, these enterprises have been, directly or indirectly, beneficiaries of state protection (e.g. via implicit industrial policies, NPF ownership, Consolidation Bank support, bank lending policies), allowing them to operate without the full impact of external market constraint. It is certainly difficult to see how any of the three large enterprises could have survived without some degree of state-sponsored support and 'understanding'. Third, patterns of corporate governance in these privatized enterprises have taken a different form from the Anglo-American or German types. Available evidence from the early post-privatization period suggests that external ownership has in part become a way of assuring trading relationships and giving competitive advantage to banks, IPFs and their representatives. Fourth, and relatedly, the enterprise managers have continued to coordinate their 'market' activities using networks of contacts, founded on former Communist Party ties, which had been the basis of realizing transactions in the past. Although, as time goes by, the use of these old contacts to by-pass competitive market forces will diminish, the socio-economic networking is likely to have become a widely accepted aspect of business practice – an institutionalized feature of management. Fifth, as implied in networking as strategic behaviour, personal values and preferences have continued to play a significant role in certain spheres of internal management. Evidence of appointment and promotion practices suggests that the enterprise managers still run a relatively paternalistic regime and exercise patronage in a number of organizational domains.

The hope in 1989–90 was that once the enterprises had their private owners and the spectre of state control had vanished, the organizations and their managers would have the freedom to develop unconstrained the structures, practices and systems necessary to participate in a competitive market economy as equals. For many transition economists, this was tantamount to expecting that the process of reinstitutionalization would take hold and progress smoothly and rapidly towards Western-style models. The world of economic transformation has shown itself to be less predictable and orderly than this. There have not emerged common patterns of Czech management and organization that adequately describe enterprises of different sizes across various industries; and the patterns that have emerged in the large privatized enterprises, which make up a sizable part of the Czech economy, have not shown a singular tendency towards any Western patterns. In fact, privatized enterprises have continued to reproduce significant aspects of their state socialist past, and these coexist in awkward juxtaposition with various characteristics of Western corporate practices. The organizational and managerial legacies have not only remained part of the management reper-toire of privatized enterprises, they have also acted as inbuilt cultural and behavioural constraints to the assimilation and implementation of market-economic knowledge.

By the time the formal institutions of private property and free markets had been properly established in the economy – arguably as late as 1995 – Czech managements had developed their own distinctive patterns of response to the demands of the transitional environment. As a variable amalgam of Western and Czech knowledge and practice, managers' post-communist business recipes had their origins in their pre-1989 experiences, their social values as Czechs, their local expectations as members of a community and, for many, their motives as surviving *nomenklatura*. Being powerful economic actors, these managers have had a crucial role in transforming the institutions of management and organization, and it is likely that the redefinitions of the early transition period will have lasting effects on the microeconomic institutions of the market economy which will eventually stabilize.

Notes

1 One consequence of the transition experience has undoubtedly been the recognition that we know little about how Western market economies actually function, and the hidden assumptions and taken for granted foundations upon which they are built (see Frydman and Rapaczynski, 1994).
2 We have begun such an analysis in a recent publication (Clark and Soulsby, 1998).
3 The Czech Centre for Voucher Privatization (1995, p. 27) indicates that, following the second wave, the NPF continued to have a long-term holding of 10 per cent of the capital stock, while about 20 per cent is still awaiting private owners.

References

Abercrombie, N., Hill, S. and Turner, B. (1980) *The Dominant Ideology Thesis*, London: Allen and Unwin.

Adam, J. (1993) 'Transformation to a market economy in the former Czechoslovakia', *Europe-Asia Studies*, 45(4), 627–45.

Adam, J. (1994) 'Mass privatization in Central and East European countries', *Moct-Most*, 4(1), 87–100.

Altmann, F.-L. (1987) 'Employment policies in Czechoslovakia', in J. Adam (ed.), *Employment Policies in the Soviet Union and Eastern Europe*, 2nd edition, London: Macmillan, pp. 78–103.

Anderle, J. (1979) 'The First Republic 1919–1938', in H. Brisch and I. Volgyes (eds), *Czechoslovakia: The Heritage of Ages Past. Essays in Memory of Josef Korbel*, Boulder, CO: East European Quarterly, pp. 89–112.

Arato, A. (1982) 'Critical sociology and authoritarian state socialism', in J. Thompson and D. Held (eds), *Habermas: Critical Debates*, London: Macmillan, pp. 196–218.

Arnot, B. (1988) *Controlling Soviet Labour: Experimental Change from Brezhnev to Gorbachev*, London: Macmillan.

Batt, J. (1991) *East Central Europe from Reform to Transformation*, London: Pinter.

Berger, P. and Luckmann, T. (1971) *The Social Construction of Reality*, Harmondsworth: Penguin.

Bohatá, M. (1996a) 'The changing patterns of Czech foreign trade', *CERGE-EI Working Paper Series*, No. 95, March.

Bohatá, M. (1996b) 'Small and medium-sized enterprises in the Czech manufacturing industry', *CERGE-EI Working Paper Series*, No. 94, March.

Bohatá, M., Hanel, P. and Fischer, M. (1995) 'Performance in manufacturing', in J. Svejnar (ed.), *The Czech Republic and Economic Transition in Eastern Europe*, San Diego: Academic Press, pp. 255–83.

Brabant, J. M. van (1991) *The Planned Economies and International Economic Organizations*, Cambridge: Cambridge University Press.

Bradach, J. and Eccles, R. (1991) 'Price, authority and trust: from ideal type to plural forms', in G. Thompson, J. Frances, R. Levačić and J. Mitchell (eds), *Markets, Hierarchies and Networks: the Coordination of Social Life*, London: Sage, pp. 277–92.

Brewster, C. (1992) 'Starting again: industrial relations in Czechoslovakia', *International Journal of Human Resource Management*, 3(3), 555–74.

Brisch, H. and Volgyes, I. (1979) *Czechoslovakia: The Heritage of Ages Past*, Boulder, CO: East European Quarterly.

Brom, K. and Orenstein, M. (1994) 'The privatized sector in the Czech Republic: government and bank control in a transitional economy', *Europe-Asia Studies*, 46(6), 893–928.

Burawoy, M. (1985) *The Politics of Production*, London: Verso.

Burawoy, M. and Krotov, P. (1992) 'The Soviet transition from socialism to capitalism: worker control and economic bargaining in the wood industry', *American Sociological Review*, 57(1), 16–38.

Burawoy, M. and Lukács, J. (1992) *The Radiant Past: Ideology and Reality in Hungary's Road to Capitalism*, Chicago: University of Chicago Press.

Callinicos, A. (1991) *The Revenge of History: Marxism and the East European Revolutions*, Cambridge: Polity Press.

Čapek, A. (1994) 'The bad debt problem in the Czech economy', *Moct–Most*, 4(3), 59–70.

Cekota, J. (1995) 'Barriers to European (East–West) integration', in R. Dobrinsky and M. Landesmann (eds), *Transforming Economies and European Integration*, Aldershot: Edward Elgar, pp. 32–45.

Centre for Voucher Privatization (1995) *Voucher Privatization in Facts and Figures*, Prague: CKP.

Červinka, A. (1987) 'The State Enterprise Act', *Czechoslovak Economic Digest*, 6, 3–12.

Child, J. (1993) 'Society and enterprise between hierarchy and market', in J. Child, M. Crozier, R. Mayntz *et al.* (eds), *Societal Change between Market and Organization*, Aldershot: Avebury, pp. 203–26.

Child, J. and Markóczy, L. (1993) 'Host country managerial behaviour and learning in Chinese and Hungarian joint ventures', *Journal of Management Studies*, 30(4), 611–31.

Clague, C. (1992) 'Introduction: the journey to a market economy', in C. Clague and G. Rausser (eds), *The Emergence of Market Economies in Eastern Europe*, Oxford: Blackwell, pp. 1–22.

Clague, C. and Rausser, G. (eds) (1992) *The Emergence of Market Economies in Eastern Europe*, Oxford: Blackwell.

Clark, E. and Soulsby, A. (1995) 'Transforming former state enterprises in the Czech Republic', *Organization Studies*, 16(2), 215–42.

Clark, E. and Soulsby, A. (1996) 'The re-formation of the managerial elite in the Czech Republic', *Europe-Asia Studies* 48(2), 285–303.

Clark, E. and Soulsby, A. (1998) 'Organization-community embeddedness: the social impact of enterprise restructuring in the post-communist Czech Republic', *Human Relations* 51(1), 25–50.

Coffee, J. (1994) 'Investment privatization funds: the Czech experience', mimeo.

Crocioni, P. (1995) 'Privatization in Eastern Europe: the case of the Czech Republic', *The International Spectator*, 30(1), 79–103.

Crouch, C. (1979) 'The state, capital and liberal democracy', in C. Crouch (ed.), *State and Economy in Contemporary Capitalism*, London: Croom Helm, pp. 13–54.

Crouch, C. and Dore, R. (1990) 'Whatever happened to corporatism?', in C. Crouch and R. Dore (eds), *Corporatism and Accountability: Organized Interests in British Public Life*, Oxford: Oxford University Press, pp. 1–43.

Czechoslovak Economic Digest (1988) 'The Law on State Enterprise', *Czechoslovak Economic Digest*, 6, 5–44.

Cziria, L. (1995) 'The Czech and Slovak Republics', in J. Thirkell, R. Scase and S. Vickerstaff (eds), *Labour Relations and Political Change in Eastern Europe*, London: UCL Press, pp. 61–80.

D'Andrade, R.G. (1984) 'Cultural meaning systems', in R. Shwedder and R. LeVine (eds), *Culture Theory: Essays on Mind, Self and Emotions*, Cambridge: Cambridge University Press, pp. 88–119.

Dawisha, K. (1990) *Eastern Europe, Gorbachev and Reform: The Great Challenge*, 2nd edition, Cambridge: Cambridge University Press.

Deacon, B. (1992) 'East European welfare: past, present and future in comparative context', in B. Deacon *et al.* (eds), *The New Eastern Europe: Social Policy Past, Present and Future*, London: Sage, pp. 1–30.

DiMaggio, P. and Powell, W. (1991) 'The iron cage revisited: institutional isomorphism and collective rationality', in W. Powell and P. DiMaggio (eds), *The New Institutionalism in Organizational Analysis*, Chicago: University of Chicago Press, pp. 63–82.

Djilas, M. (1957) *The New Class*, London: Thames and Hudson.

Dlouhý, V. and Mládek, J. (1994) 'Privatization and corporate control in the Czech Republic', *Economic Policy*, 19(5), 156–70.

Dobrinsky, R. (1995) 'Economic transformation and the changing patterns of European East–West trade', in R. Dobrinsky and M. Landesmann (eds), *Transforming Economies and European Integration*, Aldershot: Edward Elgar, pp. 86–115.

Drábek, Z. (1995) 'IMF and IBRD policies in the former Czechoslovakia', *Journal of Comparative Economics*, 20(2), 235–64.

Dubey-Villinger, N. (1996) 'The management of alliances in East-Central Europe', unpublished PhD thesis, University of Cambridge.

Dyba, K. and Kouba, K. (1989) 'Czechoslovak attempts at systematic change: 1958, 1968, 1988', *Communist Economies*, 1(3), 313–25.

Dyba, K. and Svejnar, J. (1995) 'A comparative view of economic developments in the Czech Republic', in J. Svejnar (ed.), *The Czech Republic and Economic Transition in Eastern Europe*, San Diego: Academic Press, pp. 21–45.

Dyker, D. (1981) 'Planning and the worker', in L. Shapiro and J. Godson (eds), *The Soviet Worker: Illusions and Realities*, London: Macmillan, pp. 39–75.

Earle, J., Frydman, R. and Rapaczynski, A. (eds) (1993) *Privatization in the Transition to a Market Economy*, London: Pinter.

Eliás, Z. and Netík, J. (1966) 'Czechoslovakia', in W. Griffith (ed.), *Communism in Europe: Continuity, Change and the Sino–Soviet Dispute*, Volume 2, Cambridge, MA: MIT Press.

Estrin, S. (ed) (1994a) *Privatization in Central and Eastern Europe*, Harlow: Longman.

Estrin, S. (1994b) 'Economic transition and privatization: the issues', in S. Estrin (ed.), *Privatization in Central and Eastern Europe*, Harlow: Longman, pp. 3–30.

Femia, J. (1975) 'Hegemony and consciousness in the thought of Antonio Gramsci', *Political Studies*, 1, 29–40.

Fligstein, N. (1985) 'The spread of the multidivisional form among large firms, 1919–1979', *American Sociological Review*, 50, 377–91.

Friedland, R. and Alford, R. (1991) 'Bringing society back in: symbols, practices and institutional contradictions', in W. Powell and P. DiMaggio (eds), *The New Institutionalism in Organizational Analysis*, Chicago: University of Chicago Press, pp. 232–63.

Frydman, R., Rapaczynski, A. and Earle J. (1993) *The Privatization Process in Central Europe*, Budapest: Central European Press.

Frydman, R. and Rapaczynski, A. (1994) *Privatization in Eastern Europe: Is the State Withering Away?*, London: Central European University Press.

Fulcher, J. (1991) *Labour Movements, Employers and the State: Conflict and Cooperation in Britain and Sweden*, Oxford: Clarendon Press.

Garton Ash, T. (1990) *We the People: The Revolution of 89*, London: Granta Books.

Giddens, A. (1979) *Central Problems in Social Theory*, London: Macmillan.

Giddens, A. (1984) *The Constitution of Society: Outline of the Theory of Structuration*, Cambridge: Polity Press.

Glenny, M. (1993) *The Rebirth of History: Eastern Europe in the Age of Democracy*, 2nd edition, Harmondsworth: Penguin.

Globokar, T. (1994) 'The role of culture in the reconstruction of enterprises in East and Central European countries', paper presented at the 6th International SASE conference, Paris, July 1994.

Golan, G. (1973) *Reform Rule in Czechoslovakia: The Dubček Era 1968–1969*, Cambridge: Cambridge University Press.

Graziani, G. (1995) 'Threats and opportunities for Western European industry deriving from trade liberalization with Central and Eastern Europe', in R. Dobrinsky and M. Landesmann (eds), *Transforming Economies and European Integration*, Aldershot: Edward Elgar, pp. 168–91.

Greenwood, R. and Hinings, C.R. (1988) 'Organizational design types, tracks and the dynamics of strategic change', *Organization Studies*, 9(3), 293–316.

Gros, D. and Steinherr, A. (1995) *Winds of Change: Economic Transition in Central and Eastern Europe*, New York: Longman.

Hába, Z. (1988) 'Waves of unequal height', *Czechoslovak Economic Digest*, 6, 45–61.

Habermas, J. (1976) *Legitimation Crisis*, London: Heinemann.

Hakansson, H. and Johanson, J. (1990) 'Formal and informal cooperation strategies in international industrial networks', in D. Ford (ed.), *Understanding Business Markets*, London: Academic Press, pp. 459–67.

Hare, P. (1991) 'The assessment: microeconomics of transition in Eastern Europe', *Oxford Review of Economic Policy*, 7, 1–15.

Hasager, L. (1986) *The Czechoslovak Economic Planning System*, Copenhagen: Institute of Finance, Copenhagen School of Economics and Business Administration.

Havlik, P. (1995) 'Trade reorientation and competitiveness in CEECs', in R. Dobrinsky and M. Landesmann (eds), *Transforming Economies and European Integration*, Aldershot: Edward Elgar, pp. 141–62.

Haynes, M. (1992) 'Class and crisis – the transition in Eastern Europe', *International Socialism*, 54, 45–104.

Hegewisch, A., Brewster, C. and Koubek, J. (1995) 'Different roads: changes in industrial and employee relations in the Czech Republic and East Germany since 1989', *Industrial Relations Journal*, 27(1), 50–64.

Héthy, L. (1994) 'Tripartism in Eastern Europe', in R. Hyman and A. Ferner (eds), *New Frontiers in European Industrial Relations*, Oxford: Blackwell, pp. 312–36.

Hrnčíř, M. (1993) 'Financial intermediation in former Czechoslovakia and the Czech Republic: lessons and progress evaluation', *Economic Systems*, 17(4), 301–27.

Huczynski, A. (1993) 'Explaining the succession of management fads', *International Journal of Human Resource Management*, 4(2), 443–63.

Ionescu, G. (1967) *The Politics of the European Communist States*, London: Weidenfeld and Nicolson.

Jancar, B. (1971) *Czechoslovakia and the Absolute Monopoly of Power: A Study of Political Power in a Communist System*, New York: Praeger.

Janeba, V. (1988) 'Experience gained from the comprehensive experiment', *Czechoslovak Economic Digest*, 4, 44–50.

Janyska, P. (1992) 'Imperfect but right: the Screening Act: anti-communist or antidemocratic?', *East European Reporter*, January/February, 59–60.

Jeffries, I. (1990) *A Guide to Socialist Economies*, London: Routledge.

Jeffries, I. (1993) *Socialist Economies and Their Transition to the Market*, London: Routledge.

Jepperson, R. (1991) 'Institutions, institutional effects and institutionalism', in W. Powell and P. DiMaggio (eds), *The New Institutionalism in Organizational Analysis*, Chicago: University of Chicago Press, pp. 143–63.

Johnston, R. and Lawrence, P. (1991) 'Beyond vertical integration – the rise of the value-adding partnership', in G. Thompson, J. Frances, R. Levačić and J. Mitchell (eds), *Markets, Hierarchies and Networks: The Coordination of Social Life*, London: Sage, pp. 193–202.

Kaplan, K. (1987) *The Communist Party in Power: A Profile of Party Politics in Czechoslovakia*, Boulder, CO: Westview.

Kaplan, K. (1989) 'Czechoslovakia's February 1948', in N. Stone and E. Strouhal (eds), *Czechoslovakia: Crossroads and Crises 1918–88*, Basingstoke: Macmillan, pp. 147–68.

Kaser, M. and Zieliński, J. (1970) *Planning in East Europe: Industrial Management by the State*, London: Bodley Head.

Kavan, J.(1992) 'Imperfect but wrong: the Screening Act: anti-communist or antidemocratic?', *East European Reporter*, January/February, 61.

Kenway, P. (1993) 'The role of the state in privatization in Poland and Czechoslovakia', *Moct–Most*, May, pp. 59–72.

Kerner, A. (1988) 'Reflections on the Draft Bill on the State Enterprise', *Czechoslovak Economic Digest*, 2, 47–65.

Kieżun, W. (1991) *Management in Socialist Countries*, Berlin: de Gruyter.

Kiss, Y. (1993) 'Lost illusions? Defence industry conversion in Czechoslovakia, 1989–92', *Europe-Asia Studies*, 45(6), 1045–69.

Klein, G. (1979) 'The Czechoslovak economy', in H. Brisch and I. Volgyes (eds), *Czechoslovakia: The Heritage of Ages Past. Essays in Memory of Josef Korbel*, Boulder, CO: East European Quarterly, pp. 147–58.

Kornai, J. (1980) *Economics of Shortage*, Volumes A and B, Amsterdam: North Holland Publishing.

Kosta, J. (1989) 'The Czechoslovak economic reform of the 1960s', in N. Stone and E. Strouhal (eds), *Czechoslovakia: Crossroads and Crises 1918–88*, Basingstoke: Macmillan, pp. 231–51.

Kotrba, J. (1995) 'Privatization process in the Czech Republic: players and winners', in J. Svejnar (ed.), *The Czech Republic and Economic Transition in Eastern Europe*, San Diego: Academic Press, pp. 159–98.

Kotrba, J. and Svejnar, J. (1994) 'Rapid and multifaceted privatization: experience of the Czech and Slovak Republics', *Moct–Most*, 4(2), 147–85.

Kouba, K. (1994) 'Systemic changes in the Czech economy after four years (1990–1993)', *Acta Oeconomica*, 46(3–4), 381–8.

Koubek, J. and Brewster, C. (1995) 'Human resource management in turbulent times: HRM in the Czech Republic', *The International Journal of Human Resource Management*, 6(2), 223–47.

Köves, A. (1992) *Central and East European Economies in Transition*, Oxford: Westview.

Koźmiński A. (1990) 'Market and state in centrally planned economies', *Current Sociology*, 38, 133–55.

Kupka, M. (1992) 'Transformation of ownership in Czechoslovakia', *Soviet Studies*, 44(2), 297–311.

Kupka, M. (1993) 'The privatization of state-owned assets', *Osteuropa Wirtschaft*, 38(2), 97–108.

Kusin, V. (1978) *From Dubček to Charter 77: A Study of Normalization in Czechoslovakia 1968–1978*, Edinburgh: Q Press.

Landesmann, M. (1995) 'The pattern of East–West European integration: catching up or falling behind', in R. Dobrinsky and M. Landesmann (eds), *Transforming Economies and European Integration*, Aldershot: Edward Elgar, pp. 116–40.

Lane, D. (1976) *The Socialist Industrial State: Towards a Political Sociology of Socialism*, London: Allen and Unwin.

Lane, D. (1987) *Soviet Labour and the Ethic of Communism: Full Employment and the Labour Process in the USSR*, Brighton: Wheatsheaf Books.

Laštovička, R., Marcinin, A. and Mejstík, M. (1995) 'Corporate governance and share prices in voucher privatized companies', in J. Svejnar (ed.), *The Czech Republic and Economic Transition in Eastern Europe*, San Diego: Academic Press, pp. 199–209.

Laughlin, R. (1991) 'Environmental disturbances and organizational transitions and transformations: some alternative models', *Organization Studies*, 12(2), 209–32.

Lavigne, M. (1991) *International Political Economy and Socialism*, Cambridge: Cambridge University Press.

Lavigne, M. (1995) *The Economics of Transition: From Socialist Economy to Market Economy*, Basingstoke: Macmillan.

Lewis, P.G. (1994) *Central Europe since 1945*, Harlow: Longman.

Linz, S. (1988) 'Managerial autonomy in Soviet firms', *Soviet Studies*, 40(2), 175–95.

Lízal, L., Singer, M. and Svejnar, J. (1995) 'Manager interests, breakups and performance of state enterprises in transition', J. Svejnar (ed.), *The Czech Republic and Economic Transition in Eastern Europe*, San Diego: Academic Press, pp. 211–32.

Lodge, G. and Walton, R. (1989) 'The American corporation and its new relationships', *California Management Review*, 31, 9–25.

Lukes, S. (1974) *Power: A Radical View*, London: Macmillan.

McAuley, A. (1991) 'The economic transition in Eastern Europe: employment, income distribution, and the social security net', *Oxford Review of Economic Policy*, 7(4), 93–105.

McDermott, G. (1993) 'Rethinking the ties that bind: the limits of privatization in the Czech Republic', paper presented at the Conference on the Social Embeddedness of the Economic Transformation in Central and Eastern Europe, Berlin, September.

Mann, B. (1993) 'Privatization in the Czech Republic', *Business Lawyer*, 48(3), 963–73.

Mann, M. (1970) 'The social cohesion of liberal democracy', *American Sociological Review*, 35, 423–39.

Markóczy, L. (1993) 'Managerial and organizational learning in Hungarian–Western mixed management organizations', *International Journal of Human Resource Management*, 4(2), 277–304.

Mason, D. (1992) *Revolution in East-Central Europe. The Rise and Fall of Communism and the Cold War*, Boulder, CO: Westview Press.

Matejka, J. (1989) '1,134 new state enterprises to be formed', *Hospodářské noviny*, January 1989, as reported in JPRS-EER-89-044, 20 April 1989, pp. 10–11.

Meaney, C.S. (1995) 'Foreign experts, capitalists, and competing agendas: privatization in Poland, the Czech Republic and Hungary', *Comparative Political Studies*, 28(2), 275–305.

Mejstřik, M. (1993) 'Privatization in Czechoslovakia', in V. Ramanadham (ed.), *Privatization: A Global Perspective*, London: Routledge, pp. 124–40.

Mejstřik, M. and Hlávaček, J. (1993) 'Preconditions for privatization in Czechoslovakia, 1990–92', in J.S. Earle, R. Frydman and A. Rapaczynski (eds), *Privatization in the Transition to a Market Economy: Studies of Preconditions and Policies in Eastern Europe*, London: Pinter, pp. 46–74.

Meyer, J. (1994) 'Rationalized environments', in W.R. Scott *et al.* (eds), *Institutional Environments and Organizations: Structural Complexity and Individualism*, London: Sage, pp. 28–54.

Meyer, J. and Rowan, B. (1991) 'Institutionalized organizations: formal structure as myth and ceremony', in W. Powell and P. DiMaggio (eds), *The New Institutionalism in Organizational Analysis*, Chicago: University of Chicago Press, pp. 41–62.

Meyer, J., Boli, J. and Thomas, G. (1994) 'Ontology and rationalization in the Western cultural account', in W.R. Scott *et al.* (eds), *Institutional Environments and Organizations: Structural Complexity and Individualism*, London: Sage, pp. 9–27.

Mickler, O. (1992) 'Innovation and the division of labour in state socialist and capitalist enterprises', in C. Smith and P. Thompson (eds), *Labour in Transition: The Labour Process in Eastern Europe and China*, London: Routledge, pp. 73–99.

Mitov, L. (1995) 'Discussion of Chapter 8', in R. Dobrinsky and M. Landesmann (eds), *Transforming Economies and European Integration*, Aldershot: Edward Elgar, pp. 163–7.

Mládek, J. (1993) 'The different paths of privatization: Czechoslovakia, 1990–?', in J.S. Earle, R. Frydman and A. Rapaczynski (eds), *Privatization in the Transition to a Market Economy: Studies of Preconditions and Policies in Eastern Europe*, London: Pinter, pp. 121–46.

Mládek, J. and Hashi, I. (1993) 'Voucher privatisation, investment funds and corporate governance in Czechoslovakia', *British Review of Economic Issues*, 15(3), 67–95.

Murrell, P. (1992) 'Evolution in economics and in the economic reform of the centrally planned economies', in C. Clague and G. Rausser (eds), *The Emergence of Market Economies in Eastern Europe*, Oxford: Blackwell, pp. 35–54.

Murrell, P. and Wang, Y. (1993) 'When privatzation should be delayed: the effect of communist legacies on organizational and institutional reforms', *Journal of Comparative Economics*, 17(2), 385–406.

Musil, J. (1995) 'The Czech housing system in the middle of transition', *Urban Studies*, 32(10), 1679–84.

Myant, M. (1989) *The Czechoslovak Economy 1948–1988: The Battle for Reform*, Cambridge: Cambridge University Press.

Myant, M. (1993) *Transforming Socialist Economies: The Case of Poland and Czechoslovakia*, Aldershot: Edward Elgar.

North, D. (1990) *Institutions, Institutional Change and Economic Performance*, Cambridge: Cambridge University Press.

Oberschall, A. (1994) 'Protest demonstrations and the end of communist regimes in 1989', *Research in Social Movements, Conflicts and Change*, 17, 1–24.

Oliver C. (1992) 'The antecedents of deinstitutionalization', *Organization Studies*, 13(4), 563–88.

Parker, D. (1993) 'Unravelling the planned economy: privatization in Czechoslovakia', *Communist Economics and Economic Transformation*, 5(3), 391–404.

Paul, D. (1979) *The Cultural Limits of Revolutionary Politics: Change and Continuity in Socialist Czechoslovakia*, Boulder, CO: East European Quarterly.

Pelikan, J. (1976) *Socialist Opposition in Eastern Europe: The Czechoslovak Example*, London: Allison and Busby.

Perotti, E. (1994) 'Corporate governance in mass privatization programmes', in S. Estrin (ed.), *Privatization in Central and Eastern Europe*, Harlow: Longman, pp. 54–68.

Pick, M. (1993) 'Quo vadis – homo sapiens? Results and alternatives for the transformation strategy of the CSFR', *Europe-Asia Studies*, 45(1), 103–14.

Polišenský, J. (1947) *History of Czechoslovakia in Outline*, Prague: Bohemia International.

Pollert, A. and Hradecká, I. (1994) 'Privatization in transition: the Czech experience', *Industrial Relations Journal*, 25(1), 52–63.

Powell, W. (1991) 'Neither market nor hierarchy: network forms of organization', in G. Thompson, J. Frances, R. Levačić and J. Mitchell (eds), *Markets, Hierarchies and Networks: The Coordination of Social Life*, London: Sage, pp. 265–76.

Powell, W. and DiMaggio, P. (eds) (1991) *The New Institutionalism in Organizational Analysis*, Chicago: University of Chicago Press.

Radice, H. (1995a) 'The role of foreign direct investment in the transformation of Eastern Europe', in H.-J. Chang and P. Nolan (eds), *The Transformation of the Communist Economies*, London: Macmillan, pp. 282–310.

Radice, H. (1995b) 'Organizing markets in Central and Eastern Europe: competition, governance and the role of foreign capital', in E. Dittrich, G. Schmidt and R. Whitley (eds), *Industrial Transformation in Europe*, London: Sage, pp. 109–33.

Reed, M. (1984) 'Management as a social practice', *Journal of Management Studies*, 21, 273–85.

Reed, Q. (1995) 'Transition, dysfunctionality and change in the Czech and Slovak Republics', *Crime, Law and Social Change*, 22(4), 323–7.

Renner, H. (1989) *A History of Czechoslovakia since 1945*, London: Routledge.

Rothschild, J. (1993) *Return to Diversity: a Political History of East Central Europe since World War II*, 2nd edition, Oxford: Oxford University Press.

Rutland, P. (1993/94) 'Thatcherism, Czech-style: transition to capitalism in the Czech Republic', *Telos*, 25(94), 103–29.

Rybczynski, T. (1991) 'The sequencing of reform', *Oxford Review of Economic Policy*, 7, 26–34.

Rychetník, L. (1981) 'The industrial enterprise in Czechoslovakia', in I. Jeffries (ed.), *The Industrial Enterprise in Eastern Europe*, Eastbourne: Praeger, pp. 114–28.

Rychetník, L. (1992) 'Industrial reform in Czechoslovakia', in I. Jeffries (ed.), *Industrial Reform in Socialist Countries: From Restructuring to Revolution*, Aldershot: Edward Elgar, pp. 111–28.

Sacks, P.M. (1993) 'Privatization in the Czech Republic', *Colombia Journal of World Business*, 28(1), 189–94.

Schapiro, L. and Godson, J. (eds) (1981) *The Soviet Worker: Illusions and Realities*, London: Macmillan.

Schein, E. (1985) *Organizational Culture and Leadership*, San Francisco: Jossey-Bass.

Schutz, A. (1966) 'Some structures of the life-world', in A. Schutz, *Collected Papers, Volume 3*, The Hague: Nijhoff, pp. 118–39.

Schwartz, G., Stone, M. and van der Willigen, T. (1994) 'Beyond stabilization: the economic transformation of Czechoslovakia, Hungary and Poland', *Communist Economies and Economic Transformation*, 6(3), 291–313.

Scott, W.R. (1991) 'Unpacking institutional arguments', in W. Powell and P. DiMaggio (eds), *The New Institutionalism in Organizational Analysis*, Chicago: University of Chicago Press, pp. 164–82.

Scott, W.R. (1994a) 'Institutions and organizations: toward a theoretical synthesis', in W.R. Scott *et al.* (eds), *Institutional Environments and Organizations: Structural Complexity and Individualism*, London: Sage, pp. 55–80.

Scott, W.R. (1994b) 'Institution analysis: variance and process theory approaches', in W.R. Scott *et al.* (eds), *Institutional Environments and Organizations: Structural Complexity and Individualism*, London: Sage, pp. 81–99.

Scott, W.R. and Meyer, J. (1991) 'The organization of societal sectors: propositions and early evidence', in W.R. Scott *et al.* (eds), *Institutional Environments and Organizations: Structural Complexity and Individualism*, London: Sage, pp. 108–40.

Scott, W.R. *et al.* (eds) (1994) *Institutional Environments and Organizations: Structural Complexity and Individualism*, London: Sage.

Seal, W., Sucher, P. and Zelenka, I. (1996) 'Post-socialist transition and the development of an accountancy profession in the Czech Republic', *Critical Perspectives on Accounting*, 7, 485–508.

Seeger, M. (1981) 'Eye witness to failure', in L.Shapiro and J. Godson (eds), *The Soviet Worker: Illusions and Realities*, London: Macmillan, pp. 76–105.

Selznick, P. (1949) *TVA and the Grass Roots*, Berkeley: University of California Press.

Seton-Watson, H. (1956) *The East European Revolution*, 3rd edition, London: Methuen.

Seton-Watson, H. (1960) *A Pattern of Communist Revolution: A Historical Analysis*, 2nd edition, London: Methuen.

Shafik, N. (1995) 'Making a market: mass privatization in the Czech and Slovak Republics', *World Development*, 23(7), 1143–56.

Šik, O. (1993) 'Problems in making the transition to a market economy', in J. Child, M. Crozier, R. Mayntz *et al.* (eds), *Societal Change between Market and Organization*, Aldershot: Avebury, pp. 189–202.

Šimečka, M. (1984) *The Restoration of Order: The Normalization of Czechoslovakia 1969–1976*, London: Verso.

Skilling, H.G. (1976) *Czechoslovakia's Interrupted Revolution*, Princeton, NJ: Princeton University Press.

Sobell, V. (1988) 'Czechoslovakia: the legacy of normalization', *Eastern European Politics and Societies*, 2(1), 35–68.

Soulsby, A. and Clark, E. (1995) 'Privatization and the restructuring of enterprise social and welfare assets in the Czech Republic', *Industrial Relations Journal*, 26(2), 97–109.

Soulsby, A. and Clark, E. (1996a) 'The emergence of post-communist management in the Czech Republic', *Organization Studies*, 17(2), 227–47.

Soulsby, A. and Clark, E. (1996b) 'Economic restructuring and institutional change: post-communist management in the Czech Republic', *Journal of Socio-Economics*, 25(4), 473–96.

Soulsby, A. and Clark, E. (1998) 'Controlling personnel: management and motive in the transformation of the Czech enterprise', *International Journal of Human Resource Management*, 79–98.

Stark, D. (1992) 'Path dependence and privatization strategies in East Central Europe', *East European Politics and Societies*, 6(1), 17–54.

Stark, D. and Bruszt, L. (1995) 'Network properties of assets and liabilities: patterns of inter-enterprise ownership in the postsocialist transformation', paper presented at the EMOT Workshop, Dynamics of Industrial Transformation: East Central European and East Asian Comparisons, Budapest University of Economic Sciences, May.

Stern, R. (1995) 'Putting foreign direct investment in Eastern Europe into perspective: turning a macroeconomic failure into a microeconomic success story', in R. Dobrinsky and M. Landesmann (eds), *Transforming Economies and European Integration*, Aldershot: Edward Elgar, pp. 297–310.

Stone, N. and Strouhal, E. (eds) (1989) *Czechoslovakia: Crossroads and Crises, 1918–88*, Basingstoke: Macmillan.

Strang, D. and Meyer, J. (1994) 'Institutional conditions for diffusion', in W.R. Scott *et al.* (eds), *Institutional Environments and Organizations: Structural Complexity and Individualism*, London: Sage, pp. 100–12.

Suchman, M. (1995) 'Managing legitimacy: strategic and institutional approaches', *Academy of Management Review*, 20(3), 571–610.

Suda, Z. (1980) *Zealots and Rebels: A History of the Communist Party of Czechoslovakia*, Stanford, CA: Hoover Institution Press.

Šuhan, I. and Šuhanová, M. (1995) 'The macroeconomic situation in the Czech Republic', in J. Svejnar (ed.), *The Czech Republic and Economic Transition in Eastern Europe*, San Diego: Academic Press, pp. 119–35.

Svejnar, J. (ed.) (1995a) *The Czech Republic and Economic Transition in Eastern Europe*, San Diego: Academic Press.

Svejnar, J. (1995b) 'Introduction and overview', in J. Svejnar (ed.), *The Czech Republic and Economic Transition in Eastern Europe*, San Diego: Academic Press, pp. 1–19.

Svejnar, J. and Singer, M. (1994) 'Using vouchers to privatize an economy: the Czech and Slovak case', *Economics of Transition*, 2(1), 43–69.

Székely, I. (1995) 'Financial reforms and economic integration', in R. Dobrinsky and M. Landesmann (eds), *Transforming Economies and European Integration*, Aldershot: Edward Elgar, pp. 199–227.

Taborsky, E. (1979) 'Tragedy, triumph and tragedy: Czechoslovakia 1938–1948', in H. Brisch and I. Volgyes (eds), *Czechoslovakia: The Heritage of Ages Past. Essays in Memory of Josef Korbel*, Boulder, CO: East European Quarterly, pp. 113–34.

Takla, L. (1994) 'The relationship between privatization and the reform of the banking sector: the case of the Czech Republic and Slovakia', in S. Estrin (ed.), *Privatization in Central and Eastern Europe*, Harlow: Longman, pp. 154–75.

Tatur, M. (1995) 'Towards corporatism? The transformation of interest policy and interest representation in Eastern Europe', in E. Dittrich, G. Schmidt and R. Whitley (eds), *Industrial Transformation in Europe*, London: Sage, pp. 163–84.

Teichová, A. (1988) *The Czechoslovak Economy 1918–1980*, London: Routledge.

Thompson, G., Frances, J., Levačić, R. and Mitchell, J. (eds) (1991) *Markets, Hierarchies and Networks: the Coordination of Social Life*, London: Sage.

Trade Links (1993) *Privatization in the Czech and Slovak Republics*, Prague: Trade Links.

Trade Links (1994) *The Czech and Slovak Republics at a Glance*, Prague: Trade Links.

Tsoukas, H. (1994) 'Socio-economic systems and organizational management: an institutional perspective on the socialist firm', *Organization Studies*, 15(1), 21–45.

Tushman, M. and Romanelli, E. (1985) 'Organizational evolution: a metamorphosis model of convergence and reorientation', in L. Cummings and B. Staw (eds), *Research in Organizational Behaviour*, Greenwich, CT: JAI Press, pp. 171–222.

Ulč, O. (1974) *Politics in Czechoslovakia*, San Francisco: W.H. Freeman and Company.

Ulč, O. (1978) 'Some aspects of Czechoslovak society since 1968', *Social Forces*, 57(2), 419–35.

Ulč, O. (1979) 'The "normalization" of post-invasion Czechoslovakia', *Survey*, 24: 201–13.

Urban, J. (1990) 'Czechoslovakia: the power and politics of humiliation', in G. Prins (ed.), *Spring in Winter: The 1989 Revolutions*, Manchester: Manchester University Press, pp. 99–136.

Večerník, J. (1992) 'Labor force attitudes in the transition to the market: the Czechoslovak case', *Journal of Public Policy*, 12(2), 177–94.

Villinger, R. (1996) 'Post-acquisition managerial learning in Central East Europe', *Organization Studies*, 17(2), 181–206.

Volgyes, I. (1995) 'The economic legacies of communism', in Z. Barany and I. Volgyes (eds), *The Legacies of Communism in Eastern Europe*, Baltimore: Johns Hopkins University Press, pp. 42–54.

Waller, M. (1993) *The End of Communist Power Monopoly*, Manchester: Manchester University Press.

Walters, A. (1992) 'The transition to a market economy', in C. Clague and G. Rausser (eds), *The Emergence of Market Economies in Eastern Europe*, Oxford: Blackwell, pp. 99–105.

Watson, T. (1995) 'Rhetoric, discourse and argument in organizational sense-making: a reflexive tale', *Organization Studies*, 16(5), 805–21.

Weber, M. (1964) *The Theory of Social and Economic Organization*, New York: Free Press.

Wheaton, B. and Kavan, Z. (1992) *The Velvet Revolution: Czechoslovakia, 1988–1991*, Oxford: Westview.

White, S., Gardner, J., Schöpflin, G. and Saich, T. (1990) *Communist and Postcommunist Political Systems: An Introduction*, 3rd edition, Basingstoke: Macmillan.

Whitley, R. (1994) 'The internationalization of firms and markets: its significance and institutional structuring', *Organization*, 1(1), 101–24.

Whitley, R. (1995) 'Transformation and change in Europe: critical themes', in E. Dittrich, G. Schmidt and R. Whitley (eds), *Industrial Transformation in Europe*, London: Sage, pp. 11–29.

Whitley, R., Henderson, J., Lengyel, G. and Czaban, L. (1995) 'Continuity and change in an emergent market economy: the limited transformation of economic actors in Hungary', paper presented at EMOT Programme The Social Constitution of Economic Actors, 22–24 April.

Williamson, O. (1975) *Markets and Hierarchies: Analysis and Anti-trust Implications*, New York: Free Press.

Willmott, H. (1987) 'Studying managerial work: a critique and a proposal', *Journal of Management Studies*, 24(3), 249–70.

Wilson, D. (1992) *A Strategy for Change: Concepts and Controversies in the Management of Change*, London: Routledge.

Wilson, D. and Mummalaneni, V. (1990) 'Bonding and commitment in buyer–seller relationships: a preliminary conceptualization', in D. Ford (ed.), *Understanding Business Markets*, London: Academic Press, pp. 408–20.

Wiskemann, E. (1967) *Czechs and Germans: A Study of the Struggle in the Historic Provinces of Bohemia and Moravia*, 2nd edition, London: Macmillan.

Wolchik, S. (1991) *Czechoslovakia in Transition: Politics, Economics and Society*, London: Pinter.

Wolchik, S. (1995) 'The Czech Republic and Slovakia', in Z. Barany and I. Volgyes (eds), *The Legacies of Communism in Eastern Europe*, Baltimore: Johns Hopkins University, pp. 152–76.

Yin, R. (1989) *Case Study Research: Design and Methods*, revised edition, Newbury Park, CA: Sage.

Zemplinerová, A. and Stíbal, J. (1995) 'Evolution and efficiency of concentration in manufacturing', in J. Svejnar (ed.), *The Czech Republic and Economic Transition in Eastern Europe*, San Diego: Academic Press, pp. 233–54.

Zucker, L. (1991) 'The role of institutionalization in cultural persistence', in W. Powell and P. DiMaggio (eds), *The New Institutionalism in Organizational Analysis*, Chicago: University of Chicago Press, pp. 83–107.

Index